The Crossman Confessions

*and Other Essays
in Politics, History and Religion*

By the same author

England and the Middle East: the Destruction of the Ottoman Empire

Nationalism

Afghani and 'Abduh: an Essay on Religious Unbelief and Political Activism in Modern Islam

The Chatham House Version and other Middle Eastern Studies

Nationalism in Asia and Africa

Arabic Political Memoirs and other Studies

In the Anglo-Arab Labyrinth: the McMahon-Husayn Correspondence and its Interpretations, 1914–39

Islam in the Modern World and Other Studies

Edited by the same author

The Middle-Eastern Economy
The Jewish World

Edited by the same author with Sylvia G. Haim

Modern Egypt
Towards Modern Iran
Palestine and Israel in the 19th and 20th Centuries
Zionism and Arabism in Palestine and Israel

The Crossman Confessions

and Other Essays
in Politics, History and Religion

Elie Kedourie

Mansell Publishing Limited
London and New York

First published 1984 by
Mansell Publishing Limited
(A subsidiary of the H. W. Wilson Company)
6 All Saints Street, London N1 9RL, England
950 University Avenue, Bronx, New York 10452, U.S.A.

British Library Cataloguing in Publication Data

Kedourie, Elie
   The Crossman confessions and other essays
   in politics, history and religion.
   1. Political science
   I. Title
   320   JA66
   ISBN 0–7201–1712–7

Library of Congress Cataloging in Publication Data

Kedourie, Elie.
   The Crossman confessions and other essays in politics, history, and
religion.

   Includes index.
   1. Great Britain—Politics and government—20th century—Addresses,
essays, lectures.
   2. International relations—Addresses, essays, lectures.
   3. Developing countries—Addresses, essays, lectures.
   4. Religion and state—Addresses, essays, lectures.
   I. Title.
DA566.7.K38 1984   320.941   84–7948
ISBN 0–7201–1712–7

Filmset by J & L Composition Ltd. Filey, N. Yorkshire
Printed and bound in Great Britain

Contents

Preface

THE TWENTY essays contained in this volume were written over the last quarter of a century. As the product of one mind, they naturally show unity of style, approach and preoccupation. The mind is that of an historian who examines and reflects upon political and religious ideas and dispositions which have aroused his curiosity and puzzlement, and who, while so doing, is simultaneously moved to reflect upon the character and limits of historical discourse. The unity which these essays exhibit is, moreover, a complex one in that the different and varied themes here considered cohere with one another through numerous mutual interconnections. Often explicit, these are also sometimes implicit—but not any the less evident for being unspoken.

'Development and Politics', the ninth chapter, appears here for the first time though in a sense it is the earliest to have been written, since I had jotted down a rough draft for it in the late spring of 1959. First publication of the other essays was as follows:

The American Scholar. The Jews between Tradition and Modernity, Spring 1981; History, the Past and the Future, Winter 1984.
The British Journal of International Studies. Religion and Politics, Arnold Toynbee and Martin Wight, April 1979.
Commentary. Augurs and Diviners, November 1976; A New International Disorder, December 1980.

Encounter. Lord Salisbury and Politics, June 1972; The Lure of Revolutionary Revolution, July 1972; Arnold J. Toynbee, History as Paradox, May 1974; The Crossman Confessions, December 1977; The Brandt 'Commission' and its Report, December 1980; Conservatives and neo-Conservatives, November 1982; Religion under Stress, March 1983.

The Jewish World, Thames and Hudson, 1979. The Character of Jewish History.

The Political Quarterly. Lord Halifax, Conservative, July 1966.

The Princetonian. Foreign Policy, a Practical Pursuit, 4 January 1961.

Solon. Conservatism and the Conservative Party, October 1970.

The Spectator. The History of Ideas and Guilt by Association, 1 December 1970; Politics, a Philosophical Pursuit?, 20 February 1971.

The Times Literary Supplement. New Histories for Old, 7 March 1975.

I am very grateful to the editors and publishers concerned for permission to reprint.

London School of Economics and Political Science
April 1984

The Crossman Confessions

IN THE Introduction to the first volume of his *Diaries*[1] Richard Crossman (1907–1974) tells us that in keeping such a record his purpose was to disclose the secret operations of government which are habitually concealed 'by the thick masses of foliage which we call the myth of democracy'. By disclosing the secret reality behind the deceptive appearance the *Diaries* were to make their author the Bagehot of his age. For the greater part of his life Crossman had been a don and a journalist, and the aspiration to be a twentieth-century Bagehot clearly meant a great deal to him. So much so that we find him remarking in November 1966—when he was Lord President and a prominent member of Harold Wilson's administration—that 'there's no doubt that politically too my ability to write a major book and the existence of Prescote [his country house and farm] combine to give me an increasing detachment from the Cabinet'.

Crossman died without fulfilling his ambition, but the 2500 pages of the three volumes of the *Diaries* are enough to persuade us that here is a veritable Aladdin's cave for which a latter-day Bagehot, as articulate and weighty, as concise and witty as his predecessor (and for him, truly, among today's writers on the Constitution we shall have to search with an Aladdin's lamp) will be grateful.

[1] *The Diaries of a Cabinet Minister*: vol. 1, *Minister of Housing 1964–6*; vol. 2, *Lord President of the Council and Leader of the House of Commons 1966–8*; vol. 3, *Secretary of State for Social Services 1968–70*.

In the large heap of confidential gossip, administrative anecdotes and political reflections which this priviledged chronicler has left behind him, the modern Bagehot will find much that is instructive and enlightening, and much that will give rise to wry amusement and rueful irony. One theme which emerges from the *Diaries*—no doubt unintentionally— he will find particularly striking. In 1939 the young Cross- man, then Assistant Editor of the *New Statesman and Nation*, published a small volume entitled *How Britain is Governed*.

The ideas rehearsed in this work were the common coin of Leftist argument: that Britain was a 'plutocracy' at the mercy of 'financial and industrial dictators'; that the wealthy, in the name of liberty and private enterprise, impeded the 'will of the people'; that civil servants, 'far removed from the life and ideas of the mass of the people', are employed 'to keep the present machine in running order'; and that, therefore, they are unable 'to reconstruct our society upon the principles of scientific planning.'

The ideas expressed in this opuscule are now much more familiar and prevalent than when Crossman was helping to spread them. And some of them have, appropriately enough, found dignified lodgement in a state paper produced during, and under the aegis of, the administration to which Crossman was later to belong. The view that the civil service was remote from ordinary people and unfit to carry out 'scientific planning' was authoritatively asserted by the Report of the Fulton Committee on the Civil Service which was set up in 1966. The Report, published in 1968, com- plained that the 'social and educational base' of the civil service was still too narrow, and asserted that its 'exclusive- ness' and 'isolation' hindered 'a full understanding' of con- temporary problems and of the outside world. To remedy this state of affairs, the Committee recommended a recruit- ment policy that would render the service 'more represent- ative, geographically, educationally and socially, of the nation at large than they have been in the past.'

There is little doubt that the Committee was indebted for these ideas to a social survey of the civil service which it had commisssioned from two academics, Dr A. H. Halsey and Mr

I. M. Crewe.[2] These two investigators made the discovery that the administrative class of the civil service was 'much more middle and upper class in origin than the scientific officer class or the professional workers' group', that in fact no less that 67 per cent of the administrative class and 79 per cent of its direct entrants were born into the middle and upper classes. This was not all. For while university teachers reflected 'fairly precisely' 'the social and educational composition of the undergraduate body from which they are drawn', the administrative class was—*horribile dictu*—'much more predominantly middle class.' There was an even worse revelation : to the question— which they themselves posed—'whether Oxford and Cambridge graduates are in any pejorative sense "over-represented" among those entering the administrative class', the investigators' solemn and devastating answer was, simply, 'a simple affirmative'.

What such simple affirmations assume is some kind of crude Marxist link between the origins of civil servants and their behaviour in office. The universal character and overriding significance of such a link these two investigators take to be axiomatic. Social origin, they flatly declare, 'is the most useful summary index of the complex of social forces which impinge on the upbringing of an individual', and they assert further that 'the same process of social selection which brings individuals to diverse occupational destinations also fashions and maintains norms of outlook and shared assumptions among the members of a profession'.

But such notions cannnot possibly withstand scrutiny. It is not the place of the civil service to be 'representative': representation is the affair of Parliament. The function of the civil service is rather to discharge the public business efficiently and impartially—and for this a certain aloofness, an eschewing precisely of representativeness, is necessary. The demand that the civil service should be educationally and socially 'representative', however, follows from the notion that since it is drawn from the upper and middle class, *ipso facto* it will serve

---

[2] Their memorandum is published in *The Civil Service*, vol 3 (1), Social Survey of the Civil Service, HMSO, 1969. The Memorandum runs to some 400 pages.

upper and middle class interest. But for this no evidence is adduced, nor can it be easily supplied. In fact, had the Fulton Committee remembered which university had nourished and fostered Philby, Burgess and MacLean, and had it attended to another survey which it had also commissioned, it might have been a shade more careful in its sociological asseverations. In this other survey, 'Profile of a profession',[3] Dr R. A. Chapman enquired of all the 1956 entrants to the administrative class— entrants, that is, who joined the service in its unreconstructed and unenlightened days—how they had voted in the 1966 general election. All of them answered, and their answers were as follows:

Labour	17
Conservative	6
Liberal	4
Scottish Nationalist	1
Did not vote	2

We may add that the 57 per cent of the first division civil servants who, ten years afterwards, voted to affiliate to the TUC serve to confirm the picture disclosed by Dr Chapman's questionnaire.

Even on their own assumptions, therefore, the Fulton Committee—and the young Crossman—are both misled and misleading. But this is not only becasue a large number (perhaps a majority?) of higher civil servants have sympathies which their social origins ought, on the Fulton doctrine, to rule out. The assumptions not only turn out to be wrong in fact, they are also irrelevant in principle. Whatever their private sympathies and inclinations, intelligent men of business will soon find out that public affairs and their efficient despatch are not easily bent to a political doctrine.

What the *Diaries* of the old Crossman establish—in confutation both of Fulton and of the young Crossman—is that the conduct of civil servants has little to do with their origin or party-political sympathies. The reality is that for at least four

[3] *The Civil Service*, vol. 3 (2), *Surveys and Investigations*, HMSO, 1968.

decades now—ever since the outbreak of the Second World War—the civil service has acquired habits which have ended by becoming ingrained. It has learnt the ambition to fine-tune the aconomy, to manage demand, and control supply[4], and bestow on each citizen no more and no less his fair share of income—or rather of pocket money—and of 'welfare'; to be, in one word, for the British people what their counterparts in the Indian civil service had been for the ryot: a very father and mother. It is this frame of mind, that of (shall we say?) a benevolent despotism which, more than vulgar partisanship or social origin, makes civil servants so ready to undertake the 'scientific planning' after which the young Crossman hankered, and to be so responsive to the interventionist and dirigiste proclivities of British governments, whether Labour or Conservative.

The first volume of the *Diaries*, dealing with Crossman's period in the Ministry of Housing, will supply the evidence. The Ministry, by no means the invention of a Labour Government, may be seen as an exemplar and monument of official interventionism. When Crossman became Minister, the permanent head of the Ministry was Dame Evelyn Sharp with whom, as is well known, his relations were not easy. What emerges from the *Diaries* is thus all the more significant, since beneath the tension and the disagreements, what we may discern is a remarkable congruence of instinct and outlook between minister and civil servant. Thus:

> She is rather like Beatrice Webb in her attitude to life, to the Left in wanting improvement and social justice quite pas-

---

[4]   *The Times* of 31 May 1977 carried an interview with Sir B. Hopkin, lately Chief Economic Adviser to the Treasury and Head of the Government Economic Service. He is reported as declaring: 'Fine tuning for full employment which I believed in has contributed to the problem of inflation. It was the natural result of planning for full employment.' The interview also revealed that Hopkin had been closely involved in the first attempts to introduce indicative planning on the French model in the early 1960s. What has bedevilled economic policy making, Hopkin is reported to have declared, has been the ambivalent attitude of the British people towards growth. The Arabic proverb tells us that the monkey, not knowing how to dance, complains that the ground is not level.

sionately and yet a tremendous patrician and utterly contemptuous and arrogant, regarding local authorities as children which she has to examine and rebuke for their failures. She sees ordinary human beings as incapable of making a sensible decision.

Again:

> She sees the New Towns as the great creations of her Ministry and she loves them because they have been created autocratically from above.

And again—here his testimony being at its most instructive:

> I spent yesterday in Cumbernauld New Town. ... built on the top of a long, high, bleak ridge. ... an enormous lot of roads and a fascinating variety of modern houses. Up-and-down houses, vertical houses, horizontal houses, and everything including the churches, fitting into the style, everything done in a tremendously austere, exhilarating, uncomfortable style. I thought Atticus this morning in the *Sunday Times* was extremely apposite when he pointed out that this was the kind of thing which Dame Evelyn and I are excited about, in contrast to the cosy garden suburb atmosphere of Stevenage or Harlow or Basildon.

Our new Minister is now ensconced in his Ministry. He finds himself, he tells us, as though in a padded cell, guarded, shielded and comfortably supported by his civil servants. At times he is appreciative of their attentiveness and efficiency, at others he lashes out in suspicion of these very same qualities. Here then they are, in their Ministry, these *frères ennemis*. What, we may ask, do they do in the Ministry? They do housing. But this does not mean that they actually build houses which people may want to rent or buy. Rather they decide housing policy. Whether or not it is because they inhabit the same padded cell, we find Ministers and civil servants talking the same language—a language the relation of which to common or garden house-building is both remote and problematic.

I have now [Crossman writes in November 1964] reached the conclusion that 400,000 houses will probably be built in the next twelve months. ... Any decision I *now* take to make a new kind of plan which shifts the balance of housing between the public and the private sector beyond the next twelve months involves me in a very complicated calculation. I am pretty clear what the long term plan should be. I am pretty clear that the decision means comprehensive urban renewal. ... A Labour Minister should impose central leadership, large-scale state intervention, in these blighted areas of cities, these twilight areas. ...

This is, and no mistake, clear-cut, decisive, purposive. The Minister is, however, aware that a financial crisis, an interruption in the supply of bricks, a bottleneck in the building industry might put his plans at nought. But if such are the imponderables relating to a period as short as a year, what is the value of the 'complicated calculation' which he would have to undertake if he were to plan beyond these twelve months? However precise its terms, such 'calculation' could be no more than a day-dream. But why 400,000 houses? No one in the bakery business would dream of planning the supply of bread without an idea of the likely effective demand. But in the padded cell of the Ministry of Housing, supply and demand—those Siamese twins—severed from one another, become free-floating, ghostly entities. Why 400,000? Why not 393,000 or 467,000? We may suspect that the only virtue of this figure is that it is a round figure. And as we read on, our suspicion seems to be confirmed.

26 May 1965

[Harold Wilson] has decided that all other social services must be cut back in order to have a magnificent housing drive and bring the annual production of houses up to 500,000 by 1970. 'This is it,' he said. 'We'll make housing the most popular single thing this Government does. We won't build another single mile of road if a cut-back is necessary in order to get that half-million houses a year. That's what I believe in,' he said.

But six weeks later lo and behold one of his officials was called to the Treasury and

> Came rushing back into the room with a quite extraordinary story. He said that when he got there a fellow called Petch had announced to all those present that the Prime Minister wished to have worked out for him a plan for a complete three-month moratorium on all new contracts. Quite literally, for three months no one should, on behalf of any Ministry, sign a new contract. Petch had indicated that the occasion for this extraordinary idea was the fear that this month's balance-of-trade figures might again be very bad and set off another run on the pound by the Gnomes of Zurich: the Prime Minister wanted to do something which would impress them with our determination to curb incipient inflation.

Arbitrariness, it is evident, is the principle which distinguishes this style of government. Of this arbitrariness, synonymous with planning, examples abound in the *Diaries*. Crossman and fellow ministers try to decide where a New Town should be sited. George Brown is in favour of the Preston-Chorley area 'because he wanted to see a new growth point in Lancashire.' Douglas Jay is opposed to this. The area, he says, 'can't be a growth point because growth must only take place in the development areas, and we must not grant industrial development certificates in the Chorley area because that will take them away from the areas of unemployment.' Since neither 'growth' nor unemployment are easily amenable to the wishes even of ministers, since no one knows in advance what will stimulate the one and diminish the other, the argument between Jay and Brown was logomachic and a decision based on it no better that a throw of the dice.

Such arbitrary decisions are no doubt taken out of benevolence, out of a desire to do good. But it does not follow that they will do good or in the end satisfy the powerful benevolent urges of those who seek to take them. The young Crossman, as we know, was a great believer in 'planning', which was to remedy injustice and improve the condition of the people. But to do good, the old Crossman comes to realize, is not easy. His,

8

as Minister of Housing, was the power to bind and loose in town and country planning:

> As a result of seeing on the spot the decisions I had taken, I was more aware than ever how impossible it is for me to judge them fairly when they come on appeal as bits of paper. But [as a civil servant pointed out to him] there is another problem. ... There is no intrinsic fairness in planning, it is *by nature* unfair. In order to decide one individual case fairly the Minister must know not only the details of that case but the whole background. ...

A minister with powers like these, then, has to be all-seeing and all-knowing. But would not the minister's omniscience lead him to a paralysing philosophical doubt, and will he not then—happy release—come to see that we live in the best of all possible worlds, with everything in it a necessary evil? But ministers are not omniscient and their 'planning' is fortunately, as we know, a crude, hit-or-miss affair.

Fortunately—but only in the long view. For 'planning', like other enterprises, may come a cropper, and because of its scale and pretensions may involve large numbers in misfortune or unhappiness:

> Wigan is enormously overcrowded and since it is determined to be better than its jokes, the council has undertaken an enormous building programme; and, as a result, thousands of council houses have been built. ... The houses are of an appalling dimness and dullness, and I am afraid they have built a Wigan that in 2000 will look just as bad as the old 1880 Wigan looks in the eyes of the 1960s'

Such a passage is one of these—and they are many—which serve to give the *Diaries* an eminent place in the literature of political confessions. And as a confession its interest is not at all diminished by the fact that Crossman—as he records—believed that 'the appalling dimness and dullness' of council housing in Wigan was occasioned by the absence in this town of a city architect or a town planner!

The arbitrariness, the high-handedness implicit in this style

9

of government comes out perhaps most clearly in the so-called prices and incomes policy. The Government takes to itself draconian powers—powers which mankind has hitherto attributed to God alone—to prescribe for each man how much exactly he may earn by the sweat of his brow, and for how much he may sell the product of his labour. And the Cabinet sitting in solemn conclave giving and taking away do seem to us to be very gods:

> We all soon agreed that the nurses should be given their full 9 per cent. I remembered how in 1962 Selwyn Lloyd gave the surtax payers their tax concession and cut the nurses' pay. Here we can prove that Roy [Jenkins] does the opposite. He gives the nurses their pay claim and the surtax payers a new tax on capital.

But the gods disappoint; they are, alas, hollow and powerless, as this entry attests:

> The main item was the Prices and Income White Paper. ... Richard Marsh with whom I have a great deal of fellow-feeling, repeated that the whole thing is absolute nonsense. ... The Chancellor himself doesn't believe in a prices and incomes policy. He believes that wages should find their own level. And yet as a Government we are in this situation and can't get out of it.

And this one:

> I know perfectly that the statutory prices and incomes policy is one of the few things which makes the difference between a socialist and a Tory Government. ... And yet whenever I sit at this Committee I come to the conclusion that a statutory policy is unworkable. When I listen to the mumbo-jumbo of nil norms and the rest of it, and criteria, I feel they're infuriatingly bogus and I am inspired by an Enoch Powellite desire to tear the whole thing to pieces. Yet in the end I have to vote for one of these legalistic formulae.

Or take, finally, the predicament of 'poor Peter Shore' at yet another meeting of the Prices and Incomes Committee. 'It's a fraud' Crossman complains, because whatever Shore proposes it is Scanlon and Jones who dispose:

> Yet this poor Minister has to struggle along, Peter Shore boldly suggested that he would work for selective control permitting those price rises that ought to soar and only keeping down prices which needed to be kept down.

Grown men, Ministers, members of the Cabinet solemnly debating how to allow only price rises 'that ought to soar' and to keep down those prices 'which needed to be kept down'! What is impossible to bring about should not be attempted. It is these desperate attempts to bring about the impossible which accounts for the futility, the levity, the feeling of make-believe, of being powerless and hamstrung which permeates, and rises from these *Diaries*. It sometimes results, no doubt unintentionally, in passages of a Marx Brothers quality. Here for instance is a conversation between the Prime Minister and the Lord President of the Council in September 1967—some two months before the Government was forced to devalue the currency. The conversation was on the subject of economic policy which the Prime Minister was now to direct, having just taken over the Department of Economic Affairs. Prior to that, he was saying, he had had no real say in economic decisions over economic policy even though people held him responsible:

> I told him he was getting the wrong idea. 'Even if your responsibility has only increased', I said, 'from 80 per cent to 100 per cent, the risks have also increased if anything goes wrong.' 'Ah', he said, smiling, 'but the chances of success have increased from 50 per cent to 130 per cent. If I can't run the economy well through D.E.A. I'm no good. I was trained for this job and I've now taken the powers to run the economy.'

This sense of unreality, of Ministers who, despite their enormous powers and their control over the legislative factory, are hemmed in by crises which they cannot control or alleviate, of being engaged in play-acting rather than in taking action is not confined to the *Diaries* or to the Labour Government of the 1960s. It is conveyed just as powerfully in *The Cecil King Diary 1970–1974* which covers Mr Edward Heath's administration.

December 1st, 1971

Sir Frank Figgures rather astonished me by saying it was curious how nobody had any power today: power had seeped away and none was now left. This was why it took so long to get anything done as so many consents were necessary. This is the same statement that Sir George Bolton [a banker] made to me many months ago. 'There is now in England no power centre'. Even so it was surprising as coming from a man who, until very recently, was Second Secretary at the Treasury.

February 16th, 1972

We have had a mini-general strike [by the coalminers] in which the Government has been defeated; intimidation by pickets at power-stations and at the House of Commons, has been permitted; no reference has been made to the Communist influence in the whole business; and the settlement is bound to be inflationary and to set the level for other inflationary claims. Carr's [the Secretary for Employment] conciliatory policy lies in ruins; Maudling's [the Home Secretary] feebleness is given further publicity, but no changes are forecast. ... the Rhodesian settlement seems to be a dead duck, and we are busy evacuating Malta.

April 23rd, 1972

Lunch with A.B. [a senior civil servant]. He says the miners' strike brought home to Ministers for the first time that a clash with the unions would mean a general strike— and the defeat of the Government. ... What is the Government to do? A.B. thought it would take fifteen years to build up an adequate police force, and to rouse popular feeling against the Communist menace. The police force is below strength, and its establishment is too low; the territorials have been disbanded. The troops that can be spared are in Ireland.

May 11th, 1972
Lunch yesterday with Dick Briginshaw [a trade-union leader]. ... He agreed that the £50 million given by the Government to the Upper Clyde Shipbuilders was a bad investment, but said they had no alternative. The situation became very ugly and they were afraid of an uprising.

Arbitrary government, however far-reaching its consequences on those who are subject to it, is sometimes literally senseless. In a conference of ministers and civil servants which reviewed, in March 1968, three years' official activity in the social services, Mr Kenneth Robinson, Minister of Health, declared that he had made only two mistakes in his career: 'one was to take the prescription charges off and the other was to put them on.' Indeed, in this style of government it becomes impossible to say what the consequences of any policy are, let alone whether or not they are beneficial. We are not surprised to see that, for all the complication of committee upon committee and working party upon working party at his disposal, Crossman still complains that 'there is no real instrument of central decision-taking' for the economy. Crossman himself is inclined to attribute this lack to 'Harold's proclivity for opportunism' and 'Whitehall's desire to prevent a coherent decision-taking body being imposed upon it.' We may suspect that the reason does not lie in a particular Prime Minister's inclinations or in a supposed collective desire by the civil service to escape ministerial control. It lies, surely, rather in the over-government—the attempt precisely to establish a 'central purposive direction' after which Crossman hankered—which demands a plethora of laws, regulations and administrative devices. But, to quote Mr Robinson's example, (which may stand for much else which is related in the *Diaries*) it is impossible to know whether it is better to impose or not to impose prescription charges. Such decisions, meant to bring about definite and precise

13

results are, in reality and of necessity, something like the lucky—or the unlucky—dip.

Crossman contrasted the lack of an instrument of central decision-making in economic affairs with the existence of such an instrument in foreign policy and defence. It is of course in no way surprising that this should be so. Foreign policy and defence involve a narrow and specific range of issues which have always been par excellence the exclusive affair of the state—a range of issues amenable to fairly precise definition and coherent debate, where by comparison housing policy, say, or demand management are trapped in a quicksand of self-contradictions and treacherously unreliable guesses. What picture, then, emerges from the *Diaries* of the manner in which Crossman and his colleagues discharged these primary and central political responsibilities? Of course in the first place it is a picture of Crossman himself confronting problems and responsibilities as a senior member of the Cabinet. Where he stood on these matters, what his tastes and inclinations were is not in doubt. He tells us that he found Nasser 'imaginative and creative', and was 'invigorated by his presence'. At a Commonwealth Conference dinner he hit it off with Makarios, 'a man of great charm', precisely because they shared this admiration for the then ruler of Egypt. He had, he also reveals, while a backbencher 'egged on the Greeks to stir up their Enosis campaign' in Cyprus. He does not reveal why he behaved in this way, but one reason may have been that he was, as he calls himself, a Little Englander. The future he envisaged for Britain was that of 'an offshore island, cutting down all our overseas commitments, getting ourselves an economic position as favourable as that of Japan in the Far East and living on our own as an independent socialist community.' He also believed that 'all our economic troubles and our difficulties at home' stemmed entirely from British commitments overseas. He admired Attlee's decision to withdraw from India 'despite the fact that it cost a million lives'. He does not refer to the other abrupt withdrawal effected by Attlee's administration, the abandonment and evacuation of Palestine, with its sequel of wars and refugees, but since he was, as he described himself,

14

'a great getter-outer' in favour of 'big withdrawals' which were 'rapid' and 'ruthless, 'abrupt' and 'sudden', we may perhaps take it that he also approved of that other episode in the record of the third Labour administration. He must of course have realized that it was not really possible suddenly and completely to get away from all overseas commitments. Thus at a Cabinet committee on overseas policy and defence he and like-minded colleagues insisted that 'as our military power declines the money we spend on information services and on psychological warfare must increase'—less action, so to speak, and more cackle. The *Diaries* record another bizarre consequence of abandoning military commitments. Because the defence budget has to be cut and a contract to buy expensive military aircraft from the U.S. cancelled, Concorde, unprofitable and burdensome as it is, must be retained: 'If we virtually abolish military aircraft we still have to believe in civil aircraft, particularly if we are concerned about jobs in the aircraft industry'.

Such are Crossman's views and inclinations in respect of foreign affairs and defence. But they are by no means peculiar to him alone. Many fellow-ministers share them, and the Parliamentary Labour Party favours them, by instinct so to speak. 'Our back-benchers', he notes in January 1967, 'not only detest our support for the Americans in Vietnam—they also resent the weight of the defence burden'. But both Crossman and the back-benchers are caught in an incoherence. To diminish 'the defence burden', to get away from all overseas commitments *ipso facto* must mean that Britain is incapable of defending her interests or asserting her views in a world made up of sovereign states which, recognizing no superior, have all to depend for safety and prosperity on their own power and influence. Why then, in the face of such an elementary fact and of his determination to whittle down the armed forces, does Crossman bitterly bemoan 'this Government's impotence' and its subservience to American policies? Again, the coercion of Rhodesia was a popular policy among the back-benchers. But how, without overseas bases, and a powerful army and navy, was Rhodesia to be coerced?

Rhodesia loomed very large in the foreign policy of the

Labour administration of 1964–70. It is puzzling to know exactly why this should have been so. No great public interest, whether strategic or economic, hung on the principle of 'one man one vote' being enforced in Rhodesia. In Crossman's judgment, the reason had more to do with the Prime Minister's personal preoccupations:

> in this Rhodesian affair [he writes in December 1966] his main concern is to prove himself right: to prove that he can win this as Kennedy won his Cuba. It's winning that matters here, whether by settlement or by defeating Smith. He can't make up his mind, but he's going to go on hammering, manoeuvering, intruding, evading to prove himself right.

What is at any rate the case is that Rhodesian affairs are treated at very great length in Harold Wilson's *The Labour Government 1964–1970*. By contrast, two other foreign policy issues with which his administration had to deal get very scant mention. These two issues were those of Aden (which became critical in 1967) and of the Persian Gulf (which came to the fore in 1968). These two issues, both at the time and in retrospect, could be seen to have great, not to say vital importance—an importance for Britain, far transcending that of Rhodesia. The colony of Aden was in a very disturbed state, being prey to terrorism fomented, financed and armed by the Egyptians who from 1962 onwards maintained sizeable armed forced in the neighbouring Yemen. The disturbances were such that a state of emergency was declared in September 1965. But in February 1966 the Government announced as part of the 'defence cuts' withdrawal from Aden in 1968. This naturally gave the Egyptians and the terrorists they supported every incentive to intensify disorders. This was to make sure that the British would really withdraw, to intimidate all those in Aden and in the adjoining Protectorates who might stand in their way, and to ensure that when the British withdrew, the territory would fall to them. These terrorists eventually split into two factions, the Front for the Liberation of Occupied South Yemen (FLOSY) and the National Liberation Front (NLF). The Egyptians supported FLOSY and opposed NLF. The Six-Day War led to Egyptian retreat from the Yemen, and the terrorists of the NLF gained the upper hand. It is to them that the British gave up territories which they had long ruled, and populations for whom they were, in honour, bound to secure law, order and civilized government. Crossman's entries provide a commentary on the progress of the British abandonment of Aden Colony and the Protected Territories, a withdrawal as 'big, rapid, ruthless, sudden and abrupt', as one could possibly wish for:

12 June 1967

I went straight on to an important meeting of O[verseas] P[olicy and] D[efence] about the package for Southern Arabia, and the kind of military support we will provide for the independent regime we leave behind. It's going to have to keep Vulcan bombers somewhere in the Persian Gulf as a kind of ultimate deterrent. No wonder George Brown and Eddie Shackleton and our new man there, Humphrey Trevelyan, are all nervous lest the methods we choose for withdrawing may commit us to staying.

5 September 1967

We started O.P.D. with a discussion on Aden. George Brown says the Foreign Office now wants to negotiate with the extreme nationalists, the NLF, because FLOSY, the moderate party they'd previously backed, hardly exists now. At once George Wigg was up in arms. This meant betraying everyone in Aden who had promised to support us. George Brown says that there is no alternative and doesn't deny that the F.O. has swung in a few months from one extreme to the other. I reinforced George Wigg's argument that we shall certainly undermine the Federalists in Aden and this will be noticed by the sheikhs in Kuwait and elsewhere. But I agree with George Brown that it can't be helped. 'Anyway,' says George, 'we want to be out of the whole Middle East as far and as fast as we possibly can'. It's possible that the whole very expensive military commitment, including bombers and protective screening for the independent Aden Government, may now go by the board because that Government won't be there. George Wigg thinks it a disaster. I think is first rate and most of the Committe share my view.

27 October 1967

At O.P.D. George Brown started a discussion on Aden by apologizing for having to tell us that we will be out in November instead of January. The rest of the Committee couldn't be more pleased. Really we've been miraculously lucky in Aden—cancelling all our obligations and getting out without a British soldier being killed. But George feels desperate because it's different from what he promised. We spent an hour trying to encourage him.

30 October 1967

The special Cabinet to authorize George Brown's decision to withdraw from Aden a month earlier than planned went according to form. Once again he spent his time apologizing for what all his colleagues considered a wonderfully lucky and fortunate result. That the regime he backed should have been overthrown by terrorists and has forced our speedy withdrawal is nothing but good fortune. It now looks as though we shall get out of Aden without losing a British soldier, chaos will rule soon after we've gone, and there'll be one major commitment cut—thank God.

At the turn of the century, the subject of decadence was very popular among writers. Salisbury, Balfour, Nordau (among many others) tried in their various was to discover what constituted its essential characteristics. Had they been fortunate enough to be acquainted with these entries they would, without doubt, have fastened on them as most precious examples of the phenomenon which fascinated them. We cannot, of course say how they would have explained or accounted for the spectacle of a British Cabinet (representing, so it is believed, a vigorous and ascending class) rubbing their hands with relief over surrender to what they knew to be a gang of terrorists. How did it ever come to this pass, they might have wondered, that a prominent member of the Cabinet, who was successively Scholar of Winchester, and Scholar and Fellow of New College, its sister foundation in

Oxford, author of such treatises as *Socrates*, *Plato Today*, *Government and the Governed*, should be thanking his God for the fortunate prospect of chaos and terrorism in lands over which, even as he was writing, the Union Jack still flew? The question will not be answered, but it will be expeditiously disposed of by the few lines allotted to the episode in the Prime Minister's retrospective:

> Sir Humphrey Trevelyan, the Governor of Aden, flew back to London to urge on the Foreign Secretary and myself a speeding up of the date of our withdrawal. It was successfully accomplished on 30th November, in good order and with no loss of life: a superb [no other epithet would do] operation in which Sir Humphrey Trevelyan and the C-in-C, Sir Micheal le Fanu, deserved high tribute, as did the Foreign Secretary, who handled it coolly and with great skill and imagination throughout. The new People's Republic of South Yemen came into being on that date.

But in Aden more than mere honour was involved. For Britain open and secure sea lanes are a vital necessity; equally vital is a secure supply at a moderate price of oil from the Middle East where British oil companies had extensive and valuable investments. Such interest were far greater than those involved in Rhodesia which looms so large in Mr Wilson's memoirs. The abandonment of Aden where the Soviets inherited the British position increased the potential threat to the sea lanes in the Indian Ocean and the Red Sea, weakened the British ability to ensure the supply of oil at an acceptable price, and put at risk British investment in the oil industry in the Persian Gulf. When the Cabinet took the decsion to evacuate Aden, a junior Minister was despatched to Iran and the Persian Gulf to give firm assurances that Britain had no intention of withdrawing from the Persian Gulf. Some three months later the same messenger was sent again to inform the recipients of his recent assurances that Britain was, after all withdrawing, and pretty quickly, from the Gulf. This was the outcome of a decision on spending cuts taken by the Cabinet at the beginning of January 1968 in which a large majority headed by the Prime Minister voted that withdrawal from the Gulf should take place by

19

1970–1. This decision, which Mr Heath's Conservative administration confirmed, made Britain powerless to resist the arbitrary and extortionate increase in the price of oil which OPEC was shortly afterwards to impose, or to protect British assets—which were quite substantial—against nationalization pretty much on terms dictated by the governments concerned. We learn from the *Diaries* that in Ocotber 1967 the Government was given a paper composed by some officials which phrophesied that when all Middle Eastern oil was nationalized the price would go up by 75 per cent. It is impossible to know why this figure was hit upon. If the production of oil was to be fully controlled by the producer states, and if these states were banded together in a cartel, then (as was shortly to be established) they could impose any price which they chose to charge for their commodity. The figure of 75 per cent was an arbitrary fancy, something plucked out of the air, and like similar meaningless figures of houses to be built and 'growth' to be attained, the concomitant of an arbitrary style of government.

The decisions on Aden and the Gulf were two of the most important, if not the two most important, foreign policy decisions taken by Mr Wilson's administration, and their consequences which are probably yet to be fully worked out, could be nothing but deleterious to British interests. It is undoubtedly true that disagreeable and perhaps even potentially disastrous decisions have sometimes to be taken, because there is absolutely no alternative—because any conceivable alternative is manifestly worse. This was not the case here. As the *Diaries* indicate the decision was the outcome of a doctrinaire conviction that overseas commitments are always both wrong and unprofitable, that money spent on defence is bread taken from the workers' mouths and of a process of crude bargaining between Ministers in which the probable consequences of staying in, or leaving Aden and the Gulf, were the last thing to be considered. Crossman's entries for 27 December 1967 and 4 January 1968, giving details of this bargaining are explicit enough. In the entry for 27 December Crossman describes how he had been brooding over the cuts in public expenditure which the sterling crisis was making necessary and how

Harold [Wilson] and Roy [Jenkins] are now firmly committed to the view that we have to slaughter some sacred
cows in order to appease the bankers. When I challenged
Roy about this the other night he said that £40 million saved
in prescription charges is worth £140 million anywhere else
because of the impression it makes on the bankers. . . . Well,
I've been thinking a lot about this slaughter of the sacred
cows and I've come to the conclusion that if we are going to
hold the Party together it is essential that we must have
some major cuts in defence, i.e. some slaughter of right-
wing sacred cows. When I gave Roy dinner at Lockets
before Christmas the idea of balance which I sold him was
withdrawal from East of Suez and cancellation of the
purchase of F-111 in exchange for two domestic cows.

Horse-trading between the Lord President of the Council
and the Chancellor of the Exchequer (not in a smoke-filled
backroom but in a posh restaurant) would no doubt be
justified as being in the public interest and as conducing to the
survivial of the Government. The two are of course not
identical, but men in power no doubt find it difficult not to
confuse the two. But the confusion is particularly incongruous
in someone like Crossman whose *Diaries* are redolent with the
confident rhetoric of self-assured philanthropy and tough
benevolence. Ministers' decisions, as they are described to us,
may be arbitrary, but their intentions are of the highest. As we
persevere with the *Diaries*, however, this shining and beautiful
picture, like the picture of Dorian Gray, suffers gradual but
drastic change. Ministers using power in the service of principle come insensibly to resemble the skilled operators of
eighteenth-century politics, come to seem as so many Wal-
poles, so many Henry Foxes dispensing Treasury favours. Of
the Prime Minister Crossman observes in December 1966 that
'His main aim is to stay in office. That's the real thing and for
that purpose he will use almost any trick or gimmick if he can
only do it.' He also succinctly formulates the conventional
wisdom—and it comes straight, as you might say, from the
horse's mouth—that a party in power can win an election from
Whitehall. And its weapons in such a contest are incomparably more powerful and far-reaching than what the Whig

oligarchs had at their disposal. The very same devices, namely of demand management, fine-tuning etc. which a beneficent providence has ordained for perpetual happiness and prosperity. But for all that modern Governments do not disdain the traditional, grosser and less scientific contrivances. Thus, we observe Crossman as Minister of Housing resorting to what is vulgarly known as the gerrymander in order delicately and simultaneously to provide for the welfare both of the public and the Party:

16 January 1965

One of the things I had been thinking about in the last fortnight is how to get the Boundary Commission's directive reshaped and refurbished, not merely politically where all I have to do is prevent thirty or forty Labour seats going to the Tories, but also in terms of the efficiency of local government.

24 August 1966

Come what may, no decision would be taken about a local government boundary without the parliamentary repercussions being fully considered and without my trying to shield the Labour position. I started by protecting Bert Bowden's position in Leicester, and then I dealt with Nottingham and Middlesbrough in the same way. All the way through I think I managed to combine a sound local government policy with an extremely shrewd defence of Labour's parliamentary interests.

Look, again, at these scenes from the bazaar of politics. In August 1965 the Minister of Power asks that the price of coal should be increased:

George Brown's reply was that at the present juncture an increase would be tantamount to political suicide. He reminded us that coal prices had not been increased for four years under the Tories. How could we risk the T.U.C. blowing up in our faces at their Congress in September? Callaghan turned round and said, 'Some time we have to face reality. That time has come now. We ought to put the prices up and keep the wages steady.' George Brown replied, 'That will be the end of the incomes policy.' Callaghan: 'There comes a point when you have to do it.' Brown: 'You've no right to talk like that to me here.'

See now the Prime Minister bargaining with the farmers about the size of their subvention by the State:

> [The Prime Minister] then launched into the inside story of the agreed agricultural price review. . . . Apparently Harold had sent for Woolley, the President of the N[ational] F[armers'] U[nion], and told him there was a chance of settlement. If he would come down from his £27 million, we would move up from our original £20 million. With this authority Peart and Woolley clinched it at £23 million.

Mercifully, this is not the politics of 'who whom'; rather the politics of 'how much', of fixers who in their coarse way reckon they know the price of everyone and have an eye for a good quick bargain, of ins and outs, of Tapers and Tadpoles. Let us look in on a Cabinet meeting in between elections of 1964 and 1966:

11 February 1965

Each Minister has been told that he is only allowed the increased estimate allocated to his Department by the Tory White Paper last year. This means that over the next four, if we keep the priorities unchanged, Transport would get an increase of 30 per cent, Education 30 per cent and Housing only 10 per cent. The reason is simple. In order to win votes in that last period before the election the Tories were prepared to announce a rapid expansion of higher education, a huge hospital-building programme, a hugh road-building programme. The one social service they felt it was popular to cut back was public-sector housing. . . .

It was my contention that whereas the other Ministers could fairly be asked to be content with the amount of money in the Tory estimates, this was quite unreasonable in the case of housing where we were pledged to reverse the Tory policy and expand council-house building.

Thus, through the open-handed distribution of welfare, housing and other benefits a pleasing harmony is established between principle and practice, between the welfare of the people and that of the Government. Godlike the Minister declares his pleasure. He gives his bounty to some and denies it to others. All-knowing, clement, merciful, when night comes, he sleeps the sleep of the just. Before his translation, when he was a journalist, his articles used to pursue Crossman in his sleep and he used to 'wake up early in the morning in a panic about whether I had done something wrong?' Now these fears and trepidations are gone: 'Indeed I sleep all the more soundly for having had those decisions to take during the day, for having written "O.K." on that policy document, for having been a man of action in that sense of the word.' When he sits in his house of Prescote near Banbury and pulls out 'a mass of papers from the red box and see that I have to decide on the boundaries of Coventry or on where to let Birmingham have its new housing land, I find these decisions easy, pleasant, and I take them in a fairly light-hearted way.' In short, 'Life for me personally is going magnificently.' But our Minister is no mere man of the closet. Like Haroun al-Rashid, he goes about among his subjects to see to their welfare and protect them from his remote and dilatory servants. In September 1969, while Secretary of State for Social Services, he makes a visitation to an outlying province:

Newcastle really was a great day, tremendous, invigorating, exciting, just the kind of thing I can do. I have shown them that a Minister does not just sit in London and sign papers, he comes to the spot and sees for himself. I think, too, that our staff have seen the appalling image they have, because everybody agreed when we discussed delay that three months in every year could be attributed to the Department's asking questions and holding things up. The officials have learnt a great deal and I think they were impressed by me and by what the Minister can do by making a personal impact.

24

Power is the elixir of youth. In the weekend following this visitation the Minister is moved to note: 'how I revel at this life of ministerial decisions, an opportunity that came right at the end of my career, when I never thought it would.'

> Is it not passing brave to be a King
> And ride in triumph through Persepolis?

And what enhances this marvellous well-being is Prescote Manor and its five hundred acres where life 'gets lovelier the longer it goes on'. Here he 'enjoys his creature comforts, his food, his drink, his fitted carpets, the sense of spaciousness on the farm, the sense of belonging to the village without any great obligation. These are the things I intensely and enormously enjoy.' 'Here,' the son of the High Court judge declares, playing at the workman who has risen in the world, 'one acquires bourgeois values'. Free from worries about money, and with a constantly accumulating capital, anxious to preserve Prescote for his posterity, he becomes

> very doubtful whether the fiscal changes introduced by Jim Callaghan with the assistance of Nicky Kaldor have not been clumsy, academic interventions in the economy. I'm becoming more and more uneasy about the fact that people like Harold are so confident they can intervene in the economy by means of investment allowances and be sure that this will stimulate private investment. The evidence at Prescote gives us support for this view. I'm still very doubtful about the new Industrial Expansion Bill which Wedgy is working out with Harold because I feel that such a Bill will enable him to take decisions which neither he nor his civil servants are really capable of taking. As someone who helps to run a small farming business, I can see rather more clearly the dangers of the kind of intervention by amateurs advised by civil servants which Harold believes in so much.

But all this does not go without some worries and scruples. How may a Socialist justify paying privately, as he does, for medical advice? Again,

How come that I, a Labour Minister, should be spending well over £400 on a family holiday, nearly £4,000 on a swimming bath and nearly £300 on a garnet necklace as a birthday present for my wife?

Crossman's answer is that he is simply joining in the flight out of money into things—a flight occasioned by the inflation which undermines the social order. But that the social order has been challenged and undermined during his period in office, he writes in April 1969, 'is what makes the life we live interesting', and makes him feel less disconsolate about the failures of the Government. It is, still, a relief that the swimming bath, which 'looks very large indeed', is 'thank goodness ... inside the garden where it can scarcely be seen'.

Are Prescote and his belief in left-wing socialism compatible? Crossman is challenged on this by his brother, a 'fierce old Tory', and his answer is that the two are compatible provided he is ready to vote for high taxation and even for a policy of confiscation. Crossman has also another excuse. His socialism, he declares, has never been based 'on a moral or egalitarian philosophy', it is all an expression of his 'bump of irreverence', of his conviction that 'governments and establishments are fools'; he hopes that perhaps this irreverence (which, as we have seen, has taken him far) will not necessarily be blunted 'by the marvellous kind of life we're able to live here at Prescote'. In any case he is not against privilege; on the contrary, he wants everybody to share in it!

Whether he himself or readers of his *Diaries* can believe this is impossible to say. But the fact is that this socialist in office gradually begins to feel as remote from the common man as any of those Whig grandees whose outlook and style (so different from Crossman's) Lord David Cecil has memorably evoked in the opening pages of *The Young Melbourne*. The 'amplitude of life' which Crossman enjoys at Prescote cuts him off, he feels, from the vast mass of people and particulary from the people of his constituency in Coventry: 'I feel it and they feel it too.' But just as running a farm led Crossman to doubt the efficacy and the good sense of the policies which his colleagues favoured, so after some years in office he began to feel that the certainties which had sustained him in his political life were a broken reed. His experience as a Minister, he writes in December 1967, 'has really shaken that ultimate faith in the political educability of man or, more deeply even, in the possibility of a government whose decisions are taken by ordinary people.' And so we take leave of the Minister, now nearing the end of his political life. His mood one of mellow and lofty disillusion, he surveys as from a great height the multitude over whose petty concerns Providence has charged him with the duty of keeping watch:

> I can't help wondering [he writes in April 1968] if the whole of my life has been lived in vain and if that is not the reason why I'm so glad to have given up adult education and journalism and taken on a spell as a professional politician—a member of the ruling establishment. How ironically suitable our position here at Prescote is to this task. Here are Anne and I, people of affluence, running a big farm and therefore just suitable for being members of the establishment. Is it hypocrisy to say this? No, because I've abandoned the aims in which I believed in the W[orkers'] E[ducational] A[ssociation] and I now accept that the settled and just management of society by a progressive oligarchy is the best we can hope for.

Whatever Crossman's doubts about the political educability of the common man, it remains an open question whether this passage testifies to the success of his own long and expensive political education.

Lord Halifax, Conservative

Let us now praise famous men
Ecclesiasticus, Chapter XLIV

EDWARD Frederick Lindley Wood, first Baron Irwin of Kirby Underdale, third Viscount Halifax, of Monk Bretton, first Earl of Halifax, Knight of the Garter, Order of Merit, was born in 1881 and died in 1959. The Earl of Birkenhead has written his biography, long and leisurely, full but not fulsome, its occasional longueurs redeemed by a wealth of curious detail and by sound judgement and common sense. Halifax's grandfather was Charles Wood, a notable Secretary of State for India who married the daughter of Lord Grey of the Reform Bill and was created Viscount in 1866. His father, the second Vicount, was a High Churchman and President of the English Church Union from 1868 to 1919. He was also a notable amateur of ghost stories. His mother was Lady Agnes Courtenay, daughter of Lord Devon of Powderham Castle in Devonshire, whose lineage was so ancient as to cause Gibbon to write, 'The purple of three Emperors who have reigned at Constantinople will authorise or excuse a digression on the origins and singular fortunes of the House of Courtenay.'

He went to Eton and then to Christ Church, where he took a First in History and was elected in 1903 a Fellow of All Souls. 'Questions as to whether Wood was merely an intensely religious young man with an average conventional mind could now be answered with finality: "He took a First History and won an All Souls Fellowship"'. 'There was already apparent

in his manner the effulgence of a devastating natural charm.'
He gave an impression not of arrogance, but of patrician
detachment, and no trace of *angst* disturbed the serenity of his
nature. 'In January 1904 he was provided with a much-needed
experience of the seamy side of life by accompanying a judge
on circuit in North Wales as marshal, an excursion which must
have considerably broadened his mind.' He wrote in a letter to
a friend: 'Here we have got some rather interesting cases,
wounding, rape, arson, etc. My judge has already done one
very good thing—given a night poacher three years. Good
job'. In 1904 he also went on a tour round the world which
must also have broadened his mind. When he came back, he
devoted himself to writing a life of Keble. 'The book is written
in adequate but uninspiring prose' and remains his only
attempt at historical authorship. He lightened his labours on
Keble by the raising and hunting of a new pack of harriers at
Garrowby, his Yorkshire estate. The pack proved undisciplined and he 'took ruthless measures against the offenders.
Five couples, the ringleaders, were destroyed by the vet, and he
began breeding his own hounds from a Devonshire strain'.

He stood for Parliament at Ripon in the Conservative
interest in the 1910 election, and won against his Liberal
opponent. He was again successful in the 1911 election. 'In
spite of his victory, Edward disliked electioneering and constituency work', and it was therefore fortunate that he was
subsequently 'spared these formalities'; he was returned unop-
posed in the elections of 1918, 1922, 1923 and 1924. In 1925
he was raised to the peerage, and thereafter sat as of right in his
country's legislature.

On the outbreak of war in 1914 he joined his regiment, the
Queen's Own Yorkshire Dragoons, in which he held the rank
of Captain, and remained on active service in France until the
autumn of 1917, when, at the invitation of Auckland Geddes,
he became Deputy Director of the Labour Supply Department
in the Ministry of National Service. He undertook this long
period of military service in spite of a serious physical dis-
ability, for he had been born with his left arm atrophied and
without a hand. He believed in fighting the war to a finish. In
October 1918 he wrote in a letter to his father 'I am dreadfully

afraid of events turning out in a sense to let the Germans off, and it goes much against the grain not to burn some of their towns, etc'. He also regarded conscientious objectors with unmitigated contempt and commended to the House of Commons the summary American practice of dressing them in scarlet and making them walk the street.

In 1920 Lord Milner offered him, and he accepted, the Governor-Generalship of South Africa, but the offer had to be withdrawn because the South African Government did not consider him eminent enough. In 1921 he was appointed Under-Secretary of State at the Colonial Office, and in this capacity made a tour of the British West Indies. When the Coalition broke up in the autumn of 1922 and leading Conservatives like Chamberlain, Balfour, Churchill and Birkenhead remained faithful to Lloyd George, Bonar Law filled the gap by promoting some of the abler Conservative Under-Secretaries in the Coalition Government. He therefore became a member of the Cabinet and President of the Board of Education.

He occupied this office twice, from 1922 to 1924 and from 1932 to 1935. But his 'imagination was not stirred by the subject of public education', 'his heart was not in it', he had 'little, if any, interest in educational problems past or present'. He was aloof towards his civil servants, used a senior civil servant to telephone the barber to arrange for his hair to be cut, and asked the Board to sanction a new Church School on his estate at Hickleton, for 'We want a school to train them up for servants and butlers'. In 1933, however, he accepted election as Chancellor of the University of Oxford. When Baldwin formed his second administration in October 1924 he became Minister of Agriculture, and it fell to him to steer through the House of Commons the Agricultural Returns Bill and the Tithe Bill; in retrospect, he looked upon his post as one 'of almost complete futility and frustration'. In November 1925 he was translated to the Viceroyalty of India.

It was George V who had suggested his name 'and the suggestion had met with the immediate approval of the Cabinet'. He reached Bombay on 1 April 1926, and was welcomed by the outgoing Viceroy and Lady Reading. 'They found viceregal life at first a trifle depressing' and the Vicereine wrote in her diary, 'It also gets on my nerves to be called "Your Excellency", which I am sure is overdone by the ex-Reading staff. One hardly ever calls the Q and K "Your Majesty"; it seems to me rather vulgar'. By encouraging these habits the Readings clearly showed that they were not patrician. In his first two years of office 'the Viceroy had followed the conventional road and attempted no sorties down its inviting by-ways'. But the latter half of his Viceroyalty was to see him take a bold initiative and invite Gandhi for talks which issued in the well-known Irwin-Gandhi Pact of 1931. The Statutory Commission on India, the Chairman of which was Sir John Simon, began its consideration of India's constitutional future in 1928 amidst the agitations and protests of the Congress Party. While it was still deliberating on its report the Viceroy became convinced that it was necessary to make a gesture drawing the Congress and its allied parties back into co-operation. His biographer writes that 'beneath a modest manner lay a strong belief in his own judgement', that 'he was not easily dissuaded from a course of action', and that he 'took a long time to reach a decision but, once made he never pondered it afterwards and was seldom deflected from its course'. He now came to believe that, as his biographer puts it, 'the old proprietary conception of Empire, that benevolent paternalism of Victorian days, had passed away for ever, to be replaced by the new Imperial ideal of partnership'. He shared these convictions with Wedgewood Benn, the Secretary of State, and he was authorized to issue an Announcement in the autumn of 1929 offering Dominion Status in some unspecified future. The recommendations of the Simon Commission, published in June 1930, which were to be the basis of a Round Table Conference, fell therefore still-born, but to no purpose, since the Viceroy's Announcement did not pacify the Congress. He then set out to win over Gandhi. It was the opinion of the Liberal leader Sastri that Gandhi had to be wooed like a capricious woman, that he was a 'philosophical anarch' who could not be caught and held by ordinary argument. 'If you told him, Sastri had said, that his actions would lead to chaos, he would reply that only by chaos would we get back to natural society. His most dominant quality, thought Sastri, was vanity, unconscious but not less real.' In the Viceroy's estimation this was not so; his biographer denies that they knelt down together in prayer, but when asked if Gandhi had been tiresome, the Viceroy replied, 'Some people found Our Lord very tiresome'. Sastri's worldly wisdom did not impress him, and in a letter to his father summed up his tortuous interlocutor thus

> I kept on asking myself all the time 'Was the man completely sincere', and I think as our conversation went on that I came to feel about this in rather double fashion. I came to have no doubt whatever that, if Mr Gandhi gave me his word on any point, that word was absolutely secure, and that I could trust it absolutely. On the other hand, I found what had always been my impression being confirmed, namely, that though intentionally he was completely sincere, yet in some matters he was the victim of unconscious self-deception.

They signed the Irwin-Gandhi Pact which called off Civil Disobedience and pledged the Congress to take part in constitutional negotiations. Barely a year later his successor, Willingdon, found Gandhi unable or unwilling to get the Congress to co-operate, and the Pact proved of no avail. Irwin's term as Vicerory ended in 1931. He came back to 'civic welcomes and freedom of cities, the acclaim of universities, honorary degrees, and an Hon. D.C.L. conferred by the Vice-Chancellor of Oxford on one he addressed as *vir sagacissime*'.

When Baldwin formed his third administration, he became for five months, from June to November 1935, Secretary of State for War, then Lord Privy Seal, then, in June 1937, Lord President of the Council in Chamberlain's administration, and on Eden's resignation in February 1938, Foreign Secretary. He was 'extremely reluctant' to accept this office; one of the first impressions of his subordinates was 'that he was ill at ease in this office', that he did not find the study of foreign affairs 'a matter of absorbing interst', that he was doing his work at the Foreign Office 'as an unpleasant duty', 'had no strong convictions about it', that he took a long time to make a decision, and once it was reached 'his mind hardened like cement'; he accepted the Foreign Office as he had the Board of Education, 'without enthusiasm', and allowed the Prime Minister to make his policy for him: on one occasion Cadogan, the head of the

Foreign Office, noted in his Diary that Chamberlain 'hypnotised' Halifax.

His knowledge of Europe was 'clearly' limited, he had never read *Mein Kampf*, and 'the seamy side of life was to him', in spite of his Welsh perambulation of 1904, 'a closed book'. While still Lord President, in November 1937, he went to shoot foxes with Goering, and asked to be received by Hitler, whom he assured that, 'taking England as a whole, there was a much greater degree of understanding of all his work on that side [*i.e.* the blocking of Communism] than there had been some time ago' and that there could be 'possible alterations in the European order which might be destined to come about with the passage of time'. He found Hitler 'very sincere' and 'believing everything he said'; Goering he found 'frankly attractive, like a great schoolboy, full of life and pride in what he was doing'. He, the patrician descended from 'three Emperors who had reigned at Constantinople', does not seem to have felt about Hitler and Goering as he felt about the poacher he had seen sentenced in his youth, or about his undisciplined hounds whom he had so severely chastised, or about the conscientious objectors whom he had wanted to parade in scarlet. He did not look down on these jumped-up scoundrels, as he had looked down on his respectable civil servants and on the yokels of Hickleton for whom he had desired just enough instruction to fit them to become servants and butlers. In 1939 he paid a visit to Mussolini, and his abiding memory was 'of passing through ranks of Blackshirts standing to attention with drawn daggers into which he felt in constant danger of running his throat'. But here, too, sincerity redeemed everything: 'The atmosphere was most friendly and easy. My impressions of what I expected to find were quite at fault. Mussolini spoke quite quietly, very reasonably, and so far as I could judge, with sincerity'. Lord Brand wrote, 'Although Edward was very clever the world was an innocent world to him'. He seems to have emerged with innocence unblemished from his odyssey among the cut-throats of Europe. 'My withers', he told John Wheeler-Bennett [*à propos* the Munich episode], with that old difficulty in pronouncing his r's, 'are completely unwung'. Not only innocent, he was also prudent and cautious. While an undergraduate, he was a member of the Christ Church club Loders. On Mafeking night each member drank a bottle of port, and all became completely drunk 'but Edward, with innate caution, went outside and tickled his throat to make himself sick'. His biographer gives an extract from a speech of 1937 made in the House of Lords on British policy towards German ambitions in Central Europe which he describes as 'containing several trap-doors of escape'. 'If we are unable to define beforehand what might be our attitude to hypothetical complications in Central or Eastern Europe', ran this admirably nubiferous speech, 'this is not to say that we disinterest oursleves in the fate of these parts of Europe. We have repeatedly maintained our determination to carry out to the best of our ability our obligations under the Covenant, and if these obligations are not capable of achievement with precise exactitiude, that is a feature, and I venture to think not an accidental feature—of the Covenant itself'. Lastly, his politic circumspection may be illuminated by a letter of his written towards the beginning of Hitler's war and quoted in Iain Macleod's biography of Chamberlain, in which he advised against Hore-Belisha's appointment to the Ministry of Information because Hore-Belisha was a Jew.

In the grim days of May 1940 there was talk of his becoming Prime Minister. A letter from R. A. Butler discloses that the Labour Party said they would serve under him: 'Dalton said there was no other choice but you'. The prospect of his becoming Prime Minister gave him 'a bad stomach ache'. Blessed queasiness.

Churchill retained him as Foreign Secretary and member of the War Cabinet. As Martin Gilbert recounts in the fifth volume of his biography of Churchill, twice in the dark days at the end of May 1940 Halifax forcefully tried to compel Churchill to negotiate with Hitler through Mussolini acting as mediator. It was an offer which simple could not be refused: 'it would save the country from avoidable disaster.' Clearly no queasiness there.

Churchill appointed him to the Washington Embassy in which he served from 1941 to 1946. In the United States he stoically endured the familiarity of newspaper reporters and the loud bonhomie of democratic politicians. He seems to have become popular.

'He really believed', writes his biographer, 'that privilege was a good thing, and that men in his position and of his world had the background that warranted their being in positions of authority'. See, however, *Daniel,* chapter V, verse 27.

Conservatism and
the Conservative Party

THE TERM *Conservative*, according to the Oxford English Dictionary, is the 'most common current designation of one of the two great English political parties, the characteristic principle of which is the maintenance of institutions political and ecclesiastical'. However out of date this definition may be today—and its refereence to the 'maintenance of institutions political and ecclesiastical' may now raise either a rueful or an ironic smile—yet it still remains the case, as it was in 1891, when this definition was published, that the Conservative party is 'one of the two great English political parties'. It is one of the historic parties in British politics, and neither these politics—which may be described as parliamentary and constitutionalist—nor the party can of course be understood apart from each other.

But if the Conservative party is one of the historic parties of British politics, yet as a party with an identifiable and continuous history in parliament and in the country it dates only from the last century, from that transformation of British society and politics of which the Refrom Act of 1832 was both the herald and one of the agents. To understand what the Conservative party is today, or has been in any period since 1832, it is necessary to have a detailed knowledge of the relevant transactions within the party, and between it and its rivals. This knowledge is no doubt laborious and difficult to acquire, but it is in principle attainable—and for certain periods is indeed already available.

This continuity, this continuous identity over something like a century and a half, as may be supposed has fostered in Conservatives certain loyalties, inculcated in them certain attitudes and expectations, and taught them to organize and interpret their political experience according to certain general notions. These loyalties, attitudes and notions taken together can loosely be called Conservatism. Conservatism, then, is the outcome of activity in various circumstances and over a long period of the Conservative party, an abridgement, and so to speak a codification, of this activity. Conservatism follows and does not precede the existence of a Conservative party. It is a natural attempt by a body with a long continuous existence to articulate and make intelligible to itself its own character. As a general rule, the history of ideas is more difficult and more treacherous than the history of events, and the generation and formulation of Conservatism—which is a body of ideas—and its influence on Conservative political activity is thus more difficult to detect and to follow than the details of the activity itself.

This abridgement and codification has to be expressed in general terms, and Conservatism therefore easily takes on the appearance of a 'theory' or a 'doctrine' governing the actions of the Conservative party and helping to explain its operations. Since at least 1832 British politics have become increasingly popular in character, in the sense that political leaders have had to address and appeal to an ever increasing mass of voters. The political rhetoric which such an audience evokes is a rhetoric of slogan and rough generalization; this leads to the temptation to explain and justify Conservative political action by Conservatism. One can go further, and yield to the even greater temptation of speaking as though the Conservative party throughout its triumphs and vicissitudes was but the emanation, or the exemplification of a permanent and unchanging Conservatism.

And if we follow the elaboration of Conservatism as a doctrine, we do in fact see attempts, more or less successful, to identify a thread of Conservatism supposed to run through British history since at least the seventeenth century. Disraeli's is probably the most influential of these attempts to endow Conservatism with an ancient pedigree. Shelburne, Bolingbroke and Charles I were those who principally formulated this Conservatism *avant la lettre* which he claimed to have discovered. But if we look at the record of these and other figures who are supposed to have put together a theory of Conservatism, we have to conclude that not only was there no continuity between them, not only were their characters and preoccupations highly different from one another, but also that the world in which they acted and the problems which they confronted were far removed from what Conservatives had to deal with after 1832. But what gave plausibility to this kind of historical account was the generally prevalent notion that the Conservatives were, in some sense, the political heirs of the Tories. This is what we gather from the language of John Miller writing in the *Quarterly Review* of January 1831, in a passage widely credited with giving currency to the term 'Conservative': '... we now are as we have always been decidedly and conscientiously attached to what is called the Tory, and which might with more propriety be called the Conservative party ...'.[1] In avowing his attachment to 'what is called the Tory party', did the writer mean to range himself with those who, in the Exclusion crises, were by their opponents derisively called Tories, or did he mean to favour Jacobite or non-juring principles? Manifestly not. To him the Tory party must have been first of all those men whose politics and political activity he so clearly admired. This kind of attachment is very natural and does not need doctrinal justification; for as Hume said, 'When men are once inlisted on opposite sides, they contract an affection to the persons with whom they are united, and an animosity against their antagonists'. The men to whom the writer was referring were chiefly the colleagues and successors of Pitt The Younger. These men who, as Namier pointed out, went by the name of 'Mr Pitt's friends', were certainly not Tories in the sense that Bolingbroke or Shippen, Atterbury or Swift, were Tories. If they were—loosely—to be called Tories, it is because Pitt's oppon-

---

[1] Although this passage has been generally attributed to J. W. Croker, according to the *Quarterly Review* of April 1909, p. 749, the article of 1831 in which the passage occurs, 'The State of the British Empire', was from the pen of John Miller.

ent, Fox, has successfully laid exclusive claim to the appellation Whig. If Fox and his friends were the Whigs, then it was perhaps natural to call Pitt and his friends the Tories. The appellation was to the Foxites all the more tempting in that it could be used to represent Pitt and his friends as the opponents of popular liberties, and thus as the heirs of those who, a hundred years before, had not resisted monarchical encroachment on these liberties.

But Pitt himself had of course been a Whig, and we may thus say that the coming together of 'Mr Pitt's friends' and their acting politically as a group, was the outcome of Whig dissensions which the new issues of the French revolution transformed into a Whig civil war. And it is at this period, surely, that a view of politics was formulated, which provided 'Mr Pitt's friends' with an articulate, systematic and cogent expression of their differences with Fox and his followers. This formulation immensely influential as it proved to be, constituted a touchstone by which to discriminate between what came to be called Conservatism and its rivals in British politics. This formulation was the work of Burke, himself a Whig, a name which he never abandoned, and indeed regarded as 'dear to the majority of the people'. That not only the Conservative party but Conservatism also is at its origin the outcome of a Whig civil war is strikingly illustrated by the title of one of Burke's writings of this period, the pamphlet, namely, which he published in 1791 and called *An Appeal from the New to the Old Whigs*.

During a long political career Burke said and wrote a multitude of things, a great many of which are quite tangential to the issues with which Conservatism was to be concerned, while others are perhaps potentially at variance with it. But what concerns us here is the steady undeviating vision he came to have after 1790 of the destructiveness of a certain kind of politics which was then beginning to be manifest in Europe, and the ravages of which have now spread over the whole world. Burke's vision of the demonic character of this politics can be concisely indicated by two short quotations. In *Thoughts on French Affairs* which he published in 1791, Burke declared that the French revolution was different from anything of this kind in Europe, which hitherto had been brought about 'upon principles merely political'; while 'the events then taking place in France constituted 'a revolution of doctrine and theoretic dogma'. Five years later, in *Letters on Regicide Peace*, he declared:

> We are in a war of a *peculiar* nature. It is not with an ordinary community, which is hostile or friendly as passion or as interest may veer about: not with a state which makes war through wantonness, and abandons it through lassitude. We are at war with a system, which by its essence, is inimical to all other governments, and which makes peace or war, as peace and war may best contribute to their subversion. It is with an *armed doctrine* that we are at war. It has, by its essence, a faction of opinion, and of interest, and of enthusiasm, in every country.

Awareness of this—of the difference between, on the one hand, ordinary politics in which conflict is the outcome of passion and interest and therefore may be settled by moderation and compromise, and on the other, the deadly, never-to-be-assuaged *acharnement* of the armed doctrine—distinguishes Conservatism from other varieties of British political thought. Distinguishes? Is the present tense really in order? That it distinguished Conservatism before 1914 is not in doubt. One has only to read Salisbury's public or private writings to be persuaded that there was here a firm grasp of the nature and limits of power, and of how destructive of order and security the activist assertion of principle can be. But does such an awareness distinguish Conservatism now? A book by Angus Maude, entitled *The Common Problem* is devoted to Conservatism and future Conservative policy. It is full of intelligent and sometimes penetrating disquisitions on the welfare state, proper educational policy, party and parliamentary politics. But the reader notes with interest that what used to be generally considered the common problem *par excellence*, namely the security of the realm, is hardly mentioned, and this in a world where armed doctrines are more than ever on the rampage. Is this, one wonders, symptomatic of Conservatism today? In another notable book on Conservatism, *For Conservatives Only*, the author, Lord

Coleraine, remarks that 'The historical importance of Suez for the British people was not that they were defeated, but that they were duped. They turned from the facts to a world of pure illusion.' Along with Pitt, as much as Pitt, Churchill who led the Conservatives in the last phase of a chequered career, must be celebrated as 'the pilot who weathered the storm'. But it can hardly be said that Conservatims as a body of thought took the full measure of these armed doctrines which, after 1917 or 1933 or 1945, appeared quite as deadly as the most rabid Jacobinism. Yalta did not call forth the equivalent of Burke's *Letters on a Regicide Peace*. This failure in modern Conservatism has perhaps helped the triumph of make-believe which Lord Coleraine deplores.

It is not easy to know why there was this failure of nerve in Conservative thought. It was not loss of empire, for it was clearly manifest in the 1920s and 1930s, at a time when the British empire was at its most extensive. It was not banishment from office, for Conservatives held office almost continuously between the wars. It could not have been the Whiggery

> That never looked out of the eye of a Saint
> Or out of drunkard's eye

which Herbert Butterfield has argued to be part of the heritage of every Englishman. For though essentially common-sensical, and thus perhaps slow to grasp the full horror of a Hitler or a Stalin, Whigs have not been diffident or apologetic over the exercise of power. One is driven to the thought that it is the war of 1914 which is to a large extent responsible. It seems to have demoralized British intellectual and official classes so profoundly that the country may still be said to be suffering from its effects today. Hence, perhaps, this readiness to escape into 'pure illusion' of which Lord Coleraine speaks.

What other form has Conservative illusion taken? As we have seen, the lexicographer in 1891 declared the term Conservative to apply to 'one of the two great English political parties'. The other political party he had in mind was of course the Liberal party. If this part of his definition still retains its truth, this is merely by accident. Through a whole chapter of accidents which no one in 1891 or 1910 could have imagined, the Liberal party was destroyed and Labour in due course confronted the Conservatives as the other 'great' political party in the state. Modifications in a body of thought like Conservatism, which arises out of, and remains concerned with practical politics, are dialectical. In other words, what Conservatism asserts or denies at any particular moment is much influenced by what rival political groups are denying or asserting. When Labour replaced the Liberals as the other 'great' political party in Britian, the effect on Conservatism was bound to be profound. What this effect turned out to be became fully manifest in the years after 1945. Nor is it necessary to describe it at great length. Suffice it to say that expenditure on 'welfare' has remained at the same level if it has not increased, under Conservative as under Labour administration, and that this is defended and justified as good Conservative doctrine. This is done by taking up and developing Disraeli's notion of Tory Democracy. Disraeli's mythopoeic activities gave Conservatism a fictitious pedigree to provide historical justification for what he believed to be the correct Conservative strategy in an industrial country with a large and increasing working-class. He wanted to show that the Conservative party was and always had been the national party, while its opponents and rivals merely pandered to narrow sectional interests. This was the case in the seventeenth century and it remained so two hundred years later. Disraeli's strategy and his doctrinal justification of it may be gathered from a brief passage in a letter of 1840. 'I entirely agree with you', he wrote to the popular leader Charles Attwood, 'that an union between the Conservative party and the Radical masses offers the only means by which we can preserve the Empire. Their interests are identical; united they form the nation; and their division has only permitted a miserable minority, under the specious name of the People, to assail all rights of property and person.' Whatever part the slogan of Tory Democracy had in Conservative successes under Disraeli and later—and it is doubtful whether it had any appreciable part—it is at least clear that Conservatives before 1945 did not use it to advocate or justify the so-called Welfare State or, as it is so expressively called in French, the *Etat-Providence*. It was far otherwise after the Second World War. In his book mentioned above, Lord Coleraine gives a brief and cogent history of Conservative welfarism during this period, and a statement by Mr Heath at the 1969 Conservative Party Conference which he reports suggests that its fortunes are as bright as ever: 'He (Mr Heath) suggested that Mr Wilson's claim thus to have increased expenditure on the social services (by between 42 and 48 per cent) did not give a true picture of the facts: the last Conservative government, Mr Heath said, was increasing welfare expenditure, at the end of its term of office, at a rate even higher than that which Mr Harold Wilson had been able to achieve.' In the 1983 elections, Mrs Thatcher similarly declared that, not the nation's health, but rather a collectivist organization, the National Health Service, was safe with the Conservatives. And not only the National Health Service, for public expenditure in 1983–4 (and the taxation to pay for it) is higher than under her predecessors, no less than 46 per cent of this expenditure going on 'Welfare'. In a modern industrial society, health and welfare should of course be assured to the citizens. But is there any reason why their provision should be centralized; why the citizens of what is, after all, a prosperous country, should be deprived of the freedom to choose; should have a large part of their income extracted from them, to be spent on their behalf at the discretion of ministers and the multitude of clerks, authorities, quangos, who crowd in their train?

But the question, which this and numerous similar post-1945 statements by Conservative leaders elude, is whether Conservative welfarism is not a contradiction in terms; whether welfarism does not inevitably issue, by way of progressive taxation and inflation, in a society in which, as Lord Coleraine strikingly says, only two classes exist: government and the governed. A regime of this kind in which 'there is no check on the one' and therefore 'no protection for the other' has long been familiar to the students of politics: these words describe the classical features of Oriental despotism. In such a society the appellation, Conservative, might still continue to be used; but it would be used in the same surrealist manner in which progressive journalists describe the unrepentant Stalinists of the Soviet Union and Eastern Europe as Conservatives. Then would have taken place what Hume called the euthanasia of the British constitution.

This euthanasia Hume thought might come about in consequence of convulsions and civil wars, themselves the outcome of parliamentary misgovernment and tyranny from which the country would find refuge in absolute monarchy. In making such a prediction Hume manifestly had in mind the Civil War and the Cromwellian interregnum, the study of which first stimulated his historical imagination and made him into a considerable historian. It was no doubt this backward glance which made him attribute the forthcoming euthanasia of the British constitution to the establishment of an 'absolute monarchy'. It did not occur to him that the euthanasia he foresaw might come, not through the agency of absolute monarchy, but rather through the workings of parliamentary government itself.

In the debates preceding the Reform Act of 1832 two rival theories of the constitution confronted one another. One was to the effect that the House of Commons as the representative of the electorate had and ought to have the supreme power in the state, and that the government was fully responsible to it and ought to be perfectly responsive to its wishes. The other theory was that the British constitution was a balanced constitution, in which executive, legislative and judiciary checked and controlled one another. It is to this theory that the opponents of the Reform Bill appealed when they repeatedly declared that the Reform Bill was incompatible with the existence of a House of Lords as an element in a balanced constitution; it is the same theory that Wellington had in mind when he told Croker shortly after its passing, 'I myself do not see how the encroaching power of the people out of doors on the House of Commons, and the encroaching powers of House of Commons on the House of Lords and the Crown, is to be checked and brought back to its fair balance.' The theory of the constitution implicit in Wellington's language has now entirely disappeared from Conservative thought, which has nothing distinctive to say on this crucial issue. Yet the rival theory now generally accepted, that of the supremacy of the House of Commons, has always been inadequate and is now delusive. For on this theory, the House of Commons, as the voice of the people, exercises control over the government. But the coming of a mass electorate, and of the mass parties which are its concomitant, has meant that the House of Commons is controlled by, rather than controls, the government. And it is through this development that the euthanasia of the British constitution has become a well-nigh accomplished fact.

The state as a universal provider, with the government in efficient control of its legislative factory, having unlimited license to print paper pounds—those tickets of despotism, as Burke described the *assignats*—: such a state the Conservatives may claim to manage and work more humanely and more efficiently than their rivals. Such, by and large, has been the claim since 1945, a claim justified and made good in their thirteen years from 1951 to 1964. After the fall of Mr Heath's administration in 1974, the claim ceased to be made, was indeed disclaimed. But if the State continues to seize and spend at its will nearly half of the gross national product, the force of the disclaimer will evaporate, and it will seem as though an iron Fate has ordained that the affairs of the citizens shall be forever regulated in those populous palaces of concrete and sheet glass which have sprung up with such profusion in Whitehall and its environs. Yet another thirteen years may then succeed the first thirteen, and the Conservtives continue a 'great' party. But it will be a puzzle to know what, under such conditions, Conservatives will come to understand by Conservatism.

Lord Salisbury
and Politics

O F ALL Queen Victoria's Prime Ministers, Lord Salisbury is, it seems to me, the only one who may be called an intellectual. The appellation can be justified by an examination, however cursory, of his writings. These writings took the form of articles and reviews published mostly in the 1860s in *The Saturday Review* and *The Quarterly Review*. Much in these articles and reviews is ephemeral and today of little intrinsic significance. Discounting all this, however, there yet remains a substantial residue which shows a reasoned and coherent view of politics being worked out and illustrated. And it is because he is so articulate about the general character of political activity, and its relation to religion and ethics, because he puts before us a theory of politics, that Salisbury may be described as an intellectual. The term has of course pejorative overtones, and Salisbury has not escaped the criticism of confusing theoretical with practical reason, of approaching politics with that rigid *esprit de système* which intellectuals sometimes mistakenly bring to bear on practical affairs. Thus Maurice Cowling, examining the role he played in Derby's administration in 1866–7, declares that he was 'dogmatic, intense and too clever by half', and that he had a desire 'to be something between [a] prig on the one hand and [a] doctrinaire on the other.'[1] It may be that, as Cowling argues, Salisbury was then utterly wrong in his assessment of

[1] Maurice Cowling, *1867*, pp. 21 and 23.

parliamentary reform and its consequences, that he failed to appreciate the character and intent of Derby's and Disraeli's policy, and that this failure was due to the doctrinaire cast of his mind. It is debatable whether such strictures are justified. But whatever his practical failings then, his understanding of political activity, free of cant and illusion, subtle and skeptical as we shall see it to be, exemplifies the *esprit de finesse* rather than the *esprit de géometrie*.

But it is not only for their own sake that Salisbury's writings on politics, sharp and original as they are, are worth examining. The student of British Conservatism does not find it easy to describe its distinguishing characteristics, the frame of mind and temperament associated with it. This difficulty has somewhat to do with the fact that there does not exist a systematic and coherent body of Conservative doctrine from which to make a start, by which to take one's bearings. To be able therefore to understand Conservatism, the temperament and *persona* associated with it, one has to examine the utterances and the record of a succession of Conservatives, who are articulate and aware of what being a Conservative implies, and who, for one reason or another, are in some fashion exemplary for their time and place. Salisbury became a Conservative Member of Parliament in 1853, and from 1885 to 1902 was the leader of the Conservative Party. It is this record, together with a strongly defined and arresting personality and the unusual amalgam in him of the theoretical and the practical mind, which serves to make Salisbury into an exemplary Conservative. He is, of course, not the only kind of exemplary Conservative. If, making use of William James's distinction, we were to divide Conservatives into those who are tender-minded and those who are tough-minded, it is the latter whom Salisbury may be said to represent and exemplify. And if today he seems to us a very remote figure, this is not only because the assumptions and conditions of British politics have changed utterly since his day, but also because during Baldwin's ascendancy and afterwards it is largely a tender-minded Conservatism which has set the tone and dominated the Party's rhetoric.

Salisbury, as is well-known, was all his life a devout Anglican. If, as has been said, the Church of England is the

Tory Party at prayer, then Salisbury by virtue of his Anglican-
ism was a natural member of the Conservative party. He
himself, in a letter to a friend in April 1867, at the height of the
controversy about the second Reform Bill, declared that
except for the suffrage and the Church of England there was
nothing of which the Conservatives were in any special way
the protectors. Some nine years before, speaking against the
Jew Bill in March 1858, he declared that he was opposed
particularly to the introduction of the sincere believing Jew
into the House of Commons, because in proportion to his
sincerity, such a Jew must take a view 'hostile to their whole
body, and to all their institutions'—must be 'opposed to all in
a religious sense that they were there to uphold.'[2] It is clear
that for Salisbury the protection of the Church of England, and
the preservation of its privileged position in the state, went
hand in hand with the protection and preservation of the
British Constitution. 'Theoretically,' he observed in an article
of 1861, 'there is no reason why the secular position of the
Church of Christ in any country should determine the precise
form of its civil polity. But, practically, the spirit which abhors
a national Church has been found also to abhor the institutions
which give political predominance to the educated classes.'
And he went on to quote with approval a speech of 1854 in
which Lord John Russell opposed the abolition of Church
rates: 'We have a national Church,' said Lord John Russell,
'we have an hereditary aristocracy, we have an hereditary
monarchy, and all these things stand together. My opinion is,
too, that they would decay and fall together.'[3]

But if defence of the Anglican establishment is a corollary,
which Salisbury accepted, of the notion that the Church of
England is the Tory Party at prayer, other corollaries of such a
position he would have rejected. Such corollaries are those
which Gladstone attempted to prove in his treatise on *The
State in its Relation with the Church*. Gladstone's propositions, it is true, have something extravagant about them, they

---

[2]   Lady Gwendolen Cecil, *Life of Robert Marquis of Salisbury*, vol I, 1921,
      pp. 126 and 264.
[3]   'Church-rates', *The Quarterly Review (QR)*, vol. 110, October 1861,
      p. 545.

are pervaded by a smell of the midnight oil, and smack of academicism. Yet if these propositons are loosely phrased, and are not taken to the logical extremes to which the zealous young Tory of 1838 felt called upon to take them, they would have, in his own and in Salisbury's time, been quite generally accepted. These other corollaries would have defended the alliance of Church and State not for Lord John Russell's, and Salisbury's, reasons, but rather on the ground that right political action was the outcome of right religious belief, that morality depended upon true Christian teaching, and that therefore the propagation of truth and discouragement of error were among the ends for which government exists.

In denying assent to such views, Salisbury was at his most unexpected and most original. In the most interesting and penetrating chapter on 'Religion' which occurs in volume one of Lady Gwendolen Cecil's biography, she declares that a permanent characteristic of her father's thought was 'the uncompromising acceptance' of the unsolved mystery of the Christian revelation. This acceptance, she writes 'rested upon a spiritual vision which had an existence altogther apart from his intellectual processes and which was more compelling of conviction than any evidence which they could produce.'[4] Learned and acute as he was in theological matters, he seems to have been rather indifferent to theological disputes, and to be quite averse, by temperament, to the imposition or propagation whether by an individual or a state (in the manner, say, advocated by Galdstone), of a particular dogma. 'If I myself', his daughter reports him as saying, 'am satisfied that I believe what is true, what can it matter to me what others worshipping beside me believe!'[5]

Salisbury's religion led him to two consequences which he accepted unreservedly and affirmed boldly. He refused, in the first place, to justify God's ways to man or to comfort himself with a theodicy; and in the second place, he denied that belief in Christ necessarily entailed acceptance of the Christian ethic. God's action in the world was to him utterly inscrutable, and human reason was quite unable to explain it

4 Cecil, *Life*, I, pp. 113–14.
5 Cecil, *Life*, I, p. 117.

satisfactorily. His daughter quotes an entry from a notebook which he kept between the ages of twenty-three and twenty-five in which he expresses his scepticism of any claim to discover the ways of Providence: 'When our Saviour was dying the death of a felon,' Salisbury wrote, 'the spectators thought they saw in the event a proof that God's providence was against Him. But they were mistaken; the reaction on that murder has by His grace filled the world ... In the great French Revolution, when her altars were overturned and her Head was in prison, men thought that the hour of the Church of Rome had come, but it was only a winter to be followed by a more vigorous spring of life than she has seen since the days of Loyola. Which was the aim of Providence? Her foes said the stroke; her friends say the rebound ... What folly, then, to shape our conduct according to a rule of which it is quite clear that it is precisely an even chance whether it takes us with God or exactly against him.' The entry is a long one and in it Salisbury argues vehemently against the fallacy involved in the attempt to discern divine facts from human analogies. This seems to have become a lifelong attitude. His daughter reports a discussion in which he exclaimed 'with almost defiant energy': 'God is all-powerful and God is all-loving—and the world is what it is! How are you going to explain *that*?'[6]

Divine purpose then cannot be fathomed; but also there can neither be discerned a pattern or meaning in the purposes of men, their actions and the consequences of these actions, nor can we see much congruence between what men desire and what in the end comes to pass. This led him to be sceptical regarding the worth or beneficence of any action or its outcome. He was asked for advice in the case of a young man who, in deciding his future profession, was anxious to be guided by the 'good that he might do'. Salisbury 'deprecated this attitude with the greatest earnestness ... "He is preparing himself for a most bitter disappointment." ... it was urged that, after all, good was done in the world. He answered back, with the rapid, intense utterance which characterised his rare moments of unreserve, "yes, but not by

[6] Cecil, *Life*, I. pp. 113–13.

you,—never by you—never allow yourself to believe that for an instant".'[7]

But such scepticism did not lead to a passive fatalism. On the contrary, liberating him as it did from the burden of consequences over which man has so little control, it seeems to have given him a blithe assurance in his decisions and sure-footedness in his actions. His daughter has fixed for us a memorable scene in which Salisbury, standing in a doorway at Hatfield distinguished between the burden of decision which was real, and the burden of responsiblity, which was an illusion. The burden of decision depends, the statesman declared, 'upon the materials for decision that are available and not in the least upon the magnitude of the results which may follow ... With the results I have nothing to do.'[8]

Christianity, then, implies and commands no theodicy. Even more boldly, Salisbury held that the Christian ethic was no argument for the truth of Christianity: 'He disputed its value ... He declared that while he had never known what it was to doubt the truth of Christian doctrine he had all his life found a difficulty in accepting the moral teaching of the Gospels. He added that, in fact, the process relied upon was reversed in his case and that, even then, his acceptance of Christ's moral teaching was an act of faith due to the divine authority upon which it rested.'[9] Salisbury's difficulty in accepting the Christian ethic, as expressed in this remarkable passage, may seem, at first sight, perverse and paradoxical, but enquiry reveals that on ethics he had worked out a position at once subtle, delicate and imaginative. What he seems to object to in the Christian ethic is a rigorism which fails to do justice to the variety of moral decision we are called upon to make, and which serves therefore to make it unfit as a guide to conduct. Anyone scrupulously watching his own conduct, Salisbury observed, will soon be aware of the delicacy of the gradations by which right and wrong fade into each other. A moral rigorism which, of necessity, requires that the boundaries between right and wrong should be 'sharp, clear, and easily

[7] Cecil, *Life*, I, p. 118.
[8] Cecil, *Life*, I, p. 119; *see also* III, 1931, pp. 120–1.
[9] Cecil, *Life*, I, p. 102.

discernible' itself becomes a demoralizing fiction, and ends by throwing doubt on the existence of right and wrong altogether: 'A man who is taught to believe in the dividing line (between right and wrong) when he finds in pracice that it is a pure figment of his teacher's imagination, soon begins to doubt whether there is, in reality, anything to divide. Such an inference is very absurd. The great duty of truth or the antagonism between a truthful and a false character, is not destroyed by the fact that there are falsehoods which it is consistent with truthfulness to tell ... To teach a child, in the name of truth, that all falsehoods are equally guilty, and that he is to pass through life without ever being in duty bound to tell one, is a lie which can hardly be called white; for when the child finds out the real state of the case, he is very apt to infer that all falsehoods are equally innocent.'[10] It was the same dislike of moral rigorism which led him to attack the Northcote–Trevelyan report on civil service reform, with its notion that merit ascertained by means of examinations ought to be the sole test for fitness in public employment. He quotes from William Godwin's *Inquiry concerning Political Justice* a statement to the effect that 'I *ought* to prefer no human being to another because that being is my father, my wife, or my son, but because, for reasons which equally appeal to all understandings, that being is *entitled* to preference.' The doctrine, he remarks, is 'manifestly repugnant to the commonest and not the worst feelings of our nature'. Is this seemingly stern morality, he asks, true morality or not? 'Is it an evil that ... a certain *prima facie* preference should be conceded to a man who is connected with those who are already known and trusted ...? Why should favour and friendship, kindness and gratitude, which are not banished by men from private life, be absolutely excluded from public affairs?'[11]

Just as his denial of a theodicy liberated him from the useless burden of consequences, so his refusal of rigorism freed his discourse from sententiousness or censoriousness. As his daughter remarks:' ... he never laid claim in his speeches, even

---

[10] 'White Lies', *The Saturday Review*, XIV (1862), p. 591.
[11] 'Competitive Examinations', *QR*, 108, October 1860, pp. 569 and 572–3.

obliquely, either for himself or for his auditors any peculiar right of moral condemnation or special loftiness of moral standpoint.'[12]

Salisbury's difficulties with the Christian ethic increase when social and political issues are particularly in question. 'No formal code of ethics ever put forth', he observes, 'has been found to be really applicable to the ever-varying circumstances of human life'. This is particularly true of 'the purposely informal records of our own revelation', which centuries of casuistry has tried and in the end failed to make applicable to great variety of circumstances which Christians have encountered during the passage of two millenia. Consider, for instance, poverty. In the New Testament it is looked upon as highly favourable to religious excellence but, observes Salisbury, it is difficult for an Englishman of today to believe that it can conduce to the reception of truth or the practice of morality: 'Excepting the faults of mere intellect, there is no crime and scarcely any vice, to which the poorest have not more motive than those above them.' The reason must be, he concludes, that the 'capacity for an enthusiasm more powerful than any pressure of care, or toil, or want, which was possessed by the poor in other climates or ages, is wanting in our own.' But the most difficult problem raised by the Christian ethic was that it was incompatible with the life of politics. No one would dream of conducting politics according to this ethic; the 'meek and poor-spirited among nations', Salisbury observes, 'are not considered to be blessed, and the common sense of Christendom has always prescribed for national policy principles diametrically opposed to those that are laid down in the Sermon on the Mount.'[13]

The problem raised by this incompatibility becomes compounded in modern times by the fact that more and more private individuals participate in politics, even if only through their votes, and the painful dichotomy which a small number

---

[12] Lady Gwendolin Cecil, *Biographical Studies of the Life and Political Character of Robert Third Marquis of Salisbury*, privately printed, n.d. (1962), p. 10.
[13] 'Moral Entrenchments', *The Saturday Review*, 19 (1865), p. 533; 'Poverty', *ibid.*, 17 (1867), pp. 129–30.

of statemen had to face and accept in the past, now has to be wrestled with by the multitude. But the multitude cannot bear much reality, and is unlikely to show the strength and fortitude necessary to enable one to accept and live with such a dichotomy. What is more likely is that it will gloss over and ignore this conflict, and insist on dealing with politics in quite inappropriate language. As is well-known Salisbury was at his best in foreign affairs; one reason was that he considered it, as his daughter has written, free from 'the atmosphere of falsity which penetrates democratic politics from the surface to the centre.' This falsity was incomparably greater than the 'restrictions of candour or even the rarer and more direct violations of verbal truth' which occur in diplomacy. The falsity is the outcome of the confusion whereby nations are personified under a singular pronoun, and the teachings of the Sermon on the Mount indiscriminately applied to their actions and the actions of those who officially represent them. The falsity arises from the failure to see that the conjunction of Christianity and politics necessarily involved a tragic paradox: for while it is true, as Salisbury held, that the action of the statesman, whether public or private, always remained subject to the Christian law of morals, yet 'by that very law' he was bound to place the interests of which he was the guardian 'in front of all others which he might have to consider.'[14] It is also the case that Christianity and politics are antithetical. For the necessity of the statesman acting against the Christian law of morals is imposed not only by 'that very law' but also by 'every obligation of honour and loyalty'.[15] In Salisbury's writings on politics, honour is a recurring *motif*. Tories, he affirms, in an article of July 1860, must not think chiefly 'how they may "take office"'. Such a preoccupation is 'a degrading error which has squandered away the fair fame of parties and made a byeword of the honour of public men.'[16] Peace without honour, he also remarks, is a disgrace.[17] Again, discussing British policy towards Denmark in the Schleswig–Holstein question, he remarks: 'Denmark is but a weak state to struggle

[14] Cecil, *Biographical Studies*, pp. 45 and 72.
[15] Cecil, *Biographical Studies*, p. 72.
[16] 'The Conservative Reaction', *QR*, 108, July 1860, p. 296.
[17] 'Foreign Policy of England', *QR*, 115, April 1864, p. 484.

against the unwieldy but still huge enemy that menaces her independence. She needs every aid that chance, or promptitude, or strategical advantages can give her. If, in deference to our officious counsel she foregoes those aids, and then, abandoned by us, is crushed in the unequal conflict, a stain, which time could not efface, would lie upon England's honour.'[18] But, as Churchill acutely remarked, it is 'baffling to reflect that what men call honour does not correspond always to Christian ethics.'[19] This is because the desire to act honourably is inspired by pride, and pride is the first of the seven capital sins, a vice particularly repugnant to God as is declared in the first Epistle of Peter (V.5): 'God resisteth the proud and giveth grace to the humble.' But one can be more specific. In many cases 'the policy of honour is also the policy of peace.'[20] In other cases, however, to uphold one's honour, and the honour of the state on behalf of which one is acting, one must go to war. Wars are 'not made with rose-water'[21] and wars sometimes end in victory, and in the advantages which victorious wars sometimes bring. 'In some sense', Salisbury declares, 'every seizure of territory, or of anything else, is a crime. If the ethics of private life are to be applied rigorously to the acts of nations, it is quite clear that any nation appropriating to itself that which belongs to another is decidedly guilty of violating the direct language of the Eighth Commandment, and therefore may be pronounced guilty of a great crime.'[22] The magnitude of the crime varies of course with the circumstances, but that even in the best circumstances war involves a crime Salisbury does not doubt. And as he also believed that 'There is nothing abiding in political science but the necessity of truth, purity, and justice',[23] we might well conclude that here is a man who was perpetually torn between right and expediency, and thus condemned to political impotence. Or else, since he

[18] 'The Danish Duchies', *QR*, 115, January 1864, p. 286.
[19] Winston S. Churchill, *The Second World War*, vol. I, 1948, p. 251.
[20] 'The Danish Duchies', p. 286
[21] 'Poland', *QR*, 113, April 1863, p. 452. Salisbury applies this remark to wars of aggression, but it is clear that he would not have dissented from its being applied to any war whatever.
[22] 'Poland', p. 451.
[23] 'Lord Stanhope's *Life of Pitt*', *QR*, 109, April 1861, p. 559.

was manifestly successful as a statesman, that he had somehow forgotten or put behind him such dilemmas. It is of course
true that the statements quoted here come from writings
published before Salisbury became a prominent politician, but
the testimony of his daughter shows that in this later period,
too, Salisbury remained quite as fully aware of the tension
between religion, ethics and politics. This tension, and his
awareness of it, are in striking contrast with the outward poise
and solidity which is the hallmark of his style in politics. Such a
tension might have condemned others to a feeling of guilt and
to impotence, but in him it served to sustain decisiveness and
readiness to act as and when necessary.

A well-known passage of his which is sometimes cited as
though it illustrates his own attitude in fact expresses strong
objection to a government waiting passively upon events
instead of seeking to control them. Galdstone's government,
he noted in an article of 1871, lacked that decisive policy
'which each man in his own private affairs would consider
indispensable to success': 'They are content to float sleepily
down the stream, letting it carry them whither it lists, only
stretching out a hand now and again to avoid some obstacle
that is close upon them or avert some immediate danger. And
so we comfortably drift on, little heeding the reckoning that
awaits all, nations or men, who prefer to indulge in the
pleasing illusions of the present rather than bear the pain and
discipline of foresight.[24] He himself saw nothing wrong with
fighting, even with seemingly hopeless prospects. 'Did the
great classes whose battle had been so fierce' he asked after the
passage of the Reform Act of 1867, harking back to what
happened after 1832, 'respect each other less when it was once
lost and won? Did Sir Robert Peel, who fought it to the end,
lose by his tenacity in the estimation of his countrymen? Did
the cause he represented suffer through his temerity? He was
indeed beaten down in 1832, vainly struggling for a hopeless
cause. But before six years had passed he was at the head of
half the House of Commons ...[25]

This calm decisiveness might of course be attributed to his

---

[24] 'Political Lessons of the War', *QR*, 130, April 1871, p. 281.
[25] 'The Conservative Surrender', *QR*, 123, October 1867, p. 543.

class, to the self-confidence which its position in the mid- and late Victorian period gave him. But Salisbury's view of society and politics—whether at home or abroad—was far from confident. The striking fact about him is how impressed he was with the fragility of the social order, with the extent to which the position of the upper classes, and of the propertied classes in general, was threatened by the democracy which ever since the revolution in France had become bolder, the claims of which seemed to impress, and the strength of which to cow, those who had every reason to be its resolute opponents. 'Intellectually speaking, we live in one of those periods of anarchy which are the consequence and the sure punishment of a period of civil war.'[26] This intellectual anarchy, the outcome of the struggle between Christianity and its various modern opponents, is now accompanied by another, equally fateful kind of warfare, occasioned by 'that ancient and perennial source of animoisty which, unhappily, has never ceased, and never will cease, to flow in every civilised community—the quarrel of the poor against the rich.'[27] In the last article which he wrote for *The Quarterly Review*, which appeared in October 1883 and was entitled 'Disintegration', he does not disguise his pessimism over the outcome of this battle: 'By a process of political evolution, which affects not us only, but the whole western world, ultimate power is passing into the hands of much larger multitudes than ever exercised it before.'[28] This Salisbury believed quite disastrous. Democracy is a wholly vicious mode of government: 'In the collective deliberations of any body of men, reason gains the mastery over passion exactly in proportion as they are educated and as they are few. Passion is fostered equally by the two main characteristics of the democratic sovereign—ignorance and numbers.'[29] 'Moderation, especially in the matter of territory, has never been characteristic of democracy. Wherever it has had free play, in the ancient world or the modern, in the old hemisphere or the new, a thirst for empire, and a readiness for

[26] 'The Bicentenary', *QR*, 112, July 1862, p. 262.
[27] 'The Commune and the Internationale', *QR*, 131, October 1871, p. 578.
[28] *QR*, 156, p. 570.
[29] 'Democracy on its Trial', *QR*, 110, July 1861, p. 269.

aggressive war, has always marked it.'[30] Freedom in the democratic view means 'the supreme unchecked power of the majority'[31] and must therefore in reality signify despotism: 'The bestowal upon any class of a voting power disproportionate to their stake in the country, must infallibly give to that class a power *pro tanto* of using taxation as an instrument of plunder and legislation as a fountain of gain ... and when universal suffrage was reached, it would be a simple despotism.'[32] And if it were said, as Gladstone said, that there is no reason to fear the way in which the poor would use the vote, 'that they are fellow Christians, our own flesh and blood, and so forth', then Salisbury's answer would be that the 'depositaries of absolute power have often been fellow Christians, and have generally been composed of flesh and blood akin to that of those over whom they ruled. The Emperor Paul, Robespierre, Ferdinand of Naples, were all baptised, and all of the same race as their subjects: but those circumstances did not make the absolute power which has been lodged in their hands less of a calamity to their fellow men.'[33] Salisbury was all the more convinced of the despotic tendencies of democracy by what he took to be happening in the United States during the Civil War. He has a passage in which he compares the proceedings of the government during the Jacobite rebellion of 1745 with those of Lincoln's administration, greatly to the latter's disadvantage: 'the English Government of that day did not think themselves justified, by the imminence of the public danger, in suspending, of their own authority, every guarantee for civil liberty. They did not suppress hostile newspapers, or enforce a conscription, or establish martial law, by Royal proclamation, or forbid any Englishman to leave English shores, or throw men into prison for twelve months without cause assigned or hearing granted, or send men to the Tower for expressing, within hearing of a policeman, a pity for the volunteers who were marching to the war. Still less did they venture to arrest judges for giving

---

[30] 'The Danish Duchies', p. 239.
[31] 'The United States as an Example', *QR*, 117, January 1865, p. 284.
[32] 'The House of Commons', *QR*, 116, July 1864, p. 269.
[33] 'The Reform Bill', *QR*, 119, April 1866, p. 542.

judgements which were not to their mind.'[34] All this happened in the United States, because it was a democracy. A democracy is moved by passion; it will therefore compromise nothing and will give no quarter to a minority. Again, a democracy *ipso facto* seeks to establish and maintain equality and must thus be despotic in its character and operations: 'Old King Tarquin knew what he was about when he symbolised the surest way of enslaving a community by striking off the heads of the tallest poppies.'[35]

Salisbury was aware that there was great advantage in a people feeling at one with its government, that a feeling of 'participation' increases the cohesiveness of the state: '... it may be said', he wrote in his first long essay, 'that the best form of Government (setting aside the question of morality) is one where the masses have little power and seem to have a great deal.'[36] Under modern conditions possession of great power by the masses is an illusion, and cannot but be so. Government, he pointed out in an essay on 'Equality' published in 1864, have at their disposal 'the costliest apparatus of warfare that science can supply', and they are therefore 'becoming more and more powerful to set insurrection at defiance.'[37] If this is so, then democracy does not mean direct rule by the people. The despotism which democracy means is in fact exercised by a handful of fanatics such as those at the head of the Commune who would go to any extremes to make their views prevail: 'If the combat is once commenced, one or others of the combatants must perish. It is idle to plead that the schemes of these men are their religion. ... The Thugs had a religion of their own, with a goddess to preside over it: and its tenet was this—that anybody who possessed anything they wished to have must die.'[38] Or if it is not fanatics who are in control, it is the methodical and systematic controllers of mass organizations. Electoral reform has been opposed from

---

[34] 'The Confederate Struggle and Recognition', *QR*, 112, October 1862, p. 561.
[35] *Ibid.*, p. 562.
[36] 'The Theories of Parliamentary Reform', *Oxford Essays*, 1858, p. 66.
[37] *The Saturday Review*, 18, 29 October 1864, pp. 530–1.
[38] 'The Commune and the Internationale', p. 563.

the fear that it might lead to greater corruption of the voters, but Salisbury on the whole 'pray[ed] for King Publican and his merry rule. . . . Elagabalus is more tolerable than Caligula. All the evils that we inveigh against in the constituencies where freemen prevail, the chronic corruption, the sickening debauchery, the wide-spreading fraud and wholesale perjury . . ., would be ill-exchanged for the strong, steady, deadly grip of the trades' unions.'[39]

Another conclusion follows from the observation that under modern conditions, the multitude does not prevail against an existing government: if such a government is nonetheless overthrown, it is because the rulers have chosen either to make concessions or actually to run away. This is what Louis Philippe did in 1848. But it is in making concessions that the failure of nerve which sometimes afflicts rulers most commonly manifests itself. Revolutions start with the unwitting help of the ruling classes: 'the one point of similarity which distinguishes all revolutions of a democratic tendency is this, that they are invariably started with the aid of sanguine and benevolent people, who have not the slightest thought of bringing about the confusion to which their efforts ultimately lead. Any one who in 1640 should have prophesied the horrors of 1649 as the probable result of the early proceedings of the Long Parliament, might have been truly assured that no person could attach greater importance to the rights of the Crown and the integrity of the Constitution than Hyde and Falkland.'[40] Hyde and Falkland stand for all those who think that reform, redress of grievances and improvement of government constitute a sure recipe for averting revolution. It was this delusion which possessed the French nobility in 1789 'with all their ablest and most earnest members at their head, who in a wild philosophic delirium kindled the conflagration in which they perished.'[41] The goodness or badness of a government has in fact no necessary connection with its stability: 'There was no danger of revolution under Louis XV, though his court, his nobility, and his people, were tainted with every vice that can

---

[39] 'The Budget and the Reform Bill', *QR*, 107, April 1860, pp. 539–40.
[40] 'The Coming Session', *QR*, 119, January 1866, p. 271.
[41] *Ibid.*, p. 272.

debase a nation. It was not till the strength of the Government had been paralysed by the amiable concessions of the vacillating Louis XVI, that the catastrophe came.'[42] Again, the condition of Ireland during much of the eighteenth century was quite wretched, the laws in force then against Roman Catholics were 'a byword for blind ferocity', and the commercial restrictions, adopted at the bidding of English mercantile interests 'exaggerated the same selfish policy as that which had inspired the Navigation Laws'. Yet during this period Ireland was quiet. But after 1780, when there began a steady stream of concessions to the Irish, the history of Ireland 'has been a continuous tempest of agitation, broken by occasional flashes of insurrection.' Catholic emancipation, in particular, has utterly failed to fulfil the expectations which its advocates entertained: 'Lord Melbourne is reported to have said before he died, "Everybody but the fools was in favour of Roman Catholic Emancipation; but it has turned out that the fools were right".' In Ireland as in France before 1789, the cycle of concession, discontent and insurrection was initiated not by the downtrodden, but by members of the dominant group, 'by the Irishmen of English and Scotch extraction—by those whom the Nationalist newspapers of today now revile as "West Britons". It was the worst day's work for themselves they ever did in their history. They little dreamt for whose use they were establishing the maxim, that England's necessity is Ireland's opportunity.'[43]

Catholic emancipation in 1829 was the doing of a Tory government, and a decisive part in the episode was played by Peel who, when he obtained office in 1828, was generally believed to hold Protestant opinions. This action, Salisbury held, demoralized the Tory party, and contributed to the passing of the first Reform Bill three years afterwards. In spite of his strenuous opposition to it, the Reform Bill was in effect as much his work as Lord Grey's 'because if the strong fortress of Toryism had not been carried, the Reform party would have achieved a less overwhelming and less destructive victory, and would have done the work they had to do in a less democratic

---

[42] 'Parliamentary Reform', *QR*, 117, April 1865, p. 551.
[43] 'Disintegration', *QR*, 156, October 1883, pp. 585–7.

spirit. It is true,' Salisbury points out 'that Sir Robert Peel did not lead the assault; but he made the breach. And the worst of the case was that he made it from inside.'[44] As in Ireland, as in France, therefore, surrender of power—for this, not 'reform' is what in the end is involved—is the outcome not of a successful assault on those who held it, but of their own failure of nerve. The Reform Bill of 1832, in spite of what was said at the time, could not be a lasting settlement. Lord Grey had attempted to create a provisional aristocracy out of the trading and manufacturing classes, but such an aristocracy has no staying-power: 'They were too timid heartily to resist the assaults of the lower classes, too jealous of their antagonists to combine cordially with the upper.' The middle class could not be a governing class: 'It is not a class militant; it has no internal cohesion—no consciousness of unity to enable it to maintain political predominance ... The revolution of 1832 was, therefore, in its ultimate results, a democratic revolution'.[45] This democratic revolution must eventually put the wealthy few at the mercy of the numerous poor. This of course was the basis of Salisbury's opposition to the Reform Bill of 1867. Conservative democracy, i.e. the notion 'that the poorer men are the more easily they are influenced by the rich' and that the working class, being antagonistic to its middle class employers 'must on that account love the gentry'—this notion is a 'phantom'. The plain truth established by experience is that working-men, organized in trades unions, will act in unison to advance their own pecuniary interests: 'Armed with political privileges, these organisations would wield a power against which no other political influence could make head. The power of any organised body of men depends upon the fidelity with which they obey their leaders ... Of all the arguments that can possibly be used to reconcile us to the preponderance of the working men in the constitution, the plea that they will not act *en masse* is the most absurd that can be devised. They act *en masse* with a success which no class or order of men not

---

[44] 'Parliamentary Reform', pp. 551–2.
[45] 'Political Lessons of the War', p. 279.

bound together by religious ties has ever succeeded in attaining to before.'[46]

The prospect, then, is of a multitude whose representation in Parliament is out of all proportion to its real stake in the country and, as has been said, using taxation as an instrument of plunder and legislation as a fountain of gain. Salisbury notices also another aspect of this apprehended dominance, namely its effect on the constitution and on the working of Parliament. Throughout his writings Salisbury takes for granted, and sometimes explicitly states a theory of the Constitution which was current among all shades of political opinion in the eighteenth century, and which the Conservatives themselves invoked in opposing the Reform Bill of 1832. But the widespread acceptance of Utilitarian dogmas and categories thereafter did much to discredit this particular theory, which is now only rarely invoked by writers on the Constitution (a variant of it occurs in Amery's *Thoughts on the Constitution*, and attempts to revive it—which have so far not met with much success—have been recently made in various ways by M. J. C. Vile and by Geoffrey Marshall).

This theory has many facets and variants. It can be evoked (but by no means fully described) by some such expression as 'the balanced Constitution': balanced either in the sense that it took account of, reflected and produced a balance between the various interests which exist in the country, or in the sense that no one branch of the government was able to dominate the other branches. Neither notion is of course exclusive of the other, and indeed Salisbury invokes them both. 'The principle ... of constitutional perfection', he declared in the House of Commons in 1859, 'was to check every class by another class.'[47] The best and most adequate form of representation was therefore—he wrote in 1858—that which sought 'to represent men not places: the classes and interest into which mankind are divided, not merely the bits of soil on which they dwell', and indeed 'nothing can be more rude and irrational than a geographical representation'. Geographical represen-

---

[46] 'The Past and the Future of Conservative Policy', *QR*, 127, October 1869, pp. 541–2, and 'The Reform Bill', pp. 543–5.

[47] H. C. Debs., 3rd Series, CLIII, col. 479, 21 March 1859.

tation combined with an extensive or, *a fortiori*, a universal franchise must lead to the 'great and monstrous anomaly' of wealth being given no security whatever. Conservatives, he declared in 1866, do not object to an extension of the franchise as such: 'Their doctrines are not adverse to the claims of any particular class, except when that class is aiming to domineer over the rest. And, therefore, there is nothing inconsistent with their principles in any system of representation, however wide its scope may be, so long as it does not ignore the differences of property which exist in this country, and maintains, with an even hand, the balance of power among the various classes of which the nation is made up.'[48]

The destruction of the balance of power between the classes in the country in turn has a fateful consequence on the character and functioning of political institutions. In the eighteenth century there was a system of checks and balances operating on and controlling the action of Ministers and of the Houses of Parliament. This is no longer the case, for the House of Commons has attained 'a supremacy in the State more decided than it ever possessed before'. But at the same time, Salisbury points out, it seems to 'be entirely losing one of the most necessary attributes of a ruler. The broad distinction between a civilized and an uncivilized community is this –' Salisbury goes on, 'that in a civilized community individuals or bodies of men who quarrel submit their difference to an arbitrator, while in a savage state they fight it out ... It is of the essence of the civilized system that the arbitrator should be in the main impartial; and the kings or chiefs, to whom in ruder times the power of arbitration was confided, satisfied, or were believed to satisfy, the requirement ... Assemblies have inherited the function of political arbitration where it has dropped from the hands of kings; and while their power was undeveloped, or while they were drawn from a limited portion of the community, their impartiality, though not quite unimpeachable, has sufficed for the preservation of their moral authority, and of the confidencce reposed in them. With us, as in other Anglo-Saxon societies, the Representative Assembly is

[48] 'Theories of Parliamentary Reform', pp. 56 and 75; 'Parliamentary Reform', p. 572.

no longer taken from a limited section of the community, and it has succeeded with us, far more than any assembly in America, in shaking itself free of all restrictions upon its power. But with this development of its character and strength, the loss of its fitness to arbitrate has become apparent. The movement of society is reversed; we are going back to the ancient method of deciding quarrels. Our ruler is no longer an impartial judge between classes who bring their differences before him for adjustment; our ruler is an Assembly which is itself the very field of battle on which the contending classes fight out their feuds. The settlement by arbitration has given place again to the settlement by civil war; only it is civil war with gloves on. Of course the decisions thus given vary in their character without limit; and all confidence in fixed principles or a determinate policy is gone.'[49] This precarious, unstable and arbitrary mode of government results from the fact that the House of Commons 'has come into its position, as it were, by accident. It is like the junior member of a great mercantile firm, who has suddenly become all-powerful, not in pursuance of any articles of the partnership, but simply because the senior partners have fallen into poor health, and have retired. No provision was made in the articles to meet such a contingency; and his power is absolutely unrestricted.'[50]

It is in such terms, then, that Salisbury would describe, and condemn, the theory of the Constitution which became accepted in his day, and which is still dominant, the theory which—to borrow Dicey's description—holds that the (unrestricted) legal sovereignty belongs to the Queen-in-Parliament, and that it is in turn governed and controlled by the equally unrestricted political sovereignty of the electorate. On such a theory, the freedom of the individual, property and contract alike become precarious. Salisbury held that it was not the business of Conservatives to promote and lend authority to such a theory: 'An organic change proposed by Conservatives, with no one to check it except those who were by profession bound to aggravate it, was a phenomenon

[49] 'Disintegration', pp. 565–6.
[50] *Ibid.*, p. 568.

hitherto unknown to the Constitution.'[51] For the Conservative Party to assume such a role aggravates the disorder and
instability which the coming of democracy has introduced into
the Constitution. It also demoralizes the Party and makes it
unfit to pursue its role. Catholic Emancipation, Repeal of the
Corn Laws, the Reform Bill of 1867 were either good measures or bad measures. If bad, 'they ought not to have been
passed at all; if good, they ought to have been passed by other
men.'[52] This, because just as the conservatism of Liberals will
be hypocritical, so the liberalism of Conservatives will be
'clumsy and probably extravagant.' For the 'Conservatives
have their special duties to the Constitution; and finding
forced labour to assist in Radical demolitions is not among
them.'

The special duties of the Conservatives lie in resistance to
change because the 'perils of change are so great, the promise
of the most hopeful theories is so often deceptive, that it is
frequently the wiser part to uphold the existing state of things,
if it can be done, even though, in point of argument, it should
be utterly indefensible.'[54] Resistance to change is justified on
two grounds, one which holds in every age, and another
particularly relevant to the present day. In the first place, 'It is
possible, as the celebrated dictum of Tacitus records, that a
nation may not be strong enough to bear the immediate
remedy of even intolerable evils. New wine will burst old
bottles; a healthy diet will kill a sick man outright. Sir Robert
Walpole's bribery saved his country; Necker's purity ruined
his,' Again, 'a violent isolated artificial improvement in the
institutions of a community, undertaken without regard to the
condition of the other portions of the machinery in concert
with which it is to work, is a danger so great that no improvement at all is almost to be preferred.'[55] In the second place, the
present age is taken with 'the assurance that constant future
progress is a certainty, and that there must be within reach of

---

[51] 'The Budget and the Reform Bill', p. 547.
[52] 'The Position of Parties', *QR*, 133, October 1872, p. 575
[53] *Ibid.*, pp. 582 and 584.
[54] 'Parliamentary Reform', p. 550.
[55] 'Competitive Examinations', pp. 573–4.

legislation some remedy for every evil . . .' and the 'alternative of not changing at all has been put out of court as beyond discussion.'[56] This 'optimist view of politics assumes', Salisbury also wrote in discussing Ireland, 'that there must be some remedy for every political ill, and rather than not find it, will make two hardships to cure one.' 'But is not the other view', Salisbury asks, 'barely possible?'[57] What Salisbury would have said in answer to his own question is not in doubt. If the question, which he put in 1872 were to be put today to Salisbury's Party, it is equally not in doubt that they would unite with their opponents in dismissing out of court his own answer to it.

---

[56] 'The Commune and the Internationale', pp. 570–1.
[57] 'The Position of Parties', quoted in Cecil, *Life*, II, p. 38.

Conservatives
and neo-Conservatives

THE TERM neo–conservatism has, in recent years, become quite current in United States political debate. There is now even a fairly large book by Peter Steinfels (*The Neoconservatives: The Men Who Are Changing America's Politics*, 1979) which deals, in a generally unfriendly and logic-chopping manner, with the views principally of Irving Kristol, Daniel Patrick Moynihan and Daniel Bell, whom the author considers to be the chief proponents of this trend of thought. These writers—and others who are also labelled as neo-conservative —are, of course, very different from one another. What makes it nevertheless reasonable to give them this common label is the hositility they all, in greater or lesser measure, evince to official policies and intellectual currents which became dominant in the United States in the last two decades. Neo-conservatism constitutes a reaction to such policies as President Johnson's Great Society, affirmative action, the civil rights movement and women's liberation. Neo-conservatism is hostile to these policies or movements on the score that they are the outcome of ideologies which misapprehend the character of society and which prescribe aims impossible to fulfil, and the attempt to fulfil which produces greater evils than those it was desired to cure.

One prominent feature of neo-conservatism is that associated with so-called supply-side economics. The contention here is that economic growth and continuing prosperity— which Western societies have come to desire and expect—

depend on entrepreneurial initiative, inventiveness and risk-taking. The business of government is to ensure that these qualities and modes of behaviour are not maimed or destroyed by punitive fiscal policies, imprudent monetary policies or vexatious administrative practices. The very name of this theory—supply-side economics—emphasizes the fact that it is directed against policies and tendencies that purport to derive from Keynsian economic analysis. This analysis is taken to show that economic stagnation and recession, and the un-settling and disruptive character of the business cycle in modern industrial economics, result from a failure in demand. The duty of government, it follows, is to stimulate failing demand and, in general, to pursue an anti-cyclical policy of demand-management. This, in turn, is carried on with the help of economic indicators, which are sets of statistics from which skilled and experienced econometricians predict future economic trends, thus enabling their political masters to fine-tune the economy, and to shield it from the mishaps of the trade-cycle. It is obvious that this must lead to an interven-tionist and *dirigiste* style of government. It is a self-confident and ambitious style, given to active strategies of public invest-ment, of manipulation of the supply money, and of interest and exchange rates. Like virtuoso organists, the minister of the economy, and his learned and expert calculists, pressing these keys, pulling those stops, and depressing those other pedals produce a happy economy and a harmonious body politic. But this ambitious style has proved far too ambitious. Government direction of the economy, supply-side critics have not failed to point out, far from being beneficent fine-tuning has proved to be a blundering hit-or-miss affair, the result of which has been to debauch the currency, to misdirect investment, and to encourage a cacophony of popular demands and sectional claims ruinous for any government to satisfy.

Economic interventionism has gone hand in hand with an equally ambitious policy aiming to abolish poverty and to promote equality of condition among various classes and ethnic groups, as well as between the sexes. The attempt to realize theses aims has led to an enormous increase in the number of clerks, social workers and other officials deemed necessary to administer 'welfare', promote 'social planning' and enforce equality, non-discrimination and 'affirmative action'. It has also led to a great waste of public funds, and—what is worse and in the long run much more danger-ous—to the coming to be of a mass of clients dependent on public subventions, in whom any sense of enterprise and self-respect, any desire for self-help, rapidly disappears. Such policies, the neo-conservatives have pointed out, have not abolished poverty or diminished social tensions, nor can they possibly do so.

The failure of demand-management so-called and of welfar-ism constitute, then, the gravamen of the neo-conservative indictment of the ruling ideas and policies of the last few decades. Supply-side economics, and a social policy which promotes self-help, preserves the self-respect of the bread-winner and hence protects the family and the social fabric, are the counterpart of this critique of Keynsian interventionism and of Great-Society activism. But policies are by definition a matter of practice, and here the proof of the pudding is in the eating. Suppose then that supply-side economics, either be-cause it is timidly pursued or for some other reason, seems to fail of its promise, or at least seems to take longer to yield its fruit than politicians, with an eye on election timetables, are willing to wait. Suppose again that, for similar reasons, poli-ticians will flinch from the outcry which may follow an attempt to move away from the jungle of subsidies and the swamp of welfarism. Can neo-conservatism offer reasons and arguments able to withstand the chances and changes of political and economic life, which can explain and thus trans-cend and make acceptable the vicissitudes which any body politic from time to time inevitably undergoes?

It is clear that economic science is not to be looked to here. This science constituted a system of deductions from various hypotheses. As in any other science, its practitioners will always dispute among themselves as to the validity of deduc-tions and reasonableness of hypotheses. The route, further-more, which purports to lead from the propositions of the science to the activities of the market-place and the expedients of Treasury officials, is roundabout, treacherous and some-times even non-existent. 'Monetarism is not enough'; neither is Keynesianism. They are not enough because politics is not economics. The policies associated with Keynesianism, for instance, in their hit-or-miss fashion implicitly hint at a vision of society and its governance much more far-reaching than technical issues relating to failure of demand or pump-priming and the like. In this vision, there is hostility to the private accumulation, management and transmission of capital. Keynes looked forward to the euthanasia of the *rentier*, and dismissed the long run because in the long run we are all dead. The longest stretch of human life this outlook is concerned with is no longer than a generation—one's own. Here is the vision of a society composed of ephemeral individuals who, like butterflies, flutter for a brief spell in the bright air and then are gone—to be replaced in an endless cycle by other multitudes who in turn have their brief hour. Our Economist surveying from the heights these perishable, evanescent generations will, with a judicious priming of the pump here, a gentle restraint of demand there, enable these masses to live out, painlessly, comfortably, even pleasurably, their allotted span.

There is a connection between this partronizing conception of economic management and the outlook described in Keynes's celebrated essay, 'My Early Beliefs'. He there confessed that in their youth he and his circle had completely misunderstood human nature and disastrously so; that their view of human nature led to a thinnness, a superficiality not only of judgement, but also of feeling; that they were like 'water-spiders, gracefully skimming, as light and reasonable as air, the surface of the stream without any contact at all with the eddies and currents underneath'. They were 'not aware that civilisation was a thin and precarious crust erected by the personality and the will of a very few, and only maintained by rules and conventions skilfully put across and guilefully preserved'. They 'repudiated entirely customary morals, conventions and traditional wisdom'. 'We were, that is to say,' Keynes declared, 'in the strict sense of the term, immoralists'. But he added, describing his own attitude at the time he wrote his memoir, in 1938, when he was fifty-five years old, 'I remain, and always will remain, an immoralist'.

What may have started out by being a youthful, naive feeling of superiority, a conviction of having seen through, and been liberated from, obscurantism and hypocrisy, became with the passing years something distincly coarser and more complacently corrupt and cynical, the original feeling of superiority hardening into the self-certain and brittle arrogance of the intellectual. The Keynes who appears in the first volume of Robert Skidelsky's biography and in Michael Holroyd's biography of Lytton Strachey with his sleazy and disorderly train of life gives us an inkling of the deterioration. In any case, Keynes's daring immmoralism was incoherent. As has been said, its social time span did not extend beyond one generation, and with it one may associate this narrow and distorted vision. For a generation, taken on its own is an inherently self-contradictory notion. Any generation has forebears and descendants. This fact underlies, and makes sense of, innumerable activities which would never have been undertaken if men had not been intimately convinced of the utter irrlevance—and essential untruth—of the proposition that in the long run we are all dead. On the contrary: in the long run there is an endless chain of living generations, one generation giving life to and transmitting its capital, material and spiritual, to the following generation. But Keynes's very mode of life was a daily negation of this truth.

Considerations having to do with the maintenance, the stability and the continuity of a society are among the properly political ones, and a level of discourse pitched at their level may enable political men to see that economic theory and its prescriptions large as they loom, are yet subordinate issues, to be approached with a doubly sceptical frame of mind: scepticism about the relation between analysis and prescription, and scepticism about the lasting efficacy of any policy in a world where a multitude of diverse agents make their individual decisions in constantly changing conditions.

A similar point is to be made about welfarism, the other great issue about which neo-conservatives have written a great deal. The case for welfarism rests on two assumptions: that equality ought to be the proper condition of society, and that government can institute equality. But there is no way of establishing that equality is more just or more natural than inequality. The very attempt to specify a state of society in which equality reigns soon breaks down, so multitudinous and so various are the qualifications and the exceptions which have

73

to be introduced, and so incommensurable are the qualities which produce inequalities. A case of sorts, shaky and riddled with various absurdities which make it ultimately untenable, has been made out for the progressive taxation of incomes. But how is one to deal with good looks or great native intelligence which raise their possessors above the general condition, but in ways which escape the criteria of the Inland Revenue? Equality requires, in fact, constant and detailed official intervention in the most private affairs, in order for it to be instituted and maintained—intervention which must, in turn, involve perpetual disturbance of existing relationships and expectations, and thus perpetual exacerbation of social tensions. Equality which aims at the creation of a more wholesome and peaceable society thus paradoxically leads to querulousness and contention. This is the significance of Epicurus's injunction to his disciples—to which Hegel has drawn attention—against holding property in common, because this shows distrust, and distrust is destructive of friendship. Again, since equality is not part of the natural order, it requires an equalizer who will bring it about and maintain it. And appropriately enough, in slang the equalizer signifies the cosh or the gun. The equalizer must be more powerful than those whom he compels to be equal; to establish equality paradoxically demands inequality. And this, in a nutshell, describes the Soviet world.

Welfarism is also predicated on the notion that society can be 'planned'. That it cannot is a truth which both theory and practice proclaim. 'Planning' simply engenders a bureaucratic labyrinth in which arbitrariness and irrationality flourish. What is largely lost in this labyrinth is the possibility to bring under control, and make accountable to the citizens, the host of public servants who draft, interpret and administer the numerous detailed rules and their equally numerous exceptions which 'planning' necessitates. Public responsibility is thus dissipated, and the very notion of responsibility emptied of real meaning. The authority of government is likewise lost as it becomes the prisoner of these procedures and processes, and of the organized groups whose well-being and livelihood have become bound up with the large and complex structures which 'planning' conjures up.

Authority is also dissipated and lost in the attempt to formulate policy over matters where policy is utterly rebellious to formulation: what is the proper size of the British car industry? how many nurses will be necessary ten years hence? how many universities should there be in Great Britain? Answers to such questions (which various British Governments have asked in recent decades) might as well have been chosen with a pin or drawn out of a hat, for by their very nature they could not but be arbitrary and whimsical. Sudden expansion of university education two decades ago and its sudden contraction now are an admirable case in point. In 1961 a Conservative administration decreed, in the privacy of its own counsels, that university expansion—advocated in the Report of a well-known Committee—was the thing to go for. The decision committed a large—and increasing—amount of taxpayers' money to an enterprise the desirability, extent and shape of which no minister or official had the means of determining except by flimsy and hazardous guesswork. The same kind of arbitrariness which presided over expansion, now necessarily presides over contraction. 'Cost-benefit analysis' was declared to justify the expenditure, and 'cost-benefit anyalysis' likewise to justify the cut in the expenditure. But such analysis is, from the nature of things, as watertight as a sieve; for the cost of educating a university student is open to endless debate, while the benefits to be set against the cost are even more problematic. In any case, is not such analysis itself largely out of place in this kind of activity? Here then is one class of decisions which ministers, and *a fortiori* Conservative ministers, should have been eager not to take; but rather to leave to students and their parents. This would have had the advantage of preserving and enhancing the citizen's freedom to spend his own money, rather than having it extracted from him and spent on his behalf. It would have increased freedom of choice, and promoted the citizen's feeling of responsibility for himself and his family—a feeling to strengthen which is to strengthen the body politic itself.

University policy, so-called, is only a small example of the misconceived enterprises to which the desire to do good, the love of power and the itch for busyness lure public men. Another, much more glaring and serious, example may be found in the promise, so blithely given, that full employment shall be instituted and forever maintained. The world being what it is, such a promise could not possibly be kept. This is like the government promising perpetual sunshine. It is, of course, the case that in a modern industrial economy, the link between one's own livelihood and the general state of the economy is neither visible nor readily comprehensible. Remote causes like the unit cost of a Japanese car and the price exacted for OPEC oil will make workmen in Coventry and Detroit workless. But it is natural that loss of work, disappointed expectations and impoverishment should be laid at the door not of these remote causes, but of a government dependent on the popular suffrage. In these circumstances governments will do what they have to do and what they can do to alleviate and to remedy. But they bring great trouble on themselves and on the societies for which they are responsible by employing the rhetoric of omnicompetence, by which even Conservative governments have been seduced in the last few decades.

Is this activist style of government now inescapable for administrations which call themselves Convervative, and is it the case that between conservative ideas and a political party calling itself Conservative there need be no enduring or necessary connection? In a parliamentary regime parties are in competition to gain and preserve power. Competition may stimulate product differentiation; but the differentiation can sometimes turn out to be a mere difference in labels, the article produced by one party becoming essentially the same as that marketed by its competitors. The rhetoric of a Conservative party becomes umbilically related to the slogans of its rivals. The phenomenon is well known: the Whigs went bathing and the Conservatives ran away with their clothes. The Reform Bill of 1867 illustrates the dialectic whereby Tweedledum ends up by being Tweedledee's mirror image. Again, for three decades after 1945 varieties of Butskellism proliferated, and Taper and Tadpole prospered mightily.

There is another inherent reason why Tweedledee should set the pace and Tweedledum find it difficult not to follow. Since 1945 Ministers have found themselves the ostensible masters of a civil service in whom the experience of world war has perpetuated habits of centralization, and instilled *dirigiste* and interventionist instincts. With all its weight and complexity, the administrative machine may give Ministers the feeling of being at the controls of a powerful engine which responds obediently and punctually to their bidding. But perhaps the term, control, is misleading here, and symbiosis more aptly describes the relation between politicians and administrators. In this cosy symbiosis, we wonder whether scope is left for a political idiom which can create and maintain a recognizably conservative universe of discourse common to political leaders and those whom they represent—a universe of discourse which might make the contingencies of politics both intelligible and manageable.

A common conservative idiom of politics has other dangerous enemies to contend with. Man's misfortune, as Pascal said, is that he cannot for long sit still in an empty room. Silence and stillness have become more difficult than ever to secure. We are daily and hourly overwhelmed by a cataract of 'news', views and opinions, which has never happened before in the history of the world. It must issue in a craving for novelty which feeds upon itself. This is inherent in the operation of the communication media, the unenviable *raison d'être* of which must be the perpetual provision at all costs of distraction and entertainment. In the media politics must become a drama, a spectacle, a show in which the viewer finds it difficult, if not impossible, to distinguish between political action and actors playing at politics. This drains all reality and seriousness out of politics, and transforms it into the floating world of the media men, the hallmark of which is frivolity, volatility and instability.

Neo-conservatism discerns other issues which affect the stability and good government of a modern industrial society. Irving Kristol, for instance, has touched on and discussed these themes in two collections of essays (*On the Democratic Idea in America*, 1972; and *Two Cheers for Capitalism*, 1978). Capitalism, he considers, is a spiritually impoverished civilization; it is morally and intellectually unprepared for calamity. The dynamics of the capitalist economy engender nihilism in which free spirits emptied of spiritual substance are still driven by primordial moral aspirations. The attempt to realize these aspirations, in a society the traditions of which have been emasculated, can wreak a frightful havoc. In any case, there is now a yawning gap between personal values and social institutions which, as a result, become drained of all moral legitimacy. The predicament, as Kristol sees it, is summed up in the eloquent last paragraph of an essay on equality included in *Two Cheers*:

The real trouble [Kristol declares] is not sociological or economic at all. It is that the 'middling' nature of a bourgeois society falls short of corresponding adequately to the full range of man's spiritual nature, which makes more than middling demands upon the universe, and demands more than middling answers. This weakness of bourgeois society has been highlighted by its intellectual critics from the very beginning. And it is this weakness that generates continual dissatisfaction, especially among those for whom material problems are no longer so urgent. They may speak about 'equality'; they may even be obsessed with statistics and pseudo-statistics about equality; but it is a religious vacuum —a lack of meaning in their own lives, and the absence of a sense of larger purpose in their society—that terrifies them and provokes them to 'alienation' and unappeasable indignation. It is not too much to say that it is the death of God, not the emergence of any new social or economic trends, that haunts bourgeois society. And *this* problem is far beyond the competence of politics to cope with.

If, as Kristol argues, the problem of assimilating the moral authority of tradition into capitalism is beyond the competence of politics, the scope of Neo-conservative thought has to be very narrow indeed. But, in fact, conservative discourse is considerably broader. Even if issues such as the meaning of religion in the modern world are left aside, conservative thought does encompass themes much wider than economics —and has to, unless it is to be completely defenceless in the face of powerful and wide-ranging ideological claims. It may of course prove to be the case that the obstacles to its inculcation and dissemination are too great to surmount. However

78

this may be, conservatism defines itself in contrast, and disagreement, with four ways of thinking about politics which, in one form or another, have been, and still are, widely prevalent in the West.

The first is liberalism. At its broadest, this view sees the body politic as made up of individuals each endowed with natural rights. But the notion of an individual is an incoherent abstraction. For there can be no individuals, understood literally and strictly as such. We may start in search of the individual, but instead of him, we will find fathers and sons, husbands and wives, members of religious congregations, employers and employees, artists and patrons, authors and readers ... The individual can only know and define himself when acting and reacting within such networks which are made, kept in repair, and modified by him and his fellow-individuals. Taken to its extreme, the notion of an individual leads to the search for authenticity. Authenticity is taken to be that which a human being possess when all the artificial accretions of society and social restraints are removed. Hence authenticity is the only possible self-fulfilment. This search of authenticity is anarchic and nihilistic since it involves the rejection of all institutions, of all customs, of all traditions. It must thus lead to self-destruction.

The 'contractarian' mode is a second, inadequate, way of thinking about politics. According to this view, the body politic functions in terms of a contract between the citizens, or between the citizens as a whole and the government, which defines the rights and duties of each side. But to belong to a polity is not the outcome of a contract. People are either born into polity or declare allegiance—which is unconditional—to a polity which they join. 'Contractarianism' cannot accommodate or account for the idea of allegiance, or those of loyalty and patriotism, ideas without which it becomes difficult, if not impossible, to sustain for long a political discourse.

A third way of thinking about politics by contrast to which conservatism defines itself is utilitarianism. The worth of everything, including political institutions—utilitarians hold —is judged (or rather computed) by its utility to someone or other, whether in the short or the long run. This is simply untrue. The most important and enduring human relations are not initiated or maintained for the sake of some utility extrinsic to these relations. Love, friendship, family affection, loyalty to a community or a state, art and scholarship, are all pursued for their own sake and their value lies in themselves. Utilitarianism makes discourse about such pursuits and relations impossible or else, finding it difficult not to say something about such manifestly essential features of humanity, it ends by tying itself up in hopeless knots.

Marxism is the latest, and today the most formidable, adversary, against which conservatism has to measure itself. Formidable, not because of its intellectual merits, but because it can be so easily boiled down into slogans of slick simplicity and specious profundity, irresistible in its appeal to multitudes whose innate common sense provides little defence against the corruptions of literacy. And formidable, not least because the extensive resources of powerful despotisms are employed relentlessly to reiterate and drum the message in.

As for the intellectual merits of Marxism, there is none in claiming that all social relations necessarily depend on the ownership of means of production; that politics is simply expropriation, and the expropriation of expropriation; that the disappearance of private property will lead to the classless society and the consequent disappearance of the state. All these propositions are historically false and philosophically flawed. It is, of course, true that human beings are not properly human unless they possess property. It does not, however, follow that politics is no more than a quarrel about property. On the contrary, it is politics, and law, which mediate quarrels about property and enable them to be settled—and nothing but law, and the state which maintains it, can possibly discharge this function. This is because property cannot, inherently, provide security for itself, just as the market is, equally inherently, incapable of policing itself. State and law are logically prior to family, property and the market. The necessity and authority of law and the state emanates neither from a contract nor from their ability to promote a particular pattern of property (or the absence of it). They arise from the very character of human activities in all their variety, originality and contradictoriness which the law mediates and the state protects. Anything beyond this, the state cannot do well, or at all. This is true of economic management, of the establishment of equality, or the hundred and one enterprises with which governments think they have to busy themselves.

Protection for the citizens only the state can provide, and this is particularly true of protection against outside threat. Such protection requires forces to be made ready, to be husbanded, and to be used whenever danger threatens, prudence dictates, or advantage requires. These kinds of considerations will force themselves on anyone who has charge of a state, whatever the political discourse with which he is familiar or in which he is at home. But the political discourse of liberalism has no way of accommodating itself the realities of a world where many states exist which have no common superior, and conflict between whom is always liable to break out. Contractarianism and utilitarianism likewise do not know how to speak about, let alone deal with, international conflict or international order which, in its precariousness, depends on the balance of power, to restore and maintain which itself requires power, decisiveness and skill. As for Marxism, conflict is, naturally, of its essence. But it labours under the fallacy that all conflict is really and ultimately class conflict. The doctrine thus hinders discrimination between the great variety of conflicts which can oppose state to state. It is also barbarous in that it sees no end to, and no remedy for, conflict until the last expropriator is annihilated and class domination for ever abolished. Conservatism is thus most at home with international relations as they really are. It is least prone to fancifulness most able to cope with a world where perpetual peace is a destructive illusion, but where conflict is by no means perpetual, and its assuagement not a hopeless illusion. In fact, of all modes of political discourse available to the modern world, conservative discourse is the one which hugs most closely the shape of this world, and is least problematic in understanding, and coping with, its dangers and its promise.

But here too, it does not necessarily follow that conservative discourse will be favoured or used by a Conservative administration. The Falklands affair is a case in point. It is of course true that in this as in any other conflict all kinds of arguments are employed, usually without much regard to their provenance, entailments or implications, provided they serve to

81

buttress one's case, and persuade the world of its justice. But unregarded implications have a way sometimes of springing back on one in disagreeable or inconvenient ways.

In the Falklands conflict the Government stressed quite frequently that they were opposing the Argentinian invasion because the inhabitants of the Falklands desired to live, not under Argentinian, but under British rule. Suppose then that the Falklanders were to change their minds, or that the inhabitants of Birmingham or Cardiff, or Ulster, were to aspire to independence. Would that be sufficient reason for the Queen's Government to abdicate its authority without further ado? Simply to ask the question is to realise its absurdity. A government's title to rule cannot simply depend on a plebiscite. At a given moment, this may go one's way, but plebiscites are shifting sands and the stability and good order of a society cannot be erected upon them. It is of course true that plebiscites and the right to self-determination constitute the foundation of the Covenant of the League of Nations and of the United Nations Charter. But these documents exemplify all that is most alien to conservative discourse. They proceed from a visionary, radical, levelling impulse. They aspire to an international order which simply cannot be established or be made endure on such contradictory and paradoxical premises. The situation of Central and Eastern Europe between the wars, and that of much of Asia and Africa after 1945 is a monument to the illusions of Woodrow Wilson, Smuts, Lord Robert Cecil, and F.D. Roosevelt.

In the Falklands conflict, again, the Security Council of the United Nations and the authority of its resolutions were much invoked. But the Security Council is no more than a collection of Powers whose votes are not judicial verdicts, but expressions of what, for the time being, they conceive to be their interest. To speak as though action against an opponent is justified and made lawful by such votes is no doubt to show deference and obeisance to the Charter. But the Security Council is in no sense an impartial tribunal; in the final analysis no state will, if it can help it, obey a Security Council resolution which imperils its existence—hence a ruinous gap between the aspirations of the Charter and the actual reality.

Through this gap humbug insinuates itself—and it is precisely humbug which conservative discourse ought to be at pains to root out and banish.

Augurs and Diviners

IN THE COURSE of the last few years the intellectual classes of the West have been giving voice to doom-laden prophecies about Western civilization, lamenting (or rejoicing at) the decay of 'capitalism', denouncing (somberly or gleefully, as the case may be) the weakness and corruption of 'democratic' government. Such warnings have not been confined to publicists and commentators. They have also figured in the writings of novelists primarily interested not in public distempers but in private confusions and intimate disasters. Thus, in a recent novel *Au delà de cette limite votre ticket n'est plus valable* ('Ticket not valid beyond this point'), Romain Gary draws the picture of an ageing man of affairs who finds himself the victim of business and sexual worries. The hero's intimate crisis is presented as the analogue and reverberation of the crisis of the Western economy, touched off and made manifest by the oil embargo and the great increase in oil prices following the Arab–Israeli war of October 1973. Another recent novel, Muriel Spark's *The Takeover*, dealing with the affairs of a very rich woman and the various cooks who cheat her, presents the oil crisis of 1973 as a climacteric in the life of the West: 'a complete mutation not merely to be defined as a collapse of the capitalist system, or a global recession, but such a sea-change in the nature of reality as could not have been envisaged by Karl Marx or Sigmund Freud.'

To judge by these two examples, public events in the early 1970s, through some ominous quality they are thought to possess, have conjured up a threat not only to a society and a way of life, but also to the very core of being, a threat which imaginative and intelligent writers have tried to convey through the medium of their fictions. What these events are is not in doubt: not only the Arab–Israeli war and the oil embargo but also Watergate; the *coup d'état* in Portugal which bade fair to result in a Communist regime in Lisbon, and which did in fact hand over Mozambique and Angola to clients of the Soviets; Britain in the throes of an inflation which looked as though it was being deliberately used to destroy a society hitherto stable, prosperous and well-governed; the pitiful debacle in Vietnam; and the horror in Cambodia. Truly, it seemed, these last few years, as though it was 'closing time in the gardens of the West'.

The particular expression of despondency I have just quoted, however, was not elicited by the disasters of the early 1970s but was rather a reaction to earlier disasters, those of the 1930s and of World War II. Its author, Cyril Connolly, was oppressed with the decadence and futility of Western society, which greed and philistinism were destroying. Indeed, a defeatist mood, we may suspect, was then and is now justified and made plausible not only by public events which are catastrophic enough, but also by the widely prevalent theory that the crisis of 'capitalism' is at hand, that the system is a gigantic 'self-destruct' mechanism which finally has to explode.

It is worth recalling that the earlier prophecies derived their plausibility from the terribly attractive simplifications of Marxist doctrine which offered one grand and unique explanation for a large number of disparate phenomena. May the similar forebodings of the 1970s ultimately have for their basis the same doctrine, which today more than ever is without serious rival as the opium of Western intellectuals?

The catastrophes which have befallen Western interests in the early 1970s—the oil cartel and the ruinous rise in oil prices, the debacles in Vietnam and Angola, the government-manufactured inflations—may, of course, precipitate other catastrophes, and may in the end prove mortal. But whatever the outcome, these misfortunes are by no means linked to one another, and cannot be any stretch of the imagination be seen to exemplify the 'contradictions' or the 'crisis' of 'capitalism'. Thus, the Arab–Israeli war of 1973 was one in a series of wars which began in 1948. The oil cartel and the rise in oil prices were the outcome of geography, of increased demand for oil (which betokens prosperity rather than crisis), of improvident energy policies in Western countries, and of pusillanimity in negotiation with the oil states since at least 1970. The young Portuguese officers who carried out the *coup d'état* of April 1974 may themselves—as Marxists—have believed in the 'crisis of capitalism', but it is clear that neither Portugal nor its colonies was in the throes of such a 'crisis'; in the colonies guerrillas armed and trained by Communist Powers and harboured by African states forced the Portuguese government to commit resources and troops in long-drawn-out hostilities, and this resulted in the politicization and radicalization of army officers.[1]

To mention these events and their attendant circumstance is immediately to see how disparate they are, and how useless to explain them are these ominous general causes, which yet engender forebodings of dissolution and disaster. For deceptive as they are,

>   all these are usual
> Pastimes and drugs and features of the press:
> And always will be, some of them especially
> When there is distress of nations and perplexity
> Whether on the shores of Asia, or in the Edgware Road

Features of the press, indeed. For the latest example we may turn to a long 'conversation' with George F. Kennan which appears in the September 1976 *Encounter* (the conversation, conducted by George Urban, bears the title 'From Containment ... to Self-Containment'). Kennan, it is true, seems quite innocent of the Marxism which, at whatever remove

---

[1] Such an outcome, we may add, is by no means inevitable, for the Algerian war fostered in the French army attitudes at the very opposite of those found among the Portuguese officers: the army which brought de Gaulle to power in May 1958 was vehemently opposed to a surrender in Algeria such as their hero, only four years later, was to engineer.

and however indirectly, ultimately dictates the belief that 'capitalism' has reached a stage in the West which must end in political collapse. But his arguments reveal the same grandiose ambition to conjoin social trends and political calculations. Thus, Kennan says that he does not 'think that the United States civilization of these last 40–50 years is a successful civilization.' He is increasingly 'persuaded that the Industrial Revolution itself was the source of most of the bewilderments and failures of this modern age.' The West is 'honeycombed with bewilderment and a profound sense of internal decay.' America has nothing to teach the world, and 'we must confess that we have not got the answers to the problems of human society in the modern age.'

It is, of course, possible that these sweeping statements are, all of them, true. What is by no means clear is why they should be thought to require the political conclusions which Kennan proceeds to draw from them. There is, he asserts, 'very little merit in organizing ourselves to defend from the Russians the porno shops in central Washington', and it is 'grotesque' to spend so much energy to save a decaying and bewildered West from Russian domination. Again, Kennan affirms, an 'absolutely certain ecological and demographic disaster is going to overtake this planet within the next, I would say, 60–70 years', and compared with this inevitable death sentence Soviet control over Western Europe would be only 'a minor catastrophe', Perhaps not even that:

> A couple of years ago, in the course of our usual summer cruise in the Baltic, my family and I put in at a small Danish port which was having a youth festival. The place was swarming with hippies—motorbikes, girlfriends, drugs, pornography, drunkeness, noise—it was all there. I looked at this mob and thought how one company of robust Russian infantry would drive it out of town.

Let us suppose that mankind is doomed to perish in some remote or near future. May a country base its present policy toward a rival, and a potential enemy, on such remote and misty speculations? Is Soviet society innocent of industrialism? Why are these exhortations addressed to the United States alone? Will not the calamity affect all mankind? And if all states become convinced that universal disaster is in the offing, can Kennan be sure that discord will then be stilled, and wars banished? The 'absolutely certain' disaster he foresees has to do with demography and ecology—that is, population, and resources and their exploitation. May it not occur to the rulers of some state to exterminate all the inhabitants of a set of rival states, and thus at one stroke obtain easement from military, and demographic, and ecological threat? For, after all, there are in the world today states for whose rulers thinking about nuclear warfare is not, automatically, to think the unthinkable. Or consider the hippies, the hideous hippies whom Kennan met on his Baltic cruise. One cannot possibly doubt that, as he says, 'one company of robust Russian infantry' would know how to deal with them. But before one's mind lie the opulent and sophisticated societies of which these hippies are the dregs, the rude products of luxury—to use an expression of Hegel's: what, one cannot help wondering, would the robust Russian infantry do to *them*, in the process of driving the hippies out of town? (Fears of this kind Kennan dismisses as unrealistic, because the Russians 'can't run an agricultural system that really works' and 'can't adequately house their population'. Similar shortcomings, we may remember, afflicted the early Arab conquerors, Ghengis Khan and Attila).

It is evident from Kennan's language that he thinks there is a straightforward connection between worth and power. America, he tells us, has 'nothing to teach the world'—hence his advocacy of 'a gradual and qualified withdrawal from far-flung foreign involvements'. And this simple monalism is reinforced by the belief in an unproblematic relation between society and politics, between, for example, the state of Soviet housing and Soviet readiness for war; or between the prevalence of 'porno shops' in Washington and the maintenance of American power in the Mediterranean. The confusion, though not identical, is similar to that which sees behind the multitude of disparate events which take place in the world a presumed 'crisis of capitalism' by which wars, revolutions, and other distresses are ultimately explained. These judgements, one might say, are the product of a peculiarly bookish outlook on the world. They depend, for their power to convince, on the acceptance of a long chain of speculation about the character of an economy or a society: speculation which, necessary to the academic enterprise as it must be, is yet always precarious and doubtful, and unfit to serve as a guide for practical action and political decision. But the prestige of academics in the modern world, and particularly in America, is such that economic and sociological disquisitions have come to be looked on as the indispensable foundation on which all serious political debate must rest.

An example of this tendency is a volume entitled *The Crisis of Democracy: Report on the Governability of Democracies to the Trilateral Commission*. According to a statement on the title page, the Trilateral Commission was formed in 1973 by private citizens of Western Europe, Japan and North America to study and seek solutions to problems common to these regions. The present report is the work of a Task Force on the Governability of Democracies which was set up in the spring of 1974, and which reported a year later. The members of the Task Force were Michel J. Crozier, director of the *Centre de Sociologie des Organisations*, Paris; Samuel P. Huntington, professor of government at Harvard; and Joji Watanuki, professor of sociology at Sophia University, Tokyo. They have each contributed a chapter, resepectively, on Western Europe, the United States, and Japan; in writing their papers, the three authors enjoyed the benefit of consulting an eminent body of (mostly academic) experts.

The considerations which prompted the Trilateral Commission to form the Task Force are set out by Zbigniew Brzezinski, former director of the commission, in an introductory note. Brzezinski begins by asking, 'Is democracy in crisis?' and then goes on:

This question is being posed with increasing urgency by some of the leading statesmen of the West, by columnists and scholars and—if public opinion polls are to be trusted—even by the public. In some respects, the mood of today is reminiscent of that of the early 1920s, when the views of Oswald Spengler regarding 'The Decline of the West' were highly popular. This pessimism is echoed, with obvious *Schadenfreude*, by various Communist observers, who

90

speak with growing confidence of the 'general crisis of capitalism' and who see in it the confirmation of their own theories.

What, then, does the Task Force say: *is* democracy in crisis? We find that it does agree with the 'Communist observers' that democracy is indeed in crisis, and also that this has to do with something very much like those observers' notion of the 'general crisis of capitalism.' At the very outset of their study, the members of the Task Force quote some 'acute observers' in support of the view that the future for democracy is bleak. One of these is Willy Brandt; in his estimation, 'Western Europe has only twenty or thirty more years of democracy left in it; after that it will slide, engineless and rudderless, under the surrounding sea of dictatorship, and whether the dictation comes from a politburo or a junta will not make that much difference.' We do not know on what ground or evidence this expression of despair is based. The Task Force refers to the rediscovery of the fifty-year Kondratieff cycle. According to this theory 1971,, like 1921, marks the beginning of a period of economic depression in the industrialized capitalist world which will not come to an end before the close of the century. The argument here is that the politics of the 1970s and the 1980s will therefore be as disastrous as the politics of the decades between the two world wars proved to be. Such a line of reasoning not only asserts a direct connection between economics and politics, but also clearly postulates that economics governs political developments.

The Task Force does not commit itself to these precise theories, but it does clearly take for granted the existence of such a connection. 'The viability of democracy in a country,' it emphasizes, 'clearly is related to the *social structure* and *social trends* in that country'; or,more pointedly, political democracy requires economic growth. The statement seems at first sight clear, indeed obvious; but it is really quite puzzling. Democracy, we take it, is a form of government in which authority to rule is deemed to be derived from the governed. As such, it is compatible with a multitude of social structures and social trends. But what the Task Force means by democracy—in a usage that is now quite prevalent—is more than a govern-

91

ment deriving its title to rule from the governed. By democracy the authors of this book mean also 'regular elections, party competition, freedom of speech and assembly'. But if they mean all these things by democracy, our puzzlement is, if anything, increased, for why then do they also say that a 'social structure in which wealth and learning were concentrated in the hands of a very few would not be conducive to democracy'? All the world knows that eighteenth or nineteenth century England, in which wealth and learning were concentrated in the hands of a few, had regular elections, party competition, and freedom of speech and assembly.

Our perplexity is not diminished as we get deeper into the report. We read in Michel J. Crozier's chapter that after World War I the need for order in Western Europe was met 'by recourse to the Fascist and Nazi regressions', but that such a 'setback' is not likely today; and this is because today there is 'no strong will, no sense of mission, no real dedication to fight for the restoration of an earlier moral order', because 'there is not so much will to fight for capitalism or even for free enterprise. No strong movement can be expected therefore,' he declares by way of conclusion, 'from a right-wing "reactionary" background'.

What seems to be put before us here is a simple and familiar Marxist schema, according to which 'capitalism' and 'free enterprise' belong to a bankrupt and moribund—a 'reactionary'—epoch, which only 'regressions' like Fascism and Nazism attempt, though foolishly and in vain, to revive. This may please the 'Communist observers' of whom Brzezinski speaks, but it sheds no light on the 'crisis of democracy'. Mussolini and Hitler did not fight in the cause of 'free enterpise', and their movements, far form being 'regressions', were (like Bolshevism) something fairly novel in European history. Here again we see confusion promoted and clarity confounded by these grandiose *tableaux* in which society, economy, and politics are made to perform in unison before our dazzled eyes.

Consider again—to take another instance—Samuel P. Huntington's chapter on the United States. According to him the 'basic' point in American politics today is this: 'The vitality of democracy in the United States in the 1960s produced a substantial increase in government activity and a substantial increase in governmental authority.' What this statement seems to mean is that there was an increase in public expenditure on 'welfare', and that certain policies and actions by the government (Vietnam, the draft) aroused vehement opposition. But in fact there is no visible connection between the increase in welfare expenditures and the decline in confidence which the government's conduct of foreign policy produced, nor is there any logical link to be discerned between these phenomena and 'the vitality of democracy', since such vitality would have been equally compatible with a decrease in welfare expenditures and with support for a government's foreign policy. Huntington, moreover, speaks as if democracy, 'participation', and egalitarianism necessarily go together. This of course is the cant of the age, and one might have hoped it would not have been accepted. For democracy—which concerns the source of government authority—entails nothing about participation which relates to the way in which government is carried on: and it does not imply that the members of a democratic polity are, or ought to be, equal.

If *The Crisis of Democracy* cannot be said to enlarge, or to enhance the clarity of political discourse—quite the contrary—, does it at least have anything to report about current conditions in the regions with which it deals? Its main message seems to be that in the United States, Western Europe, and Japan, a quarter of a century's prosperity has brought its own discontents. 'In all three Trilateral regions,' the Task Force affirms in the introduction, 'a shift of values is taking place away from the materialistic, work-oriented, public-spirited values toward those which stress private satifaction, leisure, and the need for "belonging and intellectual and aesthetic self-fulfillment."' Expectations have escalated, and their possible—probable—disappointment will create problems, all the greater by reason of the encouragement which governments of all shades have given to the idea that they have it in their power to ensure perpetual prosperity for everyone.

The crisis which is the subject of this book, then, is not so much a crisis of democracy as one of prosperity. Yet far from being a new academic discovery, the notion that prosperity spoils people and makes them difficult and flighty is a piece of immemorial wisdom: 'Yeshurun waxed fat and kicked,' as

Deuteronomy puts it, and Dryden, centuries later, echoes the theme:

> God's pampered people, whom, debauched with ease,
> No king could govern nor no God could please.

For such murmurings and discontents there may in truth be no efficacious remedy, except, ultimately, the harsh, impersonal one of scarcity and privation. To put it in the language favored by the Task Force: 'The new values may not survive recession and resource shortage.' Political science does not seem to have a universal or general recipe to offer to rulers who are faced with such problems. It may tell them to learn, if they can, from their mistakes, and to try and play it by ear—an ability which may have atrophied from reading too many books, and deferring too much to academics.

In what the Task Force proposes, however, we catch a hint of something distinctly more ambitious, and in its ambitiousness distinctly *dirigiste*. The introduction declares that the new values—private satisfaction, leisure, etc.—'pose an additional problem for democratic government in terms of its ability to mobilize its citizens for the achievement of social and political goals and to impose discipline and sacrifice upon its citizens in order to achieve those goals.' In the conclusion the Task Force similarly laments that a sense of purpose, hitherto supplied by religion, nationalism and ideology, is now in short supply. Crozier much admires the strength of European Communist parties, and goes so far as to say that they are 'the only institutions left in Western Europe where authority is not questioned', that 'their machine has remained extraordinarily efficient', and that there is now 'no other institution in Europe, not even the state bureaucracies, that can match the Communist parties' capabilities in this domain'.

Such remarks indicate clearly enough the drift of the book. The Task Force does not believe that the duty of government is to maintain the conditions in which citizens may pursue and realize their own various, spontaneous, self-chosen purposes. It seems, rather, to believe that survival requires governments to prescribe and direct the activities of their citizens. Crozier demands of West European governments nothing less than 'a basic mutation in their model of government and their mode of social control'. What precisely do these aspirations entail? The answer is not in doubt. The Task Force, for instance, believes in strong well-organized trade unions. The reason? Because otherwise 'the formulation and implementation of a national wage policy become impossible', and the authority of the government is weakened. Again, the Task Force lays it down that the control of inflation and the promotion of economic growth *must* have top priority; governments *must* establish a minmum floor of guaranteed subsistence for all citizens; and specific measures toward these ends *must* be devised by 'economists and planners'. 'Political democracy', the authors sagely conclude, 'requires economic growth; economic growth without inflation depends upon effective democratic planning.'

What, we may wonder, is the value of these unqualified, categorical assertions and prescriptions, and by what authority are they made? It is clear that such statements cannot have a basis in historical, or political, or economic science. For do we not know that a 'national wage policy' devised and imposed by government, simply because it must sooner or later break down, must also bring the authority of government into disrepute? And as for planning, promoting economic growth, and controlling inflation, can all these imperatives be simultaneously obeyed? Will they not hamstring one another? Have we not seen how many governments have come a cropper on these alleged imperatives, and should we not have been invited to consider the thought that perhaps governments can do very little, that the very attempt by them to do so much may in fact make them fit to do even less?

Doubts of this kind, doubts which are not easily stilled, lead in their turn to other doubts. For we find ourselves asking whether there has not been altogether too much of this kind of exercise, and all to the detriment of the public weal? Whether academics have any special qualification to engage in them? Whether public men are wise to pay so much attention to these heavy disquisitions? And whether they should not allow themselves to entertain—if only for a minute—the thought that three workmen discoursing of public affairs in an alehouse may perhaps display more clarity, shrewdness, and common sense?

A New
International Disorder

BEFORE 1914 world politics was very much the politics of European states. Relations among these states were fairly stable in their character, and their nature could be grasped and understood with the help of two organizing ideas. These organizing ideas were not imposed by students of international relations. They derived naturally, so to speak, from the way in which European states had come to conduct themselves toward one another. Nor were these organizing ideas simply theoretical concepts. They were also practical rules of thumb with which men of affairs were familiar, and by which they thought it prudent to be guided.

These two organizing ideas were, on the one hand, that of the balance of power, and, on the other, that of the concert of Europe. The notion of the balance of power meant that the security of each individual state, as well as the general peace, could best be preserved if the power and ambition of any state or combination of states could be counterbalanced or checkmated by a rival combination. About the operation of the balance there was of course nothing automatic. To establish and maintain a balance, which was as much world-wide as it was European, required acumen, boldness, cool heads, and moderation. Because the necessary wisdom and the requisite political skills were not always available, because miscalculations could always happen, the balance would sometimes overbalance and war would ensue. To end a war in manner such that the balance could be re-established required as much skill and wisdom as to keep an existing balance in being. The outbreak of war in 1914 proved the most serious failure in balance-of-power politics in modern European history, and the so-called settlement which followed in 1918-19 was likewise the most serious failure to re-establish a balance—a failure whose consequences have proved infinitely ruinous for Europe and the world.

Underlying the notion of the balance of power is the other organizing idea, that of a concert of European states. The idea is no doubt more complex, less clear-cut, and certainly less amenable to use as a rule of thumb than that of the balance of power. This other idea assumes and expresses the consciousness of a common civilization, common political attitudes, and a common language of international politics. The idea is no doubt met most frequently in the nineteenth century, but this is not to say that it appeared suddenly during this period. The society of states it took for granted, the body of international law that articulated the assumptions and norms according to which such a society could function and endure, were in the making from the time of Grotius in the seventeenth century, and even before. We might say that a *locus classicus* where the system can be seen operating most clearly is the period in the eighteenth century lying between the settlement of the War of the Spanish Succession (1714) and the outbreak of the Revolution in France—a period the international relations of which are magisterially described and analyzed in the first volume of Albert Sorel's *Europe and the French Revolution*.

The French Revolution posed a grave challenge to the European society of states and the assumptions on which it rested. The revolutionary ideology dismissed both balance and concert, and strove for hegemony and doctrinal uniformity. The threat was formidable and the triumph of the new order seemed at times inevitable and irresistible. But after a long struggle the threat of French hegemony was at last averted. The authors of the settlement which followed wished to look upon it as a restoration of the pre-1789 world. This of course it could not be, but it remains true that the dominant outlook within the European society of states up to 1914 accepted and took for granted the organizing ideas just described, which the French Revolution had attempted to sweep away.

The balance of power was destroyed during the war of 1914, and the Versailles settlement which followed, instead of re-establishing this balance, put the seal on its irremediable destruction. This was clearly seen when, less than fifteen years after Versailles, Germany under the Nazis embarked on an expansionist policy, and no combination of powers could be put together to act as a deterrent. At the heart of the Versailles settlement there was, it is true, an organizing idea which might look similar to that of the concert of Europe. The League of Nations was regarded as a kind of world-wide concert all of whose members accepted a commitment to act collectively against any disturber of the peace, thus making a balance of power—objected to by reason of its alleged amorality and cynicism, and its supposed tendency to encourage and justify armed conflict—superfluous. But involved in the idea of the League was an element at least as subversive of stability and peace as the Rights of Man had proved to be after 1789. This element, which was at the centre of the League covenant, was that of national self-determination.

The idea of national self-determination assumes quite simply that the world is composed of separate, identifiable 'nations', and claims that these nations are, as such, each entitled to form a sovereign state. Since, manifestly, the world is not what this theory assumes it to be, to make reality conform to the theory must involve endless upheaval and disorder. For one thing, it is by no means easy indisputably to identify these 'nations'; for another, to upset all existing arrangements in order to make national self-determination the sole and overriding aim of all political action is a recipe for perpetual war. National self-determination is thus a principle of disorder, not of order. This was clearly seen when German self-determination involved the destruction in turn of Austria, Czechoslovakia, and Poland—states which, ironically enough, had shortly before themselves been set up in the name of national self-determination.

The war of 1914 also led to the destruction of the old order in Russia and the foundation of the Soviet Union. This too introduced a potent source of disorder in international relations. Bolshevik doctrine in external affairs may quite accurately be summed up by Lenin's dictum about domestic politics: *Kto Kogo?*—'who whom?' The doctrine of class struggle which this dictum encapsulates is the simple and barbaric one that politics is nothing more than a constant and deadly struggle for absolute and complete domination. Like the principle of national self-determination, that of the class struggle is incompatible with the notion of a balance of power, since balance means precisely that no single interest or principle can assume sole or overriding importance. The ideas of national self-determination and class struggle are also incompatible with the existence of a society of states whose members, irrespective of their own varied political and social arrangements, are and recognize themselves to be part of a more or less coherent international order. It is, incidentally, quite arresting—and ominous—that nuclear weapons, and the concept of a balance of terror associated with them, should so accurately mirror Lenin's maxim. For does not the balance of terror seem the concept most fitted to international relations disordered and subverted by the sway of these totalitarian principles?

World War II, which started as a European war, ended the centrality of Europe in world politics. But the much wider, and eventually world-wide, political stage saw, in the following decades, in an even more accentuated and acute form, the same systematic disorder in international relations which had already become manifest at the end of World War I. The United Nations, even more than the League, was incompatible with international order and stability. It is true that no particularly new organizing ideas or principles were associated with the United Nations. However, by 1945, the Bolsheviks and their doctrine had attained a respectability and influence which they simply did not have in 1918. But instead of seeking to counterbalance Soviet power and influence, Roosevelt worked relentlessly to diminish his Western allies and dismember their empires. There is no indication in recent studies such as Christopher Thorne's *Allies of a Kind* or William Roger Louis's *Imperalism at Bay* that Roosevelt or other U.S. policymakers considered the consequences of doing away so completely with elements which might have helped to counter ambitions by their very nature relentless and limitless. Nor is there evidence that any thought was given to the way the new world-wide society of states was to operate.

An incident typifying the policy and its illusions was the manner in which U.S. agents were instructed to welcome and encourage Ho Chi Minh in the innocent belief that here was another George Washington rising against arbitrary and despotic rule. What is so conspicuous by its absence at the time of Yalta was any awareness by the most powerful country in the world that here was a hinge of fate; that the international disorder which World War I and the ensuing settlement created was now threatening to spread more widely and becoming well-nigh impossible to extirpate. In an earlier crisis Edmund Burke saw clearly that here was no ordinary conflict, that what was being contended with was a formidable armed doctrine. No Burke now appeared. We had instead the Atlantic Charter—toothless pieties facing the armed doctrines of Bolshevism and nationalism.

Since 1945, increasinlgy so with the passage of years, these doctrines, destructive of international order, have secured a firmer purchase over international life. In the Third World, so-called, the two doctrines have combines in a powerful amalgam which is today the most widespread and the most attractive in Asia, Africa, and Latin America. This hybrid doctrine joins the Marxist emphasis on class warfare with the nationalist vision of a humanity divided into separate nations each one of whom has a claim to full and unfettered sovereignty. This doctrine, the most recent proponents of which are Frantz Fanon and his imitator Colonel Kaddafi, divides the world into 'northern', rich, exploiting nations and 'southern', poor, exploited nations. The true class struggle, the only one of any consequence in this view, is the struggle between these two groups of nations, not between proletariat and capitalists in an industrialized society.

One corollary of this analysis is the demand for a New Economic Order, so prevalent today, and voiced in so many quarters from UNCTAD to the 'nonaligned' movement and the Brandt Commission. The demand for a New Economic Order really signifies that a massive transfer of resources from Western countries to the poor countries of the so-called South shall take place. The demand is justified by a variety of arguments among which loom large allegations about colonialism and neo-colonialist exploitation resting on Marxist–Leninist assumptions of whose character the Western advocates of a massive transfer do not always seem aware.

The majority of states now in the United Nations loudly and self-righteously propound these demands. These states, or most of them, attained sovereign status in the period after 1945, as a result of the destruction or self-liquidation of the European empires. They are what Michael Oakeshott has called imitation states. They are formally sovereign, but their rulers labour under strong feelings of insecurity generated by their lack of legitimacy. The product of fake elections or military coups d'état, their unrestrained power does not rest on the loyalty of those whom they rule, and they lack the strength and self-confidence which accrues to those who can speak on behalf of a well-established body politic.

Hence these states, where private interests are wholly at the mercy of the rulers, and the public interest entirely what the rulers decree, are condemned to instability and civil commotions, which become cumulative, and progressively more aggravated. Hand in hand with this condition goes an ideological style of politics. Plans and blueprints, ambitious and arbitrary, in the absence of constitutional restraints, are pursued by the rulers for the time being, only to be changed or scrapped at the rulers' whim, or as their fortunes dictate. Egypt under Nasser, Syria and Iraq under the Baath, Tanzania under Nyerere, are leading examples of this state of affairs.

From the mid-1950s onward, the international disorder which was now endemic in the world—and of which the United Nations may be considered the symptom and the symbol—spread rapidly throughout Africa. 'Decolonization' suddenly became the settled policy of the British, the French, and the Belgians, a policy precipitately and thoroughly applied whatever the costs and the consequences. The policy was, by and large, the outcome of a unilateral decision taken by the metropolitan authorities, rather than a response to some overwhelming or irresistible pressure exerted by the African populations. The decision was based on a judgement about the worth to the metropolitan countries of administering these colonies. It was taken in the light of assumptions about the future tendencies of world politics, of the world balance of power, and of the manner in which this balance—military as well as political—would be affected by the metropolitan countries relinquishing control over Africa.

There was in these judgements a large element of defeatism, complacency, cynicism, and sheer illusion. The defeatism is best exemplified by the stance which French ministers adopted toward Tunisia and Morocco in 1954–6 when, no doubt influenced by events in Indochina, they hastily dismantled the protectorates in these two countries. The complacency may be illustrated by Harold Macmillan's well-known 'wind of change' speech, in which the British prime minister unveiled to the world the shape of things to come. If, to pursue his own metaphor, navigation consisted in drifting with the wind, few ships would manage to reach a safe haven. In any case, was there really a 'wind of change', or was it that the words and actions of metropolitan governments were raising a whirlwind—which would undoubtedly engulf their unfortunate African wards, but also damage their own strategic stance vis-à-vis the Soviet Union?

Neither African welfare nor the geopolitical consequence of abandoning Africa, seem to have been given much weight. This may have represented intellectual failure—akin to that which led civil servants in the Foreign Office to press for British withdrawal from Aden and the Persian Gulf in 1968–70—but it was also the expression of a cynicism which was the ugly obverse of the complacency. De Gaulle may be said to illustrate this cynicism at its ugliest. Having decided that *l'Afrique est foutue et l'Algérie avec*, that these territories were not worth two cents, de Gaulle had no scruple in liquidating French rule abruptly and totally. In the case of Algeria, the abandonment was particularly scandalous. De Gaulle had come to power in 1958, the beneficiary of a coup d'état, as the one figure able and willing to maintain the French presence in Algeria. By 1960, the war against the FLN had been won on the ground. But by 1962 he had so manœuvered as to abandon a territory and its inhabitants who had been under French rule for over a century, causing in the process large numbers of his fellow citizens to be massacred by the new rulers or to become penniless refugees.

De Gaulle chose to act as he did because he looked on Algeria and the African territories as an embarrassment which hindered him in his pursuit of superpower status. He clearly did not think that giving up control, say, of Algerian oil, or the naval base at Oran, or of other territories inland would damage French military or economic interests. A mere two decades later his miscalculation is patent.

But if Western political leaders no longer harbour de Gaulle's haughty and disdainful illusions, there is still rife among them a cynicism, to be sure not as ruthlesss as that which de Gaulle was pleased to flaunt, but rather more soft-spoken and comfortable, snickering, shoulder-shrugging, and low-minded. This outlook is admirably captured in an article by Peregrine Worsthorne which appeared in the *Daily Telegraph* of London on 10 September 1979—the first day of the conference which encompassed the transformation of Rhodesia into Zimbabwe:

> The prospects of post-colonial Africa and Asia are beginning to look hideously ominous. For the time being the prevailing Western view is that this does not matter.
>
> Our statesmen and businessmen like to think that Third World raw materials, on which Western prosperity vitally depends, will always be available under whatever political and social system prevails in those parts—short of Russian domination. I have even heard it argued, by a senior Conservative Minister no less ... that the more degraded the political and social system, the easier it will be to extract the precious oil and minerals, since trade nowadays follows, not the flag, but the bribe. According to this view it does not matter a damn—the word is well chosen—who governs Africa or Asia. The more corrupt the regime, the better Britain's interests will be served. That is the new *Realpolitik*, disguised under the pretty mask of racial equality.

The policy of 'decolonization' led to the setting up of European-style parliamentary regimes, the workings of which necessarily fell into the hands of European-educated Africans who speedily found themselves in a position both despotic and precarious. Depsotic, because European-style government, whatever the paper checks and balances, quickly becomes transformed into an engine of oppression, all the more efficient for being endowed with European-style bureaucratic devices through which the life and livelihood of the ruled can be interfered with and controlled capriciously and minutely. But despotic as their powers are, the new rulers have, and are aware they have, a very precarious tenure. This is because there is little or no relation between the formal Western-style institutions of government and the traditional African society of which these new rulers, by some kind of magic, suddenly find themselves in control. This traditional society was a fragmented one, in which tribal loyalties and pre-ferences ruled supreme. These attitudes naturally lead to the 'corruption' which is the generally recognized hallmark of the new states. But the idea of corruption is intelligible only where it is believed the government is and must be a govern-ment of laws, that public office is not a piece of property, and that the public interest cannot be a respecter of persons. A society in which these notions have no hold is one in which the idea of corruption is unintelligible. All this is to say that between the norms and the institutions of the 'decolonized' states and their social realities, between the form and the content, there is great contradiction and very dangerous tension.

In order to escape this tension which threatens their powers, the new rulers have recourse to ideological mobilization. They think to bind together in this way the body politic, to imbue it with the cohesiveness and solidarity on which the European-style institutions they operate are predicated. These ideologies are also derived from Europe, and they are the very same ones which have introduced instability and precariousness in the international order, namely, nationalism and Marxism–Lenisim in one of its many varieties.

'Decolonization' has thus created an unstable and explosive situation in Africa where tribalism is at odds with European institutions of government, and where an ideological style of politics, instead of assuaging this conflict, serves to exacerbate it. Thus, the newly-created states find themselves endowed with frontiers which had been established as a result of European rivalries and compromises. A nationalist ideology predicated on the need for a cohesive, self-contained national entity is, in many places, at odds with the territorial arrangements inherited from the European empires. The civil wars in the Sudan, Nigeria, or Chad, or the war between Somalia and Ethiopia, are striking examples of conflicts which are the outcome of tribal differences now articulated—and exacerbated—by an uncompromising ideology; conflicts all the more savage and destructive now that what is at stake is the control of a state apparatus, and the enormous power such control is seen to confer. 'Decolonized' Africa is a potential minefield of similar conflicts.

'Decolonization', therefore, has not brought peace to Africa, and has probably increased the burden of insecurity and oppression which the African peoples carry. It has not made relations between the West and Africa more friendly or easier to manage. The complacency has proved to be mistaken, and the cynicism cheated of those banausic advantages the cynics profess to prize. Trade may follow the bribe, but even a child will realize that bribery can be no basis either for trade or friendship.

The world balance of power, moreover, has been seriously affected—for the worse, so far as Western interests are concerned. The new conditions have enabled the Soviet Union to manœuvre, to bargain, to hold out political and military inducements, and thus to establish itself on a continent where Russian power and influence had hitherto been unknown. In large part, the new Soviet position in Africa is the beneficiary of the voluntary Western withdrawal. But the Soviets have not purely and simply occupied vacated ground. They have brought with them an ideological style of politics which, as has been seen, has many attractions in 'decolonized' Africa. The techniques of indoctrination and mass control that go with this style not only prove as welcome as political support and military supplies, but also constitute a point of affinity between what are essentially one-party states which differ only in point of efficiency and ruthlessness, and in which power is checked neither by law nor by scruple.

In recent years it has become fashionable, in the United

States and Western Europe, to argue that world politics is no longer centred on the conflict between East and West, that the present challenge for the West lies in attracting the friendship and loyalty of the Third World. Even were the current military balance between East and West what it was ten or twenty years ago, this view would still be mistaken. In point of military or industrial power the Third World is negligible. Most of its states are not allies but clients. And, unfortunately, the reasons described above will necessarily make these unhappy regions, for as far as one can see, turbulent and the prey of a radical and deep-seated disorder. Turbulence can be held at bay or, better still, tamed. But you cannot sit down and smoke the pipe of peace with it, neither can you embrace it in friendship.

The Brandt 'Commission' and its Report

THE SO-CALLED 'Brandt Report'—*The Report of the Independent Commission on International Development Issues under the Chairmanship of Willy Brandt*—was published to the world under the title *North–South: A Programme for Survival*. The title is a good one. Its six words summarize and encapsulate the assumptions and arguments of the Report. They open up for us a window from which to contemplate the exhibition of wit and wisdom which is displayed wherever two or three men of light and leading, men such as Willy Brandt himself, Edward Heath, Olof Palme, Shridath Ramphal, Amir H. Jamal and Antoine Kipsa Dakouré (to choose at random from the list of Commissioners and the Eminent Persons who appeared before them) are gathered together in solemn conclave.

North–South: the Commission proclaims, *A Programme for Survival*. We are then to understand that survival, the survival of us all, is threatened, and that the Report is a kind of life-saving kit. What is the 'mortal danger' which threaten us, our children and grandchildren, if we are to believe Herr Brandt's emphatic, nay vatic, warnings? The fear oppressing him and his fellow Commissioners is summarized by the first two words of their title—The fear of a clash between the North and the South:

> There is a real danger that in the year 2000 a large part of the world's population will still be living in poverty. The

world may become overpopulated and will certainly be over-urbanized. Mass starvation and the dangers of destruction may be growing steadily—if a new major war has not already shaken the foundations of what we call world civilization.

A week, as Lord Wilson of Rievaulx used to instruct us is a long time in politics. But here we are invited to look forward twenty years. Twenty years! Who in 1900 could have foreseen the downfall twenty years later of the Habsburgs, the Hohenzollerns, the Romanoffs, and the Osmanlis? And who in 1920 could have foretold the monstrous apparition a few years hence of Hitler and Stalin? But Herr Brandt's Commissioners, blessed with extrasensory historical perception, can pierce and penetrate futurity. It may be said that their divination is—cannot but be—sound and accurate. For what do they prophesy but that in the year 2000 poverty will still be with us? But the point is not that poverty is always with us; for it is part of the delusive enterprise of this Report to spread the illusion that, if its advice is promptly followed, poverty need not be with us at all in the year 2000. One looks hard at the miracle-workers: Mr Robert McNamara (who first suggested this Commission), Dr Kurt Waldheim (who agreed to receive the very first copy of the Report), and the cloud of *illustrissimi* hovering and glimmering about them—and one recalls the earlier stars of earlier remakes of the anti-poverty scenario: one can almost hear the flutter of F. D. R. and Henry Wallace, Sir William Beveridge and John F. Kennedy ...

But suppose that in our benighted foolishness we fail to heed the Commissioners' wisdom—and suppose the plagues foretold by them will actually afflict what is called the South: overpopulation ... over-urbanization ... mass starvation. Is it really true that this will bring about an Armageddon to endanger utterly our survival, and that of our children and grandchildren? Anyone considering the question in a cool hour will surely conclude that on present evidence this is simply not true. It is not Mrs Indira Gandhi, even with a General Zia flanking her on either side, who can wage a war to destroy civilization; still less Kaunda or Nyerere or Mugabe or Machel or liberated Liberia's Master Sergeant Doe. To look for mortal danger in their direction is to deceive oneself and others. 'North-South' is *not* the axis of a world-shaking and world-annihilating conflict. It is not fear of the South which forces us to shoulder our feaful burden of armaments.

Why then speak of 'North–South' at all? The 'South' has always exercised a great power of attraction over the European imagination. Voluptuous langour, soft and balmy breezes, bougainvillaea and orange blossom, cicadas singing in the still and hot afternoon, passion and mystery are evoked and conjured up for the Northerner. For all this romanticism there is here substituted a drab abstraction. If one were to ask Herr Brandt, *Kennst du das Land, wo die Zitronen blühn*, he would answer with talk about development and decolonization, and about transnational corporations and a 'new economic order'. All this stodge is predicated on some kind of Marxism, albeit a heretical one. For the Report is a sermon based on the gospel of Li-Ta-chao, Sultan Galiev, Tan Malaka, Ikki Kita, Fanon, Kadaffi and Bani-Sadr—which preaches that the *real* struggle is not between capitalists and proletarians in industrial societies, but between the rich industrial nations of the North and the exploited proletarian nations of the South. Commissioner Layachi Faker of Algeria, Commissioner Amir H. Jamal of Tanzania or Commissioner Adam Malik of Indonesia may eagerly wish to assent to this view of things; but is it clear that Commissioner Katharine Graham (Chairman of the Board of the *Washington Post*) or Commissioner Edward Heath (former Leader of the British Conservative Party) or Commissioner Edgard Pisani (Senator and Minister under de Gaulle) know to what strange and barbarous propositions they are committing themselves?

Anthony Sampson, Editorial Adviser to the 'Commission' has revealed (*Encounter*, April 1981) that the Report was a 'negotiated document with an element of bargaining and compromise on all sides'. Sampson's language here discloses that the doomladen prophecy, which we took to be the inspired and agonized utterance of the truth, is in reality careful and politic calculation, circumspect bargaining, cautious compromise. We are disappointed and puzzled.

Bargaining about what? We would have been even more greatly in Sampson's debt had he lifted the curtain a tiny little bit, and revealed which issue was traded by which Commissioner against which, and who won and who lost. As it is, we have to be content with the bare text, and cannot penetrate behind the public *persona* with its carefully composed expression. The text unmistakably shows that if bargaining there was, the winner is not in doubt. The very framework of the Report, begining with its Manichean division between North and South, its assumptions, its attitudes are all collectivist, *dirigiste*, and Marxist—albeit that the Marxism is heretical. Lenin believed that capitalists will 'provide the rope' by which they will be hanged. But even with the stoutest rope in the world, the South may not quite be able to manage the execution; if this Report is any evidence, it will have to be carried out by the willing victims themselves.

Overlaying the implicit pseudo-Marxim lurking in the 'North-South' concept, a different theory can be detected in the Report. It is by no means compatible with this false vision of a world divided between North and South. This other, equally false, theory is that the world is 'one global village' in which the interests of everybody are fully compatible with those of everybody else, are perhaps even identical with one another. Mankind wants to survive, and peace (in Willy Brandt's words) is the aim of all religions, beliefs and philosophies. But just as it is untrue that there is a clear and distinct conflict which divides North and South (with all the immense variety of their circumstances) into two antagonistic blocs, it is equally untrue that peace is in fact the aim of all religions, beliefs and philosophies. Not peace, but struggle and contention is the aim and policy of the Soviet Union, of the Red Brigades, of Saddam and Asad, of the Ayatollah and his followers, of the IRA and ETA, of the ELF and the PLO.

Suppose the massive transfer of resources to the South advocated in the Report has taken place, is there any reason whatsoever to think that the world would be a more peaceful place? Huge amounts of aid have already gone to the countries of Asia and Africa. Is the world in consequence discernibly safer, significantly more peaceful? It can, on the contrary, be argued that this very transfer of resources has exacerbated international relations, and indeed has in some cases enabled the sworn enemies of the donors to prosecute all the more effectively the campaign against their benefactors.

Herr Brandt pats himself on the back for the *Ostpolitik* and claims that it has averted a 'sterile and dangerous confrontation'. Small wonder. It takes two parties to engage in confrontation; if one party becomes stronger and the other weaker, 'confrontation', no doubt about it, becomes much less likely. If one party provides sweeteners and benevolences to the other, confrontation may likewise be, for a time, averted.

This is not the only example of a deplorable tendency to avert one's eyes from realities and to go in for simplistic judgements which characterizes the Report. Readers may find this all the more surprising in a document prepared by, among others, experienced world figures who have had to deal with complex political and economic affairs. Thus, the Report blandly asserts that in Africa valuable human potentialities continue to be fettered because of the 'struggle for decolonization'. How can one, looking at the corruption, the tyranny and the massacres and the anarchy rampant today in decolonized Africa, fail to see that the great enemy of African welfare is not 'colonial rule' but those very African governments who are to benefit from the vast resources the transfer of which is now demanded? The Report, again, has very harsh things to say about the export of weapons and armaments to the South. It dallies with abstruse calculations such as that the cost of one tank would be enough to set up nothing less than 40,000 village pharmacies. Pharmacies are, on the face of it, wholly beneficent institutions; they contribute to the preservation and prolongation of life. But at the same time Herr Brandt and his fellow Commissioners are haunted by the spectre of overpopulation. These hard dilemmas are where the problem always begins. As for those expensively armoured tanks, they are clearly engines of destruction, but which of the Commissioners would like to see their country (Austria, India, Sweden, Gabon?) completely denuded of tanks? A line of armour—worth perhaps half-a-million pharmacies somewhere—once protected free West Berlin when Willy Brandt was its Mayor.

However, let us indulge the Commissioners in their old-fashioned Hobsonian indignation against 'the merchants of death'. But merchants are dealers: they sell and they buy. Doesn't the Brandt Commission recognise that if there were no buyers, there would be no sellers? It is an embarrassing subject, and the Report treads warily. Indeed it is utterly innocent of even the mildest stricture against Libya or Saudi Arabia, against Iraq or Ethiopia, and their insatiable hunger for *Migs* and *Mystères* and F-16s.

The Commissioners enjoin the governments of developing countries to share 'responsibility for restraint' in the acquisiton of arms. The injunction is itself put with sympathetic restraint. The Commissioners' delicacy becomes even more admirable in the passage which immediately follows this injunction, and which hastens to retract the mild strictures implicit in the appeal for restraint. 'But we recognize', the Commissioners declare with admirable understanding, 'the difficulties of restraining arms procurement in areas of tension where large imbalances of military capacity exist ...'. 'Especially', they indulgently add, 'where this is combined with persistent oppression such as apartheid.' But who is to sit in judgement, to recognize imbalances, certify persistent oppression, and wash away the sin of trafficking with the merchants of death? The Brandt Commissioners? This passage which some might call sanctimonious, is perhaps one of the products of the 'bargaining'. The merchants of death themselves do not seem to benefit from such gentleness:

Business has been rewarding for both old and new arms suppliers who have spread an incredible destructive capability over the globe.

The motives of power, influence and commerce—and, absurdly, prestige—that lie behind the arms trade must be harnessed to development, which would be a source of legitimate pride.

With the recession of the arms industry in the early 1970s— following the end of the Vietnam war—and the emergence of new profitable markets, particularly in the Middle East, the drive to sell weapons to the Third World was intensified, often aimed at stimulating new demand irrespective of real defence needs. These military-industrial pressures in the North are often reinforced and connected with contacts in the developing countries ...

Contacts? Is it meant that the merchants need native middle-men, compradores shall we Marxist-wise call them? In contrast with this gingerliness, the Report begins Chapter 7 (on disarmament and development) with the simple and blunt question, 'Arms or Peace?' One wonders which is the more delusive, the self-assured judgement that arms are bad and 'development' good, or this even more emphatic, catagorical, and rather demagogic affirmation that it is either Arms or Peace. Is the alternative proposition, Arms therefore Peace, so utterly beneath contempt, or irrelevant to political realities?

The moral astigmatism which condemns Northern exporters of arms but remains silent about Southern importers is also in evidence when the Report discusses the supply and price of oil. The Report recognizes the great harm done to poor countries everywhere in the Afro-Asian world by the exorbitant rise in the price of oil since 1973—a nasty blow delivered against the South by the South. It carefully avoids saying anything which would imply that far from being some incalculable, inexplicable 'act of God', this rise was shrewdly engineered by a producers' cartel. If the cartel had been coolly operated by a monopolistic European or American enterpise would it have benefited from the Commissioners' indulgent silence?

Double standards are bad enough, but the Commissioners are not content with passing the cartel mutely by. They go out of their way to endorse OPEC's apologias by arguing that the present price of oil reflects its long-term scarcity and its depletability. This presbyopia no doubt complements the Commissioners' far-sightedness in also predicting over-population and over-urbanization twenty years hence. How much less speculative—and how much more accurate—to have pointed out that there is today absolutely no shortage of oil, and that, traded in a free market, this commodity would not fetch a tenth of its current price. It is painful to have to read a document in which words and facts and values are so intolerably incongruent. For the commodity is there, physically there, and no technical obstacles stand in the way of its production. If the prices enforced by OPEC really reflected the balance of supply and demand, OPEC would have been superfluous. That the shortage is the outcome of restraint of trade is shown by the present glut, which has been prevented from having its full effect on prices by a cartel setting production ceilings and prices—a cartel which, when market forces threatened it with dissolution in 1983, was saved from extinction by the timely, sympathetic understanding shown by the British government, which has thus become a sort of honorary member of OPEC.

If such a cartel had been operated by private firms they would have been held up, rightly, to universal execration and their exactions speedily brought to an end. But, instead of seeking ways to release both North and South from the OPEC treadmill, the Brandt Report accepts the situation, endorses the apologias of OPEC, and proceeds to invent all manner of ingenious devices which must increase the influence and power of the cartel. In so doing, however, the Report is not at all as innovatory as its champions proclaim. It has only followed a trend established over more than a decade whereby the political leaders of the industrialized West gradually divested themselves of all power to curb enterprises like OPEC: by abandoning Aden and the Persian Gulf; by acquiescing in the confiscation of Western oil companies as practised by Algeria, Libya and Iraq; by acquiescing in the breaking of agreements which had been freely entered into by oil states with oil companies. This was an immense dereliction of the duty which they owed to their fellow citizens, and the greatest possible disservice to the populations of the so-called 'South' whose plight is now being so loudly lamented. The surrender to the OPEC may be symbolized by the meeting at Copenhagen in the aftermath of the Yom Kippur War then the EEC leaders found themselves compelled to receive, in humble and abject placation, the emissaries of the new Power, like Roman senators welcoming the envoys of Alaric the Visigoth. But Alaric, at least, had an army.

I feel it would be unjust to conclude on a negative note. For one suggestion made in the Report opens up, perhaps unwittingly, a promising avenue for the solution of the North-South problems. The Commissioners demand on behalf of the 'developing countries' the right to participate, the right to share in the decision-making processes of the International Monetary Fund and other Northern financial institutions. If this is a valuable and viable principle, the Commissioners would surely not oppose its universal application. As a *quid pro quo* for the massive transfer of capital resources to the South which they also demand, would they not agree that the purveyors of those resources—the treasure of hundreds of millions of diligent Western citizens—should, in all fairness, have a proportionate say in the decision-making processes of the governments of the South? Not only would justice be done, but conceivably the South might once more begin to enjoy the security and the modest prosperity banished by the Ayatollahs and the Amins, the Bokassas and the Pol Pots, the Nkrumahs and the Lumumbas to whom Afro-Asian power was cynically conveyed or nervelessly resigned.

Development and Politics

THE USE OF the term development and its concomitant term, underdevelopment, is today common in the discussion of political and particularly economic issues. To use either of the two terms immediately sets up in our mind a comparison and an implicit expectation. The comparison is between countries which are said to be developed and other countries which are said to be underdeveloped. And what is implicitly believed—what the terms implicitly assume and convey is that underdevelopment can be changed into development, that countries which are now underdeveloped can attain a state in which they are developed. We may then say that underdeveloped countries aspire to become one day developed, believe that they can take action in order to achieve such a state, that the aspiration is not foolish, and that a strategy exists which can lead them to such a state.

What is the ideal to which these countries aspire? It is that of a prosperous, stable, democratic society, the prosperity of which is usually believed to rest on manufacturing industry, because it is held that the developed world became rich precisely through industrialization.

We may personally believe, or not believe as the case may be, that such an ideal is worth attaining. We have however always to keep in mind that it is only in recent times—in very recent times—that such an ideal has received the suffrages of large numbers of men, that the great religions of the world, whether monotheistic or pantheistic which, until very recently, exclusively divided between themselves men's allegiance—that these religions recommended quite another goal to humanity, whether this goal is personal salvation, or the absorption of the individual in an all-encompassing Godhead.

We may also personally entertain varying estimates, whether optimistic or pessimistic, about the possibility of some or perhaps most of these so-called underdeveloped countries eventually achieving the state of being developed. But whatever our estimate of the likely outcome, there seem to be many reasons to believe that the very attempt to realize a developed state, if seriously undertaken, will bring about numerous and serious political predicaments escape from which will not be easy. Let us consider some of these predicaments. In the *Politics*, Aristotle discusses two desirable characteristics to look for in a polity. The first is that rule should be for the benefit of the governed, that a polity should not suffer arbitrary and self-interested rule by the one or the few over the many, or of the many over the few. The second characteristic of a desirable polity is stability. Aristotle himself is enormously impressed by the virtue and importance of political stability, believing—perhaps optimistically, since he did not live to see how pure evil became incarnate in the Nazi regime—that no polity is so devoid of goodness that its preservation is not worth some effort. Stability is indeed universally considered to be a necessary requisite in any political order—whether this order is that associated with constitutional and representative government, or whether it is associated with so-called Oriental despotism. There are many ways of accounting for the importance of political stability. We may say for instance with St Augustine that man's profoundest aspiration is peace—peace with God, with himself and with the world. But to be at peace, with the world at any rate, requires that the world around man, the world specifically which he has made for himself, should not change too violently and too frequently. If there is violent and frequent change, then the process itself becomes cumulative. Frequent and violent change produces, for some time, at any rate, change even more frequent and violent, or else a lively and overmastering fear of such a change. This cumulative process—and the savage fears which it elicits—is the simplest and most satisfactory explanation why a revolution, however laudable its ends, however crying the grievances it sets out to remedy, can never stop when it has swept away what it had set out to abolish, and why the familiar saying that the revolution devours its children is so terribly true. This saying originated in the Terror which speedily engulfed the high hopes raised by the French Revolution of July 1789, but it has also proved to be true in respect of the Bolshevik revolution in Russia, in China, in Cambodia, and in the Middle East both in relation to the Syrian and Iraqi Ba'th, and to the Islamic Revolution in Iran.

If, then, a society comes to look upon itself as under-developed, and comes to set up for itself an ideal which it believes is possible of realization through human action, conscious and planned, then we would not be wrong to expect that such a society would be in a continuous state of effervescence and its political stability to be continuously threatened by the expectant state of mind of its members, who have come to believe that change must ensue, and that out of change good will also, infallibly, ensue. A situation of this kind arose in Europe in the decades preceding the Revolution of 1789. Englightened thinkers came to believe that they had resolved the enigma of human nature, penetrated the springs of human action, and solved the riddle of history. In their own interest kings and priests had combined to establish the reign of superstition and despotism. Superstition once banished, corrupt and despotic forms of govenrnment would be infallibly reformed and humanity would attain an era of happiness. The Englightened absolutists who imbibed these ideas came to think that with the help of this new science of human nature, they could now so legislate and administer that their permissions and prohibitions, and their improvement of institutions, would inaugurate a new era in which human happiness would be infallibly assured and human progress become practically limitless. These new hopes created in the minds of the educated and official classes a predisposition to welcome change and to expect to see social and political institutions continually questioned and reformed. This state of mind so widely prevalent in 1789 ensured a wide welcome for the French Revolution at its beginnings and, for instance, gave the poet Wordsworth the feeling that it was bliss to be then alive, and to be young very heaven. Similar, though perhaps not quite as strong and tumultuous, feelings attach to the pursuit of development today, and we must therefore entertain very seriously the thought that political instability is, implicitly, inseparable form the very pursuit of this ideal.

The ideal of an industrial, prosperous, democratic society is not indigenous to the countries of Asia and Africa to which the term underdeveloped principally applies. It originated, on the contrary, in a civilization quite alien to them. Furthermore, in those countries which are supposed to approximate in their social and political development most nearly to this ideal, its practical achievement rests on the enormous technical and scientific resources which alone make an industrial civilization possible, and thus make prosperity and democracy in the modern sense also possible. Again, in Western Europe and North America, the present state of economy and society did not come about as a result of people conceiving an ideal or a plan and setting about to realize them. What exists now came about in unpremeditated fashion, more or less gradually, more or less slowly as the case may be. Its coming about was facilitated by the emergence of a scientific state of mind, and on increasing numbers of men with scientific curiosity. When these scientists made their discoveries they could have had no idea of the enormous practical significance of these discoveries. That this scientific endeavour came to practical fruition is by no means unrelated to a social structure in which an entrepreneurial and mercantile middle class was not devoid of political power and was increasingly at liberty to pursue its economic aims. But we must observe that even under such favourable conditions the transformation of West European and North American society into its present state was by no means an easy matter. The so-called industrial revolution, great as its material benefits proved to be, has created formidable stresses and strains in the body politic. It brought into being an urban industrial proletariat which had migrated from the countryside and suffered in the factories and slums of industrial cities cultural disorientation and spiritual poverty. It is only gradually that municipal facilities, and the housing stock grew and improved so that living in these modern urban conditions became tolerable, and urban neighbourhoods lost their forbidding and alienating character. Again, the Western revolution of industry brought about problems of the trade cycle, of economic crises and depressions quite new in their widespread intensity, in which masses who had come to depend on regular factory employment suddenly—and to them inexplicably—found themselves workless and utterly without resources, the disinherited stepsons, so to speak, of industrial society.

If such was the situation in the Western world, where the industrial process and industrial skills were indigenous, what may we expect when decades of Western experience and experimentation are abridged into a number of slogans or maxims or recipes and abruptly introduced into societies to whom they must be profoundly incomprehensible, and for which they are so little prepared. What are these societies, by and large? They are traditional agricultural societies where for very long periods of time the tempo of change in the conditions of life as well as in the general outlook was so slow as to be imperceptible. For many complex reasons, in the last hundred years or so these areas have found themselves undergoing a tremendous increase in population, the rate of the increase itself becoming greater with the passage of time. The orders of magnitude are eloquent enough. In 1882 the population of Egypt was under 7 million. In 1982 it is about 40 million. The natural rate of increase per thousand of population in Ceylon, for example, in the 1950s was between 25 and 28, in France between 6 and 7, in the U.K. around 4.5, and in the U.S. between 15 and 16. A consequence of these high figures in 'underdeveloped' countries is that a high proportion of the population is very young, say 40 per cent under 14 and two-thirds under 30. In other words a very large proportion of the population is not within the productive age range. By contrast in Western industrialized societies earners constitute the majority of the population, and their productivity has served to keep themselves, as well as the older and the younger generation, at an adequate standard of living, and to endow the young with the social capital represented by technical skills, scientific knowledge, and professional know-how to enable them in their turn to provide for themselves and increase the general wealth. An increase in population such as that of the U.S. in the 1950s—15 per 1000—is a blessing, while the higher increases in Egypt, India or Ceylon or China are a drag on the society and a cause of increasing impoverishment, since even when the young reach the productive age range, there is no opportunity or scope for them to produce. Hence the phenomenon of perpetual unemployment open or disguised which afflicts a very large proportion of the population of these 'underdeveloped' countries. There is one particular aspect of this overpopulation, as we may reasonably call it, which has also to be noticed: the great and growing increase in the size of cities, which is very unlike the increase that cities like London or New York or Manchester or Los Angeles have experienced in the nineteenth and twentieth centuries. In these cases the increase in population was an index of the increase in industry and in employment opportunities generally. And sooner or later as the case may be, the housing stock and the municipal facilities increased in order to keep pace with the growth of population. Cities in the underdeveloped world are by means centres of industry which can offer a livelihood to the enormous numbers who flock to them from the countryside. Cairo at the outbreak of the Second World War had less than 1.5 million inhabitants. Today it has ten or twelve million, or perhaps more. No one imagines that opportunities of employment, the housing stock or the facilities have kept pace. What is true of Cairo is also true of Tehran, Istanbul, Bombay, Calcutta and so many others. This inordinate growth of cities, this over-urbanization as it has been called, has all kinds of repercussions on the social and private lives of the inhabitants and on their governance—consequences which cut across, thwart and hamstring efforts to realize the ideal of development. In the cities of the underdeveloped world, the structure of the extended or patriarchial family which was traditional to these areas has been disrupted, and with it the traditional religions which served to give meaning and coherence to life,

124

and bind the generations together. With the disruption of the traditional family and the loss in prestige and credibility which traditional beliefs have suffered, a wide gap has opened between the young and the old, with the old uncomprehending and ridiculed, and the young disoriented, dissatisfied, open to the lure of slogans and eager to follow whatever path promises to provide a way out of the blind alley in which they find themselves caught. Abd al-Nasser's *Philosophy of the Revolution*, Abol-Hassan Bani-Sadr's Islamic economics, Sadeq Hedayat's fiction, Nirad Chaudhuri's *Autobiography of an Unknown Indian*, V..S. Naipaul's two works *An Area of Darkness* and *Among the Believers* are so many reports, direct and indirect, witting and unwitting on the moral and intellectual condition of the underdeveloped world. And we have to ask if the state of mind of a young man dabbling in terrorism like Jamal abd al-Nasir or Bani-Sadr's Pol-Potian ideals, or the Calcutta students seduced by Gandhian demagogy, or the systematic de-schooling advocated and practised by Muslim fundamentalists in Indonesia can possibly help to further the ideal of development.

The ideal of development, we have said, aspires to a society which is not only prosperous but also democratic. This democratic ideal implies in the first place a state of affairs in which there is personal freedom regulated by impersonal law. It implies further governments responsive to the desires and opinions of the governed, and responsible to them. A government regulated by law and responsible to the body politic is a constitutional government, and constitutionalism is a more adequate and a more precise appellation for this kind of government than the term democracy—a word which is now a victim of verbicide. Constitutionalism, as is well-known, derives its reality and vitality not simply from the suffrage and parliamentary arrangements. It is given reality and is underpinned by a social structure which contains a multitude of interests none of which is able to overrule or to ride roughshod over one another. This mutual checking and balancing of divergent interests is that which gives reality to the checks and balances of a constitutional manner of governing. Thus, the mediaeval theory of the English

constitution distinguished between gubernaculum and juris-
dictio, or as we might say executive and legislative power.
The first inhered in the king, and the second was exercised by
the king by and with the consent of the estates of the realm.
In this traditional framework it proved possible to accommodate various emergent interests, the latest of which is the
new proletariat conjured up by the revolution in industry. All
this is implied by the ideal which the underdeveloped
countries deem themselves to be pursuing. How does this
ideal fit in with their own political inheritance?

By and large these countries share one or other of two
political traditions. China, India, the Islamic Middle East
belong to the tradition of Oriental despotism, while in black
Africa the tradition is that of tribal rule in which an immemorial and divinely sanctioned custom is deemed to regulate
the behaviour of the members of the tribe, and to guide the
acitons of the tribal chiefs and the elders who assist and advise
them. Tribal rule can be described as primitive government.
Primitive is not to be understood in a pejorative sense, but only
to indicate that here is a kind of government which is not
intricate in its arrangements and which has shown that it does
not possess any great powers of resistance when it is faced with
more sophisticated kinds of political and military organizations. The case is far otherwise with Oriental despotism
which the record shows to be one of the most intricate, most
efficient and most lasting of political organizations. In
Oriental despotism, to adopt Karl Wittfogel's classic formulation, the state is stronger than society. How such a political
organization came to be is a matter of speculation which for
our present concerns is quite immaterial. What remains the
case is that where Oriental despotism obtains, political sociology is extremely simple: there are two social groups, those
who are ruled and those who rule, there is a population which
works, produces and pays taxes, and there is a ruling institution quite separate from it, which extracts the taxes, imposes
law and order and engages in warfare. Marx's dictum about
the relation between economic and political power is here
dismetrically reversed. You do not seek to find out who owns
the means of production in order to find out who is the
government. On the contrary, you ascertain where political

and military power lies, and it will then become apparent that economic power is non-existent, that riches are vanity, and that property has no security. It is in this sense that in Oriental despotism the state is stronger than society, that there is no interest in society which can withstand the demands of the ruling institution. Hence, the significance of the fact that feudalism as a political arrangement is here absent. As is well-known control of land in the feudal age in Western Europe meant that a state of affairs arose in which the king as a feudal monarch was bound to seek counsel and consent from the vassals, that feudalism became an intricate network of rights and obligations. This network of interests mutually checking one another is fundamental to the rise of constitutionalism in Western Europe, and constitutionalism we have said, is inherently a matter of checks and balances. The story told of a Chinese general could never have been told of a Western magnate. This general was accused of plotting against the Emperor. In order to exculpate himself and to prove that he had absolutely no interest in political matters, the general pointed to the fact that his one consuming passion was the accumulation of property in land. Hence also the precariousness of private property in Oriental despotism, where wealth can be confiscated or bestowed at the caprice of the ruler, and where to be known to be a man of substance can invite sudden and utter ruin. Ibn Khaldun recounts the instructive and moving story of the philosoper Ibn Baja who happened to recite in the presence of the ruler at an Andalusian court a poem which made the ruler so enthusiastic that he vowed that he would send Ibn Baja home walking on gold. Ibn Baja was in a predicament: to accept or to refuse the gift was equally dangerous. To refuse would offend and anger, while to accept would make Ibn Baja so rich that his life might henceforth be at risk. Ibn Baja resolved the dilemma by begging for two pieces of gold which he proceeded to insert one in each shoe and so walked home literally on gold, thus both making the ruler's vow come true, and yet preserving his own life from the perils of great wealth.

Again, in contrast with the Western situation, there is in Oriental despotism an utter absence of free municipal institutions, and in general of autonomous associations devoted to promoting within the law the interests of their members. Trade guilds have existed of course in Oriental despotism but they always were mistrusted and closely controlled by the ruler. When Oriental despotisms were rejuvenated in the nineteenth and twentieth centuries by the methods and precepts of European Englightened Absolutism, and subsequently of Leninism, the traditional guilds wilted and died in the scorching blaze of centralizing power. Municipalities, municipal institutions and organs of village self-government are then prominent by their absence in the world of Oriental despotism. Omdas in Egypt or mukhtars in the Ottoman empire or village elders elsewhere do not represent villages in which they reside, but rather act as the agents of authority. They are responsible not to the villagers but to the ruler. They are there to ensure the good behaviour of those whom they oversee. Village assemblies are also known in India and China, but such organisms were politically irrelevant in that no mechanism existed whereby the wishes and views of such assemblies could regularly, and as a matter of course, by conveyed to the central authorities,let alone be taken into account or acted upon. British officials in India thought to build on the presumed tradition of Indian village assemblies in order to prepare Indians for parliamentary self-government. But institutions of local government in India proved a dismal failure and in no way engaged the interest or the enthusiasm of those whom they were intended to benefit.

In Oriental despotism, then, there is a great barrier fixed between those in the official class, and those not in the official class. Power sits in formidable and solitary eminence, and all that the ordinary subject may aspire to is to escape the attentions of authority. A story in *The Thousand and One Nights* concerns a man who coming back from work in the evening finds a corpse near his door. He is terrified to report his discovery to the police lest they accuse him of murder. He carries the corpse and puts it over the wall into a neighbour's garden. The neighbour in his turn discovers the body and is likewise terrified; he in turn transfers it to his neighbour's property where the same story is repeated and so on and the body ends by perambulating through the whole town without anybody daring to make public its existence. A saying attributed to the Abbasid Caliph al-Ma'mun declares that the best life has he who has an ample house, a beautiful wife, and sufficient means, who does not know us and whom we do not know.

If power sits on an eminence cut off from the rest of the population, the supreme power is likewise isolated from its servants by a wall of reciprocal mistrust and fear. *Mirrors of Princes* and similar writings abound in advice to rulers and those near them about the best means of protecting their lives and safeguarding their positions. The Indian Kautilya in the latter part of the first millenium B.C.E., advises the ruler on how to take precautions against poisoning, and tells him that the king should spy on his prime minister, that he should beware of his close friends, his wives, his brothers, his heir apparent, and his progeny in general. 'Princes like crabs', says Kautilya, 'have a notorious tendency of eating up their begetter'. A Persian mirror of princes advises the vizir that 'should the ruler at any time pretend to you that you are completely secure with him, begin from that moment to feel insecure; if you are being fattened by someone you may expect very quickly to be slaughted by him.'

This is clearly not the world of Mrs Thatcher or President Reagan; nor is it something utterly remote, dead and gone. We recognize this world as a world which exists here and now, the world in fact in which the greater part of humanity finds itself, Stalin's world, Mao's world, Nasser's world, a world from which escape is a vain and delusive hope. Oriental despotism has in fact been given a new lease of life, and endowed with enhanced powers by all the new technology of communications, indoctrination, and mass control which are the off-shoots of Western scientific innovation, and which have spread to the whole world.

For the world of Oriental despotism then, the political ideal which forms part of the notion of development is not to be realized. And in so far as economic development and constitutionalism seem to go hand in hand, we may perhaps also conclude that the modernized and rejuvented system of Oriental despotism must also stand in the way of economic development itself, that the economic modernization in which all these regimes are feverishly and ostensibly involved amounts (to adopt the eloquent title of Galal Amin's book) to no more than the modernization of poverty.

But it may be said that, as indicated earlier, there is another political tradition to be met with in the underdeveloped world, namely that of tribal rule. Here there is no state apparatus which is stronger than society. Here are warrior chiefs assisted and counselled by elders, rudimentary political arrangements, an openness of relations between leader and led such that the poorest tribesman could address King Ibn Sa'ud as Ya Abd al-'Aziz! The record however shows, in the first place, that it is not true, as used to be argued by romantic historians, that constitutional representative government has its origins in the forests of Germany, or among the Beduins of the Arabian Peninsula. Tribal self-government is primitive government and cannot sustain the sophisticated legal structure without which constitutional representative government cannot exist. In the second place, the record also shows that tribal self-government, as I have said earlier, cannot withstand assault by more solidly and intricately organized political structures. Owing to the fact that their military means were limited and their empires far-flung Oriental despotisms were not always able to submit to their authority nomadic tribes within their territories. But once modern weapons and communications became available nomads were hardly in a position to resist, and their tribal institutions have been superseded. And even when administrators like Lyautey in Morocco or Lugard in Nigeria strive to preserve indigenous institutions by instituting what is called indirect rule, these very attempts at conservation drain life and significance out of what had been—within its limits—a viable political system. Indirect rule transforms tribal institutions into museum pieces. Again, tribal rule itself may change into more complex and more powerful political organizations. But these more complex organizations have evinced no tendency to become constitutional representative governments. On the contrary: the Glaoui in Morocco, the Hausa in northern Nigeria, the Bantu kingdoms in Southern Africa, the Kingdom of Saudi Arabia—all of them having their origin in tribal confederacies and tribal warfare—became despotisms more or less ruthless, more or less arbitrary, haunted by insecurity and suspicion, and schooled in those arts to which rulers have to resort when they do not enjoy the boon of governing with the consent of the citizens and under the aegis of the laws.

Whatever the political tradition to which they belong, rulers of these 'underdeveloped' countries are quite well aware of the gulf which yawns between them and their subjects. Such a state of affairs offers solid advantages to the rulers who can sleep easy in the confidence that their subjects' fear of government is such that passivity is their only political stance. But development is not compatible with passivity. Development requires that passive subjects should be mobilized into activity. Here, too, the example of Europe seems to provide the answer. Ideology and an idelogical style of politics constitute a dintinctive and powerful feature of the European political tradition. Mobilization of subjects, their integration into the enterprise of development—so rulers increasingly came to believe—would be effected by the indoctrination of subjects in some ideology or another, whether nationalism or socialism, or ujamaa or négritude. Thus passivity would be changed into activism, into enthusiasm for the common weal. But such ideologies are, on the one hand, alien to the experience and cast of mind of the inhabitants of 'underdeveloped' countries. And, on the other, they cannot produce initiative, inventiveness, or enterprise—cannot, in other words, make lively and energize these societies. To the burden of passive obedience which the subject owes to the ruler, they only add the obligation of active and demonstrative assent to official slogans and licensed doctrines.

The political inheritance of the underdeveloped countries is thus not propitious to development as this ideal is understood by them. Their economic situation is likewise not auspicious, and—what is perhaps even more serious—the planned and deliberate pursuit of development by a central authority is likely to set up powerful stresses in the body social and the body politic, and thus to put obstacles in the way of that prosperity and democracy which is declared to be the goal of development.

Foreign Policy
A Practical Pursuit

FOREIGN POLICY, it is universally agreed, is a practical pursuit. It is an activity the end of which is the attainment of advantage or the prevention of mischief. Foreign policy, in short, is action, not speculation. Is the academic fitted by his bent, his training, his usual and wonted preoccuptions, to take or recommend action of the kind which generals and statesmen are daily compelled to recommend or take?

Someone might say, in reply, that academics are the best fitted for this activity. They have, after all, a highly trained intelligence, they are long familiar with the traffic of ideas, and long accustomed scrupulously to weigh evidence, to make subtle distinctions, and to render dispassionate verdicts. Plato, it might be urged, was not far out when he pinned his hopes on philosophers becoming kings.

The good academic is indeed as has just been described, but it is not really wise to invoke Plato's shade, and exalt the scholar to such high degree. For consider: if the academic is to recommend action here and now—and in foreign policy action must be here and now—should he not have exact and prompt knowledge of situations and their changes? Is it then proposed that foreign ministries should every morning circulate to historians and 'social scientists' the reports of their agents and the despatches of their diplomats? Failing this knowledge, the academic advising or exhorting action will most likely appear the learned fool, babbling of he knows not what.

It may be objected that this is not what is meant at all: we do not, it may be said, want the academic to concern himself with immediate issues or the *minutiae* of policies; we want his guidance on long-term trends and prospects; and here, surely, his knowledge of the past, his erudition, his reflectiveness will open to him vistas unknown to the active politician, or unregarded by him. And should not this larger view, this wider horizon be his special contribution to his country's policies and to its welfare? But this appeal to patriotism, this subtle flattery, needs must be resisted. Here the man of action may be called on in support: it is related of the great Lord Salisbury that presented with a long, judicious, balanced memorandum written by one of his officials, and abounding in wise considerations on the one hand, and in equally sage considerations on the other hand, he impatiently exclaimed: 'How well do I know these hands!'

The long view, the balanced view, the judicious view, then, can positively unfit a man for action, and for giving advice on action—which, as has been said, must be taken here and now. The famed adcademic, Dr Toynbee, writing his *Study of History* in 1935 came to the conclusion, on the weightiest and most erudite of grounds, that there was no likelihood of Peking ever again in the future becoming the capital of China! Should he not have remembered the sad and moving confession of Ibn Khaldun—a writer he much admired—that his minute knowledge of prosody unfitted him for the writing of poetry?

What is true of poetry is as true of politics, and an academic's patriotic duty is not to confuse rulers with long views and distant prospects, for the logic of events seems to take pleasure in mocking the neat and tidy logic of ideas:

Think now [it is a poet who warns us]
History has many cunning passages, contrived corridors
And issues, deceives with whispering ambitions,
Guides us by vanities. Think now
She gives when our attention is distracted
And what she gives, gives with such supple confusions
That the giving famishes the craving. Gives too late
What's not believed in, or if still believed,

134

In memory only, reconsidered passive. Gives too soon
Into weak hands, what's thought can be dispensed with
Till the refusal propagates a fear.

How difficult, therefore, to be wise, except after the event, and
how every leap is a leap in the dark! To be wise only after the
event is accounted a failing in men of action; but to be wise
after the event is a virtue in historians. To leap in the dark
requires strong muscles, steady nerves, a taste for adventure,
and not too great a fear of the consequences. 'I am not
responsible for the consequences' Salisbury used to say, and he
meant that having acted to the best of his knowledge and
judgement, he could not but let the events take their course as
the fates in their caprice decreed.

Shall academics then presume to instruct a man how he shall
leap? Presumption is the pride of fools, and it ought to be the
scholar's pride not to presume. It is pursuit of knowledge and
increase of learning which gives scholars renown and a good
name. How then should they, clothed as they are in the mantle
of scholarship, yet imitate this lobby or that pressure group,
and recommend this action or that, all the time knowing full
well that in politics one is always acting in a fog, that no action
is wholly to the good, and that every action in benefiting one
particular interest will most likely be to another's detriment.
Scholars, of course, are also citizens, and as such jealous for
the welfare and honour of their country. Equally with other
citizens they can recommend and exhort, but they should take
care that a scholarly reputation does not illicitly give spurious
authority to some civic or political stance.

Of what use then are academics? The impatient, mocking
question seems to invite the short, derisive answer, which men
of action and men of business have not seldom been disposed
to give. But the scholar's existence and activity does not have
to be justified by his usefulness. Who, in the first place, shall be
the judge of usefulness, who can tell whether the useful will not
turn out to be useless and worse, and in the second, a world in
which people shall live or die according as they are useful or
not is one which men must feel to be totally estranged and
hostile. The question therefore cannot be, of what use are
academics, but rather what is it that they do. Unlike the earlier

question, this one does not plunge the enquirer into the metaphysical depths, and the answer to it is very simple. Academics seek to transmit and to increase learning, one had almost said useless learning—but one does not wish to provoke. Foreign policy they leave to those who make bold to know how to leap in the dark.

Politics
A Philosophical Pursuit?

IN THE PREFACE to his book, *History and Class Consciousness* (1923), Lukács tells us that ever since his childhood he had felt 'hatred and contempt' for life under capitalism. Luckács's childhood as is well-known, was that of a banker's son, and his hatred and contempt cannot therefore be the outcome of personally having to suffer that 'oppression and exploitation' which, according to him, characterizes this 'system of production' more than any other known to history. His book, then, like *Do It* and *The Anarchist Cookbook* may be described in words of Hegel, the master to whom Lukács frequently appeals, as a rude product of luxury. *Do It* and *The Anarchist Cookbook*, like *History and Class Consciousness*, invoke and justify violence. But Yippies and Weathermen are direct and crude, having none of the glitter and sophistication with which the cultivated and learned author of a treatise on *The Soul and the Forms* or *The Theory of the Novel* knows how to embellish such a subject.

Lukács, then, starts by making clear that Marxism is the doctrine by which history as a 'totality' and as a 'unified process' may be understood. Marxism teaches that class, which is created by a particular system of production, 'is at once cause and effect, mirror and motor of the historical and dialectical process'. Two classes and one system of production particularly interest Lukács. The system is capitalism, and the two classes are the bourgeoisie (the beneficiaries of capitalism) and the proletariat (the indispensable victims, and eventual supplanters of capitalism). The capitalist mode of production deprives man of his 'authentic' humanity. Under capitalism human labour becomes a mere commodity, to be bought and sold at a price which is determined by supply and demand in a market seemingly impersonal and beyond human control. Man is thus fragmented and destroyed because his humanity is alienated and his free activity becomes 'reified' into objects, institutions and so-called laws of economics. A superstition prevalent under capitalism, the superstition of fetishism, deludes men into thinking that these objects and institutions which they themselves have made, nonetheless exist independently of their will, and can somehow exercise power over them. Capitalism thus dehumanizes man, and its overthrow liberates man from the demonic power of fetishism and reification.

Lukács's account suffers from an illusion and a misapprehension. The illusion which he shares with Marx derives from the German romantics. It is to the effect that there once was in the past, and that there once more can be in the future, a man who is a 'perfected whole', free from 'the dichotomies of theory and practice, reason and the senses, form and content'. The misapprehension – which Lukács derives from Marx – is that this dichotomous existence, in which man reifies his own activities and then allows these reifications to tyrannize over him, is the doing of capitalism, i.e. of private ownership of the means of production. The oppressive dichotomy, in which there is an utter divorce between man's activity and the product of this activity, which so offends Lukács is clearly the effect not of capitalism, but of the industrial or factory system.

The misapprehension under which Lukács labours is clear, if not to Lukács himself, at any rate to his readers. Consider the features which he associates with capitalism, and which result in 'Oppression and an exploitation that knows no bounds and scorns every human dignity' in a manner hitherto unparalleled: Lukács quotes Max Weber with approval to the effect that what is specific to modern capitalism is 'a strictly rational *organisation of work* on the basis of *rational technology*' and himself declares that 'At every single stage of its development, the ceaselessly revolutionary techniques of modern production turn a rigid and immobile face towards the individual producer'. Is this not today a more apt description of the wage-slave economies of the 'socialist sixth of the world' than of capitalism, and does not then alienation and reification ravage Soviet society more deeply than American? Lukács also believes that these ravages extend to all aspects of life under capitalism, and says for instance of journalists under capitalism that the 'prostitution' of their experiences and beliefs 'is comprehensible only as the apogee of capitalist reification'. Remembering the unfortunates who write in *Pravda* or *Ahram* as they are bidden, or Lukács himself who, to appease the sectarian ferocities of the Comintern had abjectly to recant, and to disown this very book, we become very sceptical alike of his diagnosis and of his remedy.

Not that his remedy is particularly original. A faithful Marxist, he says that a strategy exists by which mankind can attain the 'realm of freedom', fashion a 'consciously ordered society', that 'in our deeds and through our deeds, we will be able to transform the quality of life and consciously take our history in our hands'. All this can be accomplished through the proletariat, which Marx called the universal class. The proletariat is produced by capitalism and is indispensable to it. As a class, it experiences capitalist oppression at its sharpest. This oppression leads it to class consciousness, i.e. to a knowledge of the system which inevitably produces this opppression, and hence to a determination to destroy it. And by destroying capitalism, the proletariat saves not only itself but all mankind. Reification and alienation lose their maleficent power: *homo laborans* again becomes what he had once been, *homo ludens*.

But there are problems. For class consciousness, on which so much revolves, turns out to be a very peculiar thing. For Lukács, class consciousness is not necessarily a consciousness which anybody actually has; he firmly says that class consciousness is different from psychological consciousness. Again he distinguishes it from status consciousness which, he says, can actually 'mask' class consciousness. It turns out that class consciousness in the consciousness which 'objectively' a class ought to have of its position as disclosed by historical materialism. Class conciousness, Lukács tells us, is 'imputed' consciousness. With this piece of transformative analysis, or, some might say, prestidigitation, the orthodox Marxist Lukács transforms himself into an orthodox Leninist. The fate of mankind turns on the proletariat and its class consciousness, but the proletariat does not know it. Who knows it? The Party knows it: 'The form taken by the class consciousness of the proletariat is the Party'; again, 'the Party is assigned the sublime role of *bearer of the class consciousness of the proletariat and the conscience of its historical vocation*'. In discharging this sublime role, the Party organizes and directs revolution against capitalism since, Lukács observes, the latter will change neither 'by itself' nor 'through legal devices'. It will also have to coerce peasants and drag them in the wake of the proletariat: it must come into conflict with 'certain proletarian strata' fighting on the side of the bourgoisie; it is sometimes even 'forced to adopt a stance opposed to that of the mases; it must show them the way by rejecting their immediate wishes'. The Party, again, must 'purge' its own ranks. All this is inescapable, for as Lukács says, quoting Marx with approval: 'The present generation resembles the Jews whom Moses led through the wilderness. It must not only conquer a new world, it must also perish in order to make room for people who will be equal to a new world.'

This scriptural simile leads us to another aspect of Lukács's book, namely the religious fervour which he displays towards the Party. Where the Party is concerned he is, as they say, 'stoned'. The Party, he says, is 'the first *conscious* step towards the realm of freedom'. But this freedom does not mean the freedom of the individual. It is only by fully subordinating himself to the Party, by the 'unconditional absorption of the total personality in the praxis of the movement', that the individual can hope to obtain freedom. What the Party does as a whole, writes Lukács in his last paragraph 'it performs likewise for its individual members. Its closely-knit organisation with its resulting iron discipline and its demand for total commitment tears away the reified veils that cloud the consciousness of the individual in capitalist society.' We can now perhaps understand why, like Rubadshov in *Darkness at Noon*, Lukács gladly accused himself, recanted and disowned his book when, for obscure sectarian reasons, it pleased the Party to decree its suppression – a suppression which has incongruously endowed this apology for tyranny with an aura of persecution and martyrdom. For to obey the Party, to welcome and approve this suppression is for the true believer to acquiesce in a necessity which is yet one more proof of his freedom. We may quote the master once more: as Hegel profoundly observed, nobody is coerced who does not will his own coercion.

The History of Ideas
and Guilt by Association

THE BUSINESS of the student of politics is to explain politics. It is at his own peril, therefore, that he takes for granted, or uses on his own account, terms like right and left, whig and tory, conservative and liberal. In themselves these terms have no power to explain; rather it is they that call for explanation.

For they are invented and given currency by politicians who use them as labels roughly to identify supporters and opponents, and as battle-cries to laud and magnify their own cause, and to bring into disrepute the cause of their opponents. Green and blue in Byzantine politics were such labels and battle-cries; whig and tory in seventeenth-century English politics were insulting and derogatory appellations hurled at one another by the factions of the day. In short, such words far from having timeless and universal meaning or significance are very much the creature of their day. Their outward sameness and stability masks shifts of meaning usually, but not always, slow, and to the contemporary, almost imperceptible; but which, for all their gradualness, in the end amount to considerable revolutions. Consider what gulf separates the whig Algernon Sidney in 1680 from the whig Hartington in 1880; or reflect on the problematic character of the word, tory, used to describe indiscriminately Bolingbroke and Samuel Johnson, Sacheverell and the Duke of Wellington. It is, then, only as exhibits that the student of politics can use such terms—exhibits to illustrate some particular kind of political rhetoric and the political practice to which it is related.

These reflections are occasioned by a series of books entitled *Roots of the Right* the general editor of which is Dr George Steiner, and of which three volumes have appeared.[1] The term right—with its twin, left—is of course part of the contemporary vocabulary of politics. It became current in continental Europe in the nineteenth century, and has even been introduced, in spite of some incongruity and outlandishness, into the language of British politics. It seems to have begun its life as a mere label. At the French estates of 1789, the nobles, deeming themselves entitled to the place of honour, sat on the right of the president, and their lowlier opponents were therefore relegated to the left.

The division was thus clear-cut which is no doubt a great convenience for the purpose of labelling: what is not right is clearly left, and what is not left is as indubitably right. As battle-cries the appellations were equally handy: what the right did not support it could denounce as left, and what the left did not like it could damn as right. For busy, practical men who have no leisure to be nice about words this is an ample sufficiency.

We might perhaps expect these elementary considerations to be put before us in a series purporting to lay bare the roots of the right; but our expectation is disappointed. The rough-and-ready classification of left and right, so profitable to the politician and publicist, so treacherous to the student of politics, is here uncritically adopted as a category of explanation.

Drumont's ill-bred and maniacal drivel is ranged side by side with Claudel's old-maidish effusions. Taine who was neither maniacal nor effusive is crowded into the same *galère* because he pointed out quite cogently that terrorism is the child of revolution. Maurras, who was wrong-headed, malicious and belligerent, but who had many sensible things to say

[1] *Gobineau: Selected Political Writings* edited and introduced by Michael D. Biddiss; *The French Right from de Maistre to Maurras* edited and introduced by J. S. McClelland; *Alfred Rosenberg: Selected Writings* edited and introduced by Robert Pois.

about centralization and political *mores* in the Third Republic finds himself chained to George Sorel, an apostle of proletarian violence, because Mussolini, a socialist agitator who later began murdering socialists and thus automatically became a man of the right avowed an admiration for this thinker. Alfred Rosenberg both sinister and a bore is made to cohabit in the same series with the elegant, witty and melancholy. Gobineau who in fact rather admired Jews, and whose speculations on human races—much the least interesting thing he wrote and an awful example of the pitfalls surrounding the enthusiastic autodidact—can be described as 'racist' only by doing violence to its mood and argument—which, as Dr Biddiss himself points out, is exactly what the Nazis did.

The reason why writers so various and so different in outlook, in quality and in importance find themselves forced into this curious straitjacket is that the slogans of European politics after the French Revolution have been accepted as a reliable guide to this politics.

The reasoning is obvious: de Maistre was against the Revolution and thus was of the right: Rosenberg declaimed against the Bolsheviks who are of the left and thus he and de Maistre clearly belong together. Is this guilt by association, or do they really have much in common? A preface by the general editor—which figures in every volume—purports to tell us. 'Much of the crisis of identity and society that has overshadowed twentieth-century history', declares Dr Steiner, 'comes from an impulse towards totalitarian politics'. This totalitarian politics, we are given to understand, is an attack on the theory of man 'as a rational animal, entitled to a wide exercise of political and economic decision'. Nazis, Fascists, Falangists, etc., have used the 'concept of the Fall of Man' to offer 'an alternative statement of the human condition' and this 'political and philosophical programme of the right' we are further told, has come 'near to destroying our civilization'. It is then a gallery of horrors that Dr Steiner wishes to parade before us, the private case or the *enfer* of political literature.

As if to whet our appetite for the morbid and the forbidden, Dr Steiner informs us that most of these texts have never been available in English 'and several have all but disappeared in their original language'; and goes even further, calling his series a collection of 'black books'. Their jackets are indeed strikingly and suggestively black. The colour is evocative—of the black mass, black shirt, black jackboots, black underwear?

All this will give an agreeable *frisson*, but what, as political and intellectual history, does it exactly amount to? Totalitarian government undoubtedly arose, and was perfected in Europe, half of which is today under its more or less effective control. But why associate totalitarianism with the right? If totalitarianism is to use Burke's words, the progeny of an 'armed doctrine', then it was first seen in Europe precisely at the French Revolution. Was it not precisely in attempting to give body to 'the theory of man as a rational animal, entitled to a wide exercise of political and economic decision' that Robespierre and his colleagues decreed the terror without which they believed virtue to be in danger? Was it not one of the most virtuous of this dedicated band, St Just, who announced that happiness was a new idea in Europe, and worked with merciless benevolence to establish its reign? Again, who but a simpleton—or a leftist—would see anything much to prefer between Auschwitz and Kolyma? Or, if it is true that certain doctrines about society are directly responsible for such horrors—which is most doubtful—are not the absurdities of marxism on a par with the absurdities of racism? Racism in the present context means above all anti-semitism. But even if we uncritically categorize politics according to the notion of right and left, we will observe the phenomenon surely on both sides? Holbach, Voltaire, Proudhon, Marx, Hobson—and Hitler, whose party was called the National Socialist German Workers' Party? The historical truth is that anti-Judaism and anti-semitism constitute a recurring theme in European thought, and cannot be exclusively associated with one kind of political activity.

The truth also seems to be that since the French Revolution, and particularly during this century, Europeans invented and perfected a demoniac kind of politics, whereby men of terrible and destructive energy, a Hitler or a Lenin, seduce large masses of people into the belief that political action is a passport to salvation, enjoining on their followers, to quote Nkrumah's parody of the Sermon on the Mount: 'Seek ye first the political kingdom and all things shall be added unto you.' Such a style of politics is beyond left and right, and is irrelevant to such a distinction. Irrelevant, that is, if by the right we mean those who seek to safeguard private property and prescriptive rights, and by the left those who would encroach on them. This was the original distinction at the estates general of 1789, and it is wise to keep a hold on it.

To use categories of classical political science, the right then is aristocratic or oligarchic and the left democratic. If this is the case, then what Dr Steiner in his preface calls the radical right—which he makes responsible for totalitarianism, and the millions who died in Europe and Russia in the twentieth century—appealing to, and drawing its power from the seduction of the masses, would seem to have more affinities with the left than with the right, properly so called.

Such a paradox is a measure of the intellectual confusion on which this series rests and which it must in turn promote.

The Lure
of Revolutionary Revolution

FOR ALMOST two centuries now, revolution has been a word of magic and power. Why this should be so is not readily apparent. In common speech the word takes its place within a range of expressions similar but not identical in meaning: words such as revolt, rebellion, insurrection, or *coup d'état*. The dictionary will tell us that a revolution signifies a complete overthrow of the established government, or the forcible substitution of a new ruler or form of government. The occurrences which these words describe are as old as human society, and when they take place no one except the winners and the losers ought, by rights, to rejoice or mourn, or see in them more than a contest, more or less violent, between those who have power and those who seek to acquire it. How then has the word revolution—the forcible substitution of one form of government for another—come to be so widely invested with a magical aura, and in its effects on large numbers of men, to have the potency of a powerful drug?

The answer—or at any rate the beginning of one—seems to lie in certain events in the intellectual history of eighteenth century Europe which are as yet imperfectly known, and which seem to have given new life and wide currency to ancient millenarian and gnostic speculations about the meaning of history and the salvation of man. Lessing's short work of 1780, *The Education of the Human Race*, is undoubtedly a key document in enabling us to understand these events. Lessing announces his certain belief that the epoch of perfection is coming, and describes the course of history as 'a large wheel which, in a slow movement, leads the human race to the point of its perfection', or again as a 'road on which humanity progresses towards perfection.'

Belief in these speculations, which from a Christian point of view are either of doubtful orthodoxy or downright heretical, was widely prevalent among the educated classes of Europe in the eighteenth and nineteenth centuries. These speculations in fact constituted the religion of enlightened men. The Marquis de Saint-Martin invented the motto 'Liberty, Equality, Fraternity' as part of his new religion; the Comte de Saint-Simon, who was much influenced by Saint-Martin, announced the advent of a new Christianity, the lineaments of which were sketched out in his doctrine; the poet Victor Hugo and many others devoutly believed in the speedy coming of a new age.

It is not difficult to see how this new apocalypse and the idea of revolution became conjoined. The apocalypse announced and promised a renewal of man and a renovation of his society. Since educated men in Europe were also coming increasingly to believe that man makes himself, that he can set up and work institutions which will ensure his permanent happiness, this renovation was to be effected not by divine agency, by miracles or prodigies, but by man himself. The *novus ordo saeculorum* which the revolutionaries were intent on inaugurating in the thirteen colonies was to be established on a man-made constitution and maintained by purely human virtue. Tom Paine has a passage in which the conjunction between all these ideas apears in a striking fashion:

> What were formerly called Revolutions [Paine wrote], were little more than a change of persons, or an alteration of local circumstances. They rose and fell like things of course, and had nothing in their existence or their fate that could influence beyond the spot that produced them. But what we now see in the world, from the Revolutions of America and France, are a renovation of the natural order of things, a system of principles as universal as truth and

150

the existence of man, and combining moral with political happiness and national prosperity.[1]

If revolutions are 'a renovation of the natural order of things', the word assumes, in certain contexts at any rate, a special and privileged meaning. In such a usage a real revolution cannot possibly be only the overthrow—however complete—of the established government, or the forcible substitution of a new ruler. As Condorcet affirmed—and he was, as they say, *payé pour le savoir*—only when it has liberty for its object is the revolution revolutionary. For liberty others have substituted equality or fraternity. But in all these cases where it is the object to be attained which decides whether a revolution is revolutionary, the word ceases to be descriptive or identificatory and becomes ideological. It is this ideological guise which gives the notion its extraordinary power and makes it into so intoxicating an opium for those who can read, and even more for those who can write. For, used in this way, the word serves to disclose the meaning and direction of history. It shows those who understand it properly the way to escape the lowliness and misery of the human condition, while it provides justification for all actions—whatever they are—which further the revolution. Since Tom Paine's day, the lure of revolutionary revolution in its various guises has become world-wide and men of all colours and races have felt the attractive power of this modern European apocalypse. Hardly a day passes without someone somewhere announcing the good tidings of revolutinary revolution. One example, of striking absurdity, may suffice: 'What is necessary', proclaims Ronald Segal,

> is for the need of permanent revolution to be so widely accepted, for permanent revolution to be so influential a principle of human conduct, that no revolutionaries would, or safely could, attempt to make final their particular social design. Each revolution must be seen as no more that an

[1] This passage is cited by Isaac Kramnick in an article, 'Reflections on Revolution' in *History and Theory*, vol. XI, no. 1 (1972). The article is a very useful survey of various modern approaches to the study of revolution.

experiment, from which men must move on, to experiment again and again, for the integration of their lives with their ideals. It is revolution because no aspect of society should be beyond the reach of experiment; no institution so fixed, that it may not be displaced. It is permanent because one experiment must merge into another, for a continuous process of probing deeper; developing the social imagination further; cutting yet one more ledge from which human experience can climb to the next.[2]

If revolutions are made by men, and if they are privileged events which at once show the direction of the future and speed it on its way, then by a natural development another idea emerges: revolutions have as their opposite counter-revolutions. Counter-revolutions are the work of foolish, misguided, or even wicked men who think they can stop the future or deflect its course.

An essay by Arno J. Mayer, *Dynamics of Counterrevolution in Europe, 1870–1956* attempts to define and describe counter-revolution. The author writes that he is a 'confirmed leftist critic of those Allied and American policies ... that condoned or advanced ... the counterrevolutionary side in the era of the communist revolution.' For him the communist revolution in Russia and China is 'the central event of this era', and counter-revolution 'symobiotically related' to it. The latter is the affair of 'crisis intellectuals', and of what he calls 'anxiety cartels':

> whereas the revolutionary project aims at a total transcendence, the counterrevolutionary project has a much more limited scope: the transformation of the polity for the purpose of restabilizing and maintaining the economy and society.

Counter-revolutions are 'less historically creative than revolutions.' They are 'a sectarian *levée en masse*.' Revolution 'can be conceived as a coherent idea and utopian vision that have found bayonets,' while counter-revolution 'is in the nature of

---

[2] *The Struggle against History.*

bayonets in search of a fabricated idea and a millenarian charge'. To Professor Mayer the difference may seem both lucid and illuminating; others may think that in the end it all comes down to bayonets, that creativity and transcendence are difficult to identify and measure, and that really revolution and counter-revolution are six of the one and half-a-dozen of the other.

Take, for instance, what is known as the Spanish revolution of the 1930s. What was the revolution, and who were the revolutionaries then? As a readable history of these events [3] shows, what happened in Spain between 1936 and 1939 was that the mediatory and adjudicatory function of government broke down irremediably. This left the various groups of Spanish society confronting one another face to face, 'eyeball to eyeball', with their mutual fears, ambitions, and cupidities. In such a situation, since there was no power to prevent it, these groups had no alternative to mutual repression, proscription, confiscation, and extermination. It is true that the authors of *The Revolution and the Civil War in Spain* seem to use the word 'revolution' in the privileged sense described above, and to mean by it anarchist and other Leftist seizures of power which took place in Barcelona and elsewhere. But who, except for an ideologue, would want to call anarchism revolutionary and the *Falange* counter-revolutionary, or *vice versa*? There is, of course, no harm—there is indeed advantage—in calling what took place in Spain between 1936 and 1939 a revolution, if one loosely means by it (as Aristotle and Machiavelli might have meant by it) a state of extreme violence and insecurity in which every group was for itself and the devil took the hindmost. This social dissolution and institutional breakdown in which 'things fall apart' and 'the centre cannot hold' is a state of affairs for which the word revolution seems a fitting label.

This nuance is a useful one to supplement the dictionary's reference to 'a complete overthrow of the established government'. It is a sense or a nuance with which historians will feel at home, as may be seen from F. L. Carsten's excellent work,

---

[3] *The Revolution and the Civil War in Spain.* By Pierre Broué and Emile Temime.

153

Revolution in Central Europe, describing the combined effect on Germany and Austria–Hungary of military defeat and the resulting *vacance du pouvoir* on the one hand, and of the Bolshevik example and mystique on the other. Revolution, for Professor Carsten, is what took place in Kiel and Berlin and Graz and Vienna and Budapest and Klagenfurt and other places when the existing governments lost their power to attract allegiance and compel obedience. To understand what 'revolution' meant in Central Europe in 1918–19 one must have a knowledge of the groups which tried to overthrow the lawful government, how they set about this, and the manner of their success (or failure). All these events, so well and so patiently elucidated by Professor Carsten, and nothing more or less, *were* the revolution in Central Europe.

In dealing on his own account, then, with words like revolution, the historian must be a nominalist. The word can be for him nothing but a loose and convenient shorthand term for a cluster of events having to do with the breakdown or violent overthrow of governments, and with the arbitrariness, insecurity and terror which accompany such events. As for the privileged sense of the term, he must hold it at arm's length, elucidate its meaning, enquire whether belief in it was current at a particular time and in a particular place, and ascertain whether and in what manner the currency of such a belief was associated with breakdowns of government. To do otherwise is to impose on himself the hopeless task of looking for a special kind of event called revolution, defined according to criteria which some ideology or some political rhetoric prescribes from the outside. This is what a writer like Professor Mayer, who describes himself as a 'confirmed leftist', does. But the way in which he looks at counter-revolution—and therefore at revolution—is the outcome not only of his leftist predilections, but also of another, quite as powerful, influence. His book is subtitled, *An Analytical Framework,* and the reader will notice that for a work purporting to deal with a particular period in the European past, it seems to have a curious aversion to the use of the past tense, and to be written in a flat and timeless present. A few sentences taken at random will give the flavour:

Because of its composite, interjacent, and contingent qualities the counterrevolutionary project lacks ecumenical luster ... certain political conjunctions benefit the counter-revolutionaries, particularly in times of deepening crisis ... The counterrevolutionaries realize that their partners and patrons share their deliberate misrepresentation and de-famation of reformers ... The form and intensity of counterrevolutionary movements and reforms are a func-tion of the structural conditions and conjunctural develop-ments, national and international, that impinge upon them.

What we have here, as this last sentence clearly shows, are the language, methods, and aspirations of social science. In this perspective, revolution again is no longer a cluster of events (and no more than these events); it becomes hyposta-sized, transformed into some kind of substance or stuff to be treated in the same way as a chemist, say, examines tooth-paste, notes how various samples differ in composition, thick-ness and consistency, and thence proceeds to a theory of toothpaste which, until it is falsified, must be true always and everywhere.

This is the ideal and the vision which inspire social science, and the attempt to invent under its auspices a scientific theory by which to explain revolution has already produced a volu-minous and sometimes weird literature, which Professor Kramnick has surveyed in the article mentioned earlier. The authors of this literature are not content with explaining revolution as the activity of this or that specific man or group of men, responding to the activity of other men, in this or that particular context, according to the available evidence. For them nothing is what it seems to be, and explanation to be really explanation must go beyond what men say and do. It must, rather, analyse—and pulverise?—sayings and doings so as to assimilate them into a general theory of human be-haviour. Thus, according to their various ratiocinations, 'Revolution is the extreme case of the explosion of political participation'. Or, it is that which occurs 'at the point on a J-curve when the rising pattern of expected satisfactions ... is abruptly interrupted.' Or, it is 'produced by dysfunctional social systems, *i.e.*, systems where there is a lack of harmony between the adaptive mechanisms and the value structure'. Or, it is the outcome of 'relative deprivation ... [*i.e.*] perception of a gap between what people think they deserve and what they in fact get', and is made by revolutionaries who 'have strong feelings of admiration for their fathers, but these fathers also withhold privileges, especially the most important object of the individual's early years, the mother'.

This literature is, of course, by no means devoid of interesting disquisitions or striking *aperçus*, but when we compare the amplitude of the claim it makes (which is that it can explain and account for all Revolutions) with its broken and fragmentary performance, then we see that much if not all of it is the merest book-making, the most inconsequential *littérature*; about it all that need be said is that if you do like this kind of thing, you may pay your money and take your choice.

As is notorious, one of the most influential of the theories which pretend to explain revolution—a theory which is also an ideology—is Marxism. In his book, *Modern Revolutions*, John Dunn declares that 'Marxism as a theory, a coherent body of doctrine, is false.' His scepticism is commendable, but the book shows it to be neither consistent enough nor radical enough. His very enterprise seems to assume, like the writers surveyed by Professor Kramnick, that there is a phenomenon called 'modern revolutions' which can be isolated and studied. Yet Dunn knows very well that 'modern revolutions' are nothing apart from this or that or the other revolution. This is why the bulk of this book is devoted to the examination of eight 'modern revolutions', which took place respectively in Russia, Mexico, China, Yugoslavia, Viet Nam, Algeria, Turkey and Cuba. Neither at first sight, nor on closer reading is it apparent to the reader why this miscellaneous list of civil wars and international conflicts should disclose what it is that distinguishes modern from other revolutions, or why others, of seemingly equal or greater interest, have been omitted. There is in this book nothing about Fascism or Nazism or the Persian Revolution of 1906, or the Mau Mau, or the Spanish civil war, or the post–1945 insurrections in Greece or Malaya; and if one is to appeal to history for the understanding of 'modern revolutions', then surely Hitler and Dedan Kimathi are of as great interest as Lenin and Ho? Again, how can eight brief chapters possibly do more than present an imperfect, abstract, and therefore historically useless, sketch of events both complex and obscure? These sketches cannot explain the events with which they purport to deal; for the explanation of these events means their narration, and their proper narration requires taking into account all the known evidence. If we do this, we soon discover that 'modern revolutions' as a model or ideal type is no more than a delusive construct, the pale shadow of what men, in the endless variety of their circumstances and the ever-surprising originality of their minds, do and suffer. In short to speak, as does John Dunn, of 'historical case studies' is to speak the language not of history, but of toothpaste-making.

Toothpaste-making is, of course, a useful practical occupation. Dunn's discourse also has its practical side, but whether it is useful is not so clear. He believes that there is 'certainly much social and political organization which is eminently in need of destruction in the world today'. Many régimes, again, 'are so exotically deplorable that any successor régime could hardly fail to represent a change for the better.' Also there are 'probably more countries than not governed by men with a deeper interest in the preservation of a variety of different national or international structures than they have in maximizing the economic growth of their countries' (not 'necessarily', he charitably adds, 'for unedifying reasons'), but under present demographic conditions they are, he affirms, 'a perilous luxury for any society'. As can be seen, Dunn speaks like a confident *maître démolisseur* and has no trouble at all in deciding which states are derelict and ripe for dynamiting, and his list is likely to be fairly long. He is quite as categorical in prescribing what is to take their place. He is, it will be recalled, utterly sceptical of Marxist theory. Nonetheless, he does not hesitate to affirm that

> countries which today need a revolution (of which there are not a few) would be best advised to entrust their destinies to decidely Marxist political élites and ones which (other things being equal) are better the better organized they are.

Lenin and Mao and Ho and Hoxha and Karume and Sekou Touré are good for you; they are a nasty but wholesome medicine, Dunn firmly tells the Asians and Africans, they will stand no nonsense about freedom etc., they will keep you in order, and give you the economic growth you need.

One does not know what to marvel at more: the cool patronizing presumption of the advice, or the sheer credulity about economics and politics which it betrays. We must conclude that even if revolution were as beneficial as Dunn implies, what is, on the evidence, quite doubtful is whether reading—or writing—books on revolution is really such a good thing.

New Histories for Old

DURING THE past ten or fifteen years the notion that history is in the throes of a revolution has been spreading within, and on the fringes of the world of learning. Thus *The Times Literary Supplement*, presumably in order to discharge avant-garde duties, thought it necessary to devote in 1966 no fewer than three issues to an explanation of the 'New Ways in History'. And, if readers felt at the end that these roads did not lead anywhere in particular, the impression none the less persisted that here were certainly doings and busy comings-and-goings.

The centre, one of the main centres at any rate, of this reformation was believed to be Paris. Such an impression is amply confirmed by a great many contributions to *Faire de l'histoire* (3 vols., 1974). Though its editors, Jacques Le Goff, president of Sixième Section of the École Pratique des Hautes Études, and Pierre Nora, *maître de conférences* at the Institut d'Études Politiques, rightly deny, that the book is designed to represent an orthodoxy, they nevertheless affirm that it aims at illustrating and advancing a 'new type of history'. And they go on to say:

> Si l'on retrouvera chez les auteurs ou dans l'esprit de l'ouvrage la marque souvent de la prétendue école des 'Annales', c'est que l'histoire nouvelle doit beaucoup à Marc Bloch, à Lucien Febvre, à Fernand Braudel et à ceux qui les continuent dans l'innovation.

In a work devoted to the 'new type of history' it is fitting that the names of Marc Bloch (1886–1944), of Lucien Febvre (1878–1956), and of their younger contemporary Fernand Braudel (b. 1902) should figure on the first page. But, if this is nothing less than fitting, then why do the editors speak dismissively of 'the so-called school' of the *Annales*? For, if a new movement in historical scholarship exists, then it must also be admitted that the journal *Annales* is at the heart of it.

Founded by Bloch and Febvre at Strasbourg in 1929, *Annales* was subsequently edited from the Sixiéme of the École Pratique des Hautes Études, first by Febvre and then by Braudel. The first president of this Section (which he laboured much to establish) was Febvre, his successor was Braudel, and on retirement he was, in turn, succeeded by Le Goff, one of the co-editors of *Faire de l'histoire*. These facts may give rise to the impression that here indeed is an orthodoxy, the tenets of which are safeguarded by some kind of apostolic succession. Hugh Trevor-Roper, for instance, has said of the school of the *Annales* that it 'has now passed into a period of almost bureaucratic consolidation'.

But, whatever the position today, it is by no means the case that this historical school began self-consciously as a school equipped with strict doctrines and shibboleths. If it is a school, this is above all by reason of the admiration with which the writings of Bloch, Febvre and Braudel are regarded, and of the inspiration which historians have derived from them. For these works exhibit high qualities of intelligence and imagination, and it is surely these qualities, rather than a common doctrine they supposedly apply and exemplify, which fellow historians have recognized and acclaimed. In fact, as might be expected, works of this calibre are not to be reduced to a common denominator, and the reader comes quickly to recognize in them the product of original minds, quite different and sharply distinguishable from one another.

The belief, however, that these historians constitute a school of some kind is not entirely without foundation. It is to be accounted for, in the first place, by the friendship and the intimate intellectual intercourse which linked Bloch and Febvre as colleagues in the University of Strasbourg shortly after the First World War. They seem to have been drawn together by a similar dislike of some dominant fashions in the French historiography of the time. These fashions were represented by writers such as Seignobos and Lavisse, and their dominance was accentuated and made more painful to those who disagreed with them by the centralization which was and which remains—in spite of the so-called reforms which followed May 1968—such a feature of the French academic world: Seignobos, Lavisse and those who thought like them 'tenaient' as Febvre later on put it, 'le haut du pavé sorbonnard'.

Febvre and Bloch disliked the ruling emphasis on political, and more especially diplomatic history. Such history was both dull and superficial. It neglected so much that could be used to show the past in all its marvellous complication and its rich variety: institutions, social arrangements, economic organization, states of mind and attitudes, in short all that we have to know in order to understand what a society was like.

But the dominant school not only neglected all these subjects: its attitude to historical discourse was naively positivist. It believed that to do history consisted merely in first collecting 'facts', and then in compiling narratives where the 'facts' were somehow worked in and incorporated. In a passage written half a century after his first encounter with the academic historiography of his youth, Febvre expressed with characteristic vivacity and vehemence (in the foreword to *Combats pour l'histoire*, published in 1953) what he found most to dislike in this school:

Alors, cumulant la double âpreté, 'critique, polémique et guérrière', de la [Franche] Comté et de la Lorraine—que je n'aie pas accepté avec placidité l'histoire des vaincus de 1870, ses prudences tremblotantes, ses renoncements à toute synthèse, son culte laborieux, mais intellectuellement paresseux, du 'fait', et ce goût presque exclusif de l'histoire diplomatique ... qui, d'Albert Sorel, ce demi-dieu, à Emile Bourgeois, ce dixième de dieu, obsédait les de 1895 à 1902— que j'aie réagi instinctivement et à peu près sans appui dans le camp des historiens ...; que tout de suite, pour ma part, je me sois inscrit parmi les fidèles de la

Revue de Synthèse Historique et de son créateur Henri Berr: rien d'étrange dans une telle aventure.

We may, with hindsight, say that if Febvre found Seignobos, Lavisse and Bourgeois dull and uninspiring this was simply because they happened to be dull and uninspiring, not because they were philosophically naive, or because they concentrated on political and diplomatic history. For, after all, to write economic and social history does not in itself guarantee that the writer is wise, or profound, or witty: at the drop of a hat, one could produce a string of economic and social histories which will equal if not surpass in tedium those 'manuels' of diplomatic history which made hideous the days of Febvre's youth. Again, as Jaques Barzun points out in his elegant and concise examination in *Clio and the Doctors* (1974), of what, since Fabvre's death, has well-nigh become a dominant fashion in America and elsewhere, the fates that spin have not forgotten politics, diplomacy and war, and to concentrate on social history is to empty the public mind of 'plain empirical realities'.

The two Strasbourg colleagues shared likes as well as dislikes. They both admired Pirenne, both had much to learn form the geographer Vidal de la Blache, and both came under the influence of Durkheim (1858–1917), and of Henri Berr (1863–1954) who, disliking the dominant school of historiography as much as his juniors, nursed the significant and perilous ambition of constructing, or composing, or distilling—one doesn't quite know which metaphor to choose—nothing less than a 'synthèse historique'.

And they were much impressed both by reason of their own professional interests, and of prominence of class conflict as an issue in contemporary politics, with the importance of economic and social studies. They thus decided to establish the new journal, *Annales*, modelled on the *Vierteljahreschrift für Sozial -und Wirtschftsgeschichte*. Its full title was in fact *Annales d'histoire économique et sociale*.

But, whatever ideas they held in common during their Strasbourg years, it does not seem that Marc Bloch—to judge by his publications at any rate—nourished the design to put history on a new foundation, to endow it with new methods, or to claim for the historian's work significance beyond itself, in the world, say, of practice or of some problematic social science. His unfinished and posthumous work *Apologie pour l'histoire* (1946), is a lucid and engaging description by a master of the skills which history demands and of the pitfalls which historians must avoid. His rejection of the dominant school of this youth appears not in any lengthy *réquisitoire*, but in a brief, quiet remark that there can be no autarchy in the various branches of history, and that 'la seule histoire véritable, qui ne peut se faire que par entr'aide, est l'histoire universelle.'

As for political history, one of the contributors to *Faire de l'histoire*, Jacques Julliard, reminds us that Bloch did not see why the political should be considered a synonym for the superficial, and that it was perfectly conceivable to have a history centred on the study of changes in modes of government. Nor is this surprising in the author of *Les rois thaumaturges*, and the second volume of whose *Société féodale* is subtitled 'Les-classes et le gouvernement des hommes'.

The case seems otherwise with Bloch's colleague and friend. To judge by his writings, Febvre's temperament must have been quite different from Bloch's, more combative, more entrepreneurial, perhaps, more sanguine and less sceptical. It is in character that he should entitle a collection of articles on history and historians *Combats pour l'histoire*. He wrote at some length about the theory of history, and what he wrote on this subject seems to have influenced the 'new history' a great deal. As has been said, Febvre was most impressed by the ideas of Durkheim, Vidal de la Blache, and other writers less well known in the English-speaking world: writers such as François Simiand, a great believer in the virtues and potency of comparisons, or Paul Lacombe, author of a book published in 1894 entitled *De l'histoire considérée comme science*.

It is from Berr, Lacombe and Simiand that Febvre seems to have taken the dismissive and pejorative expressions 'histoire historisante' and 'histoire événementielle'. In *Faire de l'histoire*, Julliard points out that *Annales* had a rubric which reviewed books on 'histoire politique et historisante'. This conjunction gives a clue to Febvre's meaning: political history was, ipso facto, something not serious, something concerned with the mere surface of things, with spectacular happenings to impress readers of the popular press. It is such a meaning which he—and the historians who acknowledge his inspiration—seem to give to the word *événement*. It is on the face of it a restrictive meaning, for the word need not, and does not, necessarily indicate only spectacular happenings like the divorces of film stars, or Middle Eastern coups d'état. A change in the price of salt or in the current meaning of a word is as much an *événement* as anything else. But it is this dismissal of *événements* as unworthy of the serious historian which accounts for Febvre's—surely unjustified?—irony at the expense of 'Albert Sorel, ce demi-dieu', and his attack in the manifesto launching the new *Annales* in 1946 on Ranke, who is surely, even less than Sorel to be dismissed as a Seignobos or a Lavisse:

> Eh, bien, non! Nous n'avons plus le temps. Trop d'historiens, et bien formés, et consciencieux, c'est là le pire—trop d'historiens encore se laissent égarer par les pauvres leçons des vaincus de 70. Oh, ils travaillent bien! Ils font de l'histoire comme leurs vieilles grands-mères de la tapisserie. Au petit point. Ils s'appliquent. Mais si on leur demande pourquoi tout ce travail—le mieux qu'ils sachent répondre, avec un bon sourire d'enfant, c'est le mot candide du vieux Ranke: 'Pour savoir exactement comment ça s'est passé'. Avec tous les details, naturellement

But, we may ask, does the study of *subsistances* in eighteenth-century Angers, or the fluctuations in the price of gold on the Antwerp exchange in the year 1539, involve less finicky tapestry-work than Anglo-French diplomacy under Charles II?

What is to replace this 'histoire historisante', this 'petite science de la contingence', as Braudel has disdainfully dismissed it? The impression emerging from Febvre's copious writings on historiography is that he is engaged on a paradoxical, not to say impossible, quest: it is to make history into a science like linguistics. It is not perhaps without significance that the word 'histoire' disappeared from the title of *Annales* when the journal was re-launched in 1946.

In his inaugural lecture at the College de France in 1933, which he entitled 'Examen de conscience d'une histoire et d'un historien', Febvre argued that, just as linguistics, a new science, emerged from comparative philology, so a new kind of history will emerge from the 'global study of historical wholes', a history which would be the 'static study of the facts of history'. Hence Febvre is terribly impressed with comparisons and comparative studies. Hence, in an article of 1949, 'Vers une autre histoire', he envisages large-scale enterprises of comparison:

> Enquêtes convergentes, pensées d'ensemble, lancées simultanément, de façon que tel important phenomène de circulation monétaire, j'imagine, ou de transport ou de peuplement, ou de psychologie collective soit étudié dans un mème esprit, ou bien dans des civilisations éloignées dans le temps, ou bien dans des civilisations séparées dans l'espace par de grandes distances.

These vast inquiries would be presided over and orchestrated by a

> chef d'équipe, alerte et mobile, qui, nourri d'une forte culture, ayant été dressé à chercher dans l'histoire des éléments de solution pour les grands problèmes que la vie, chaque jour, pose aux sociétés et aux civilisations, saura tracer les cadres d'une enquête, poser correctement les questions, indiquer précisément les sources d'information et, ceci fait, évaluer la dépense, régler la rotation des appareils, fixer le nombre des équipiers et lancer son monde à la quête de l'inconnu.

The question, of course, is whether this paragon, should he be found, would not rather write his own masterpieces in the manner of Sorel, or Ranke, or Febvre, or Braudel, than become the managing director and chief executive of a historical factory. But the notion of a comparative history suffers from a radical failing which is well brought out by Paul Veyne, a classicist, his book, *Comment on écrit l'histoire* (1971), which displays a philosophical sophistication, a breadth of learning, a delicacy of imagination and an energy of reasoning such as to place it in the front rank of the literature.

Veyne acutely points out that there can be no analogy between comparative philology and comparative history. When comparative philologists compare Sanskrit and Greek, it is not in order simply to deepen understanding of one or other of these languages, it is in order to reconstruct a third language, the Indo-European, from which the other two derive. However perspicacious the philologist might be, he would never have been able to detect Indo-European by examining Greek alone. On the other hand, when comparative history discusses millenarism or the city, 'it can declare no truths which are not true of the several millenarian movements and the several cities which it has taken into consideration: comparison makes understanding easier, but in principle a sufficiently penetrating mind would have been able to gather from one monograph all that comparison allows to be understood more easily.'

But for Febvre comparison was more than a heuristic device which some historians might find useful, and some others (who might be thought particularly to exemplify Hobbes's observation that thought is quick) clearly a bore. Belief in comparison went for him hand in hand with the belief that there was some kind of bedrock structure, some ultimate, more real, reality to which, with improved drills and metal-detectors, the new historian can penetrate. And this ultimate reality will not be accident-prone, or the victim of change. Febvre quotes with approval the words of Camille Jullian, a historian whom he admires, to the effect that history

> se laisse vraiment trop séduire par les accidents et tenter par les grands hommes. Tous ces bruits des individus, des combats et des révolutions la préhistoire ne les entend pas. Elle ne voit que les oeuvres d'une longue époque, les progrès de l'intelligence collective, les résultats acquis par l'humanité qui se fonde.

If historians have to shut their ears to the noise of individuals, of wars and revolutions, and avert their eyes from the seduction of accidents, how are they to spend the time? They are to explore the depths. In the end Febvre came to the conclusion that the fashionable notion of structure was too static for history, but it remained his conviction to the end that a historian worth his salt should be a diver or a tunneller penetrating deeper and deeper. In a passage of 1955 he wrote that he imagined the 'foundation' ('soubassement') of history to be

> assez semblable au sous-sol d'une de nos capitales modernes, inextricables lacis de conduites d'eau et de gaz, d'électricité, de chaleur, de tunnels par quoi circulent les hommes et leurs voitures, de câbles par quoi se propagent leurs voix, leurs messages, leur esprit ..., des déversoirs enfin et des égouts ...

This 'soubassement' which should be the fundamental concern of the historian was constituted, Febvre had no doubt, by economics. The world is not now what it was in 1848: 'Why? For political reasons? Or moral? Certainly not! For economic reasons. This is blindingly obvious.' Febvre therefore also speaks of the 'cadre indispensable', the 'cadre primordial des réalités économiques', and looks forward to minute studies of prices, wages, rates of exchange in France and elsewhere. The results of these studies would be 'so clear, so precise and certain that it would be possible to translate them into curves and graphs'. But, like comparisons, graphs and cruves can be no more than an occasionally convenient device for the historian. Sometimes they do summarize faithfully the picture emerging from counting what can truly be counted. But quite as often the rhetoric of graphs, curves and tables gives an air of spurious exactitude, of overprecision which can be very misleading.

In *Clio and the Doctors* Jacques Brazun discusses, for instance, so-called crime statistics and shows how difficult it is to know what they correspond to, let alone what they mean. As regards economics in particular, he quotes an economist, the late Ely Devons, who wrote:

> There has been much theoretical examination in recent years of the meaning and significance of what we measure

... and most of it leads to the conclusion that, except in very special and unusual circumstances, it is not possible to give any significant meaning to index numbers of real national income, produciton or price.

Barzun himself rightly points out that 'the question of exactitude is more complicated than common opinion imagines when it assumes that numbers = exact, words = inexact. The idea of exactitude implies a relation; we ought to say "exact to something", as we say "correspond to". It is by due rhetoric that a history is exact ...' And this due rhetoric of history, for many reasons, can seldom, even in economic history, be the rhetoric of numbers. Because, as Barzun puts it, the historian is engaged in the communication of many truths and not of a simple formulated truth, because he is visualizing a scene and a story rather than deciphering a code, for him words have no rivals in point of precision and subtlety. Quanto-history, cliometry, 'histoire sérielle', must be contradictions in terms.

There is yet another aspect of what might be called the scientism of Febvre as a theorist of history. He is very impressed with the science of psychology as a foundation for historical studies; he even goes so far as to speculate whether psychology is not 'à la base même de tout travail d'historien valable'. He declares that we lack a history of Love, of Death, of Pity, of Cruelty, of Happiness. He calls for a 'vast collective inquiry into the fundamental feelings of men and their modalities'. Taken at its face value, an historical inquiry of this kind can lead nowhere; it is impossible to write a history of feelings as such. As Barzun says, history deals with activity, not process, which means that it deals with men who can express their thoughts, deliberations and imaginings in speech, literature, action and artifacts. It is these which can have a history; feelings and drives to which men are subject are not as such within the historian's province. Undoubtedly there is *amour* in *l'amour courtois*, but the historian can do nothing with it unless it expresses itself in song and poetry and modes of behaviour. If there is evidence in respect of none of these, then such love, be it ever so intense and devastating, is not the historian's affair.

Febvre himself argues in such a way as to confirm this view.

168

To illustrate what he means by the history of death he directs us to the chapter on the art of dying in Volume 9 of Henri Brémond's *Histoire littéraire du sentiment religieux en France*. What the history of death amounts to, then, is the study of what men have said and done when confronted with the fact of their inescapable extinction here on earth. While the fact of death is the same always and everywhere and thus can have no history, attitudes towards death have shown appreciable changes in time and space, and can thus be studied by the historian.

But a study of this kind does not require a knowledge of the science of psychology. Febvre, as is known, was very much interested in *mentalités*, and some of his best work is devoted to their study. But *Le problème de l'incroyance au XVIe siècle* and similar studies of his in the history of ideas and attitudes would not have been, we suspect, so outstanding had they been encumbered with the technical terms and methods of the science of psychology. What, one wonders, would he have made of the psycho-history which has come to flourish since his death, the products of which Barzun reviews so trenchantly? For all Febvre's preoccupation with the real, deep, underlying forces in history, would he have welcomed psycho-history as practised in the *History of Childhood Quarterly*? This periodical, subtitled 'The Journal of Psychohistory', Barzun tells us,

> lures its readers by summarising an article in these terms: '"Childhood and The Bible" ... argues why the Bible is a coherent story of intra-family struggle and asks if the West may not more usefully be described as a part of the history of childhood rather than the other way round'.

Psycho-history, in effect, is a kind of reductionism. For it, the significance of human actions does not lie in themselves; it lies in what is behind them, in the urges, drives illusions and obsessions which, unbeknown to the agent, fatally condition and regulate his action. On this reading, an action or utterance is like a myth (no, is a myth) which the historian deciphers, demystifies, demythologizes. Alternatively, to use another vocabulary quite as influential, in this sublunary world action and utterance are the product of a false consciousness.

A neat example of such argument occurs in an article in the third volume of *Faire de l'histoire*. In this article, 'Le mythe: Orphée au miel', Marcel Detienne, of the Sixième Section of the École Pratique des Hautes Études, argues for the structural anaylsis of myth which brings out the changeless form of a myth behind its changing contents, and thus contributes to

> une histoire globale, qui s'inscrit dans la longue durée, plonge par dessous les expressions conscientes et repère sous l'apparente mouvance des choses les grands courants inertes qui la traversent en silence.

All this is alien to the 'histoire événementielle' of 'the antiquarian and the rag-picker'. Why so? Because, among other things, the study of mythology was abandoned to literary history, which chose in mythological discourse those 'éléments compatibles avec l'idéologie dominante d'une société bourgeoise dont la philologie dite classique a toujours fidèlement servi les interêts et les objectifs'. We may perhaps paraphrase Detienne by saying that the study of Greek mythology in modern classical scholarship was itself mythologized by the false consciousness of the classical philologists serving, of course, 'sans le savoir' (and thus victims of what might be called M Jourdain's syndrome), the interests and objectives of bourgois society. Psychoanalysis and Marxism are here well mixed in a modish cocktail shaker. In the fumes of this heady concoction history vanishes.

Would Febvre have relished this particular cocktail? To judge by his own historical investigations, this is hardly likely. The question, the doubt arises only when one considers his historical theories. The same is just as true of Febvre's successor as president of the Sixième Section. Braudel's work, *La Méditerranée et le monde méditerranéen à l'époque de Philippe II*, has been hailed as a great achievement. And like all great historical works it expresses a distinctive vision with eloquence and imaginative power. Given the work, the achievement, it does not really much matter how the author came to conceive it, and what notions about history sustained

170

him in his long labour. As it happens, Braudel himself tells us that while he was engaged in writing *La Méditerranée* (in a German prisoner-of-war camp) his attitude was: 'Down with occurrences, especially vexing ones!' 'I had to believe', he says, 'that history, destiny, was written at a much more profound level! Choosing a long time-scale to observe from was choosing the position of God the Father himself as a refuge.'

Such an approach, however, let us remember, in itself guarantees nothing. It may as likely produce a flop as a masterpiece. Braudel's words tell us something about his tastes, and about the kind of historical issue he personally finds exciting. But Braudel would like to convince us that the outlook and method he prefers and recommends are essential to a genuine science, as opposed to that superficial history of events, of happenings, of politics, of great men, that 'petite science de la contingence', which he found himself condemned to teach as a young historian in Constantine and Algiers. In an ariticle of 1958 (included in a useful book, *Ecrits sur l'histoire*, published in 1969) Braudel declared that 'le temps court est la plus capricieuse, la plus trompeuse des durées', and contrasted it with 'la valeur exceptionnelle du temps long'. This 'temps long' it is which, patiently followed, allows the historian to understand historical reality. Because the 'temps long' refers to the depths, the solid foundations, the fundamental structure of total history, a structure almost motionless:

> C'est par rapport à ces nappes, d'histoire lente que la totalité de l'histoire peut se repenser, comme à partir d'une infrastructure. Tous les étages, tous les milliers d'étages, tours les milliers d'éclatements du temps de l'histoire se comprennent à partir de cette profondeur, de cette semi-immobilité: tout gravite autour d'elle

For Braudel there is a historical hierarchy in which 'histoire événemetielle' is the least regarded; above it stands 'histoire conjoncturelle'; and at the very summit stands 'histoire structurale', the history of all that is stable and almost changeless in human affairs. As J. H. Hexter has asked, how coherent is this classification which depends on the time-scale? Is it really possible clearly to assign events to a particular scale, to say of one event that it is of the order of the 'événementiel', another of the 'structural'? What, again, are the relations between events of these various kinds? The answer is obscure, and one suspects that the greater the clarity the greater would be the difficulties and the more numerous the objections.

The assumptions and preferences of Febvre and Braudel, to judge by *Faire de l'histoire*, are today widespread, if not dominant, among French historians. This is of course not to say that all the contributors to the three volumes (which deal with new problems, new approaches and new objects respectively) are concerned with the theory of history, or are followers of what Paul Veyne, who contributes an article to Volume 1 on 'l'histoire conceptualisante', calls 'notre école des *Annales*'.

Veyne himself, for one, is not a follower, nor, for instance is Jean Starobinski of the University of Geneva, whose article in Volume 2 on the interpretation of literary texts is perhaps the best in the whole work and applicable to much more than literary texts. The book, again, contains a great deal of valuable information on the history and present state of various branches of historical inquiry. Notable in this respect are the articles, in Volume 2, by Jean Bouvier of Paris VIII on the study of French nineteenth century economic crises, by Pierre Chaunu of Paris–Sorbonne on recent trends in the study of economic history, and by André Burguière of the Sixième Section on historical demography.

The great variety of subjects discussed notwithstanding, the dominant theoretical influence, acknowledged, as has been said, by the editors in their introduction, is that of Febvre and Braudel, and the strongest tendency is towards making history into a kind of event-free social science, the task of which is to discover the norms of human behaviour. History helps to do so by seeking out the abnormal, the extraordinary, the exception which, as they say, confirms the rule.

This is the belief of Michel de Certeau, of Paris VII, a member of the Ecole Freudienne de Paris, whose article 'L'opération historique' opens the work. For Certeau, the particular constitutes the limit of the thinkable. History investigates this limit, as it does that of 'significant deviations'. History, again, is 'the composition of a locus which establishes in the present the ambivalent figuration of the past and of the future'.

It is obvious that de Certeau believes human activity to be subject to laws and norms which account for particular events, whether they take place in the past, the present or the future. The business of historians is to establish a relation between 'regularités' and 'particularités'. Otherwise, an event remains an opaque and inexplicable 'this'. But this way of describing the historian's activity is open to a great many objections: one is that the fundamental organizing idea of history, namely the notion of the past, becomes superfluous: a historian and a 'futurologist' become identical since both are in quest of the regularities which will explain and account for individual events; yet another difficulty lies in establishing which actions conform to, and which deviate from, the norm. Which norm, anyway? Veyne's way of accounting for an event is much more convincing: in history an event is explained and accounted for by the previous course of events—'le cours antéieur des événements', not by laws or norms.

Certeau's idea of history has another peculiarity which perhaps owes something to the notions underlying linguistics, now a very fashionable subject. Just as a distinction is made between a particular speech and the language which this speech necessarily presupposes, so Certeau states that any particular work of history presupposes the historical discourse which makes it possible and 'the relation of this discourse to the social institution'. The primacy belongs to the discourse and the institution, and the historian and the subject he studies are of little account:

> Ce discours—et le groupe qui le produit—*fait* l'historien alors même que l'idéologie atomiste d'une profession 'libérale' maintient la fiction du sujet auteur et laisse croire que la recherche individuelle construit l'histoire.

This is clear and emphatic enough, but Certeau is still more emphatic. For he goes on to compare a historical work to a motor car; just as the car is wholly the product of a factory, so a work of history 'is linked to the complex of a specific and collective process of manufacture'. Historical discourse, in other words, is a function of the institution in which it is produced. It comes, therefore, as no surprise that Certeau joins Habermas in asking for a 'repoliticization' of the human sciences. *Politique d'abord*: it is an old and recurring refrain. This sociologism, as it might be called, is identified by the editors in their introduction as one of the features of the new history.

Another feature of the new history is expounded in the article 'Le quantitatif en histoire' by François Furet, of the Sixième Section, which appears in the first volume. The most general and the most elementary ambition of quantitative history, we are told, is to convert events into a temporal series of homogeneous and comparable units, in which change may be measured periodically. Such a method is superior in rigour and efficacity to what 'qualitative methodology' offers. Events are elusive; they can only be captured and fixed by the regular repetition of data selected and constructed according to their comparability. In this way they also become scientifically measurable and the historian's subjective distortions are ipso facto banished. Again, because quantitative history gives a privileged position to long-term developments and the equilibrium of a system, it is, Furet says without irony, a good corrective to the identification of history and change. But, Furet concludes, it will not be possible to test the possibilities of this method 'tant que l'histoire tout court ne s'est pas mise à l'école des procédures de l'histoire sérielle'.

Alas! we turn over the pages and come upon the article in which Furet's colleague, André Burguière, begins by telling us that historical demography is a young science which already suffers from the illnesses of old age. We are reminded of Baudelaire's king of a rainy country who was 'Riche mais impuissant, jeune et pourtant très vieux' and wonder if Burguière's remark is not equally true of quantitative history in general.

Another member of the Sixième Section, Pierre Vilar, contributes a long article to Volume 1, 'Histoire marxiste, histoire en construction', in which he declares that the lessons taught by Karl Marx and those taught by Lucien Febvre converge. 'Historians' history' today is more like

Marx's and Ibn Khaldun's than Thucydides's. By this Vilar means that historical matter is structured and permeable by thought, and scientifically penetrable like every other reality. History in this mode is given coherence by means of a solid and common theoretical schema; it is total, leaving nothing outside its jurisdiction which may be usefully analysed; and finally, it is dynamic since it is concerned with discovering the principle of change.

History is studied not, as Raymond Aron thinks, in order to give back to the past the uncertainty which characterizes the future. On the contrary, it is studied in order to reduce this uncertainty. Marx and Febvre converge because both of them work towards a total history. Again, Marx was faithful to the principle of the 'histoire antiévénementielle'. In this total history the subjective is objectified by statistics, and comparison is at the service of 'problématiques théoriques'. This total history, this Marxist history, is, simply, 'l'histoire tout court'. This total history which knows everything, which does away with uncertainty in the future because it abolishes the uncertainty of the past, is, like all scientific thought, 'porteuse d'action'. But Vilar warns us that to practise this kind of history, 'il faut s'appeler Lénine'.

Our name is not Lenin, and such vaulting ambitions are therefore not for us. We will abandon the dizzy heights of method, modestly recognizing with Barzun that for the historian it is 'only a metaphor to say that he is rational and resourceful, imaginative and conscientious'.

Or, with Paul Veyne, we will say that history, that which is made as well as that which is written, is a matter not of science but of prudence; that it is a simple description without method; that in history *expliquer* is *expliciter* is *raconter*; that history has no depths to be plumbed or main lines to be traced out; that it does not reveal what lies hidden 'behind' what has taken place; that therefore there is no tenable distinction between *événementiel* and *non-événementiel*; that, finally, history does not need explanatory principles, but only words to tell how things were. We may, in conclusion, quote on historical method some words by G. M. Young, a historian whose contempt for diplomatic history would have gladdened Fabvre's heart:

Of historic method, indeed, nothing wiser has ever been said than a word which will be found in Gibbon's youthful Essay on the Study of Literature. Facts, the young sage instructs us, are of three kinds: those which prove nothing beyond themselves, those which serve to illustrate a character or explain a motive, and those which dominate the system and move its springs. But if we ask what this system is, which provides our canon of valuation, I do not believe we can yet go further than to say it is the picture as the individual observer sees it ... History is the way that Herodotus and Fra Paolo and Tocqueville and Maitland, and all those people, saw things happening.

History,
the Past and the Future

THE WRITING of history is an activity in which the historian
engages, here and now, an activity that is carried on in the
historian's present. But it is also an activity which has reference to, which seeks to obtain knowledge of, a past. Involved
then in the historian's activity is the implicit assumption that
past and present can be related, can come into contact with
one another, that the present can know the past. To a philosophic mind this assumption is by no means obvious; it is one
which, on the contrary, has to be established or justified or
explained. But the historian, busy with his researches into
what has been, will cheerfully take it for granted. He will
dismiss the philosopher's finicky doubts with the robust
argument that history has been, is, and will continue being
written, regardless of such logic-chopping. Confront the historian, however, with the third term in series, and ask him how
he relates the past to the future and he will, quickly enough,
find himself in difficulties. From such difficulties simple, if not
simple-minded, ostensiveness—pointing to so many and so
many shelves of historical works—will be no means extricate
him. He will have, reluctantly, either to call upon the philosopher, or himself to philosophize in order to establish whether
and, if so, how, the past is related to the future, whether
historiography has a role in relation to the future.

History is, then, about the past. It is, the *Oxford English
Dictionary* tells us, 'a relation of incidents'. To relate incidents
is to tell a story, and the word story itself indeed derives from,

is an elision of, the word *history*. All stories begin, or ought to begin, with the phrase, Once upon a time. To say 'once upon a time' is ipso facto to be sure of living in the present, a present different from what has been. This awareness is part of what we understand by self-consciousness or mind. And it would be impossible without memory. Self-consciousness, mind and memory entail one another, are concomitant with one another.

We are aware, then, of a past because we remember. This remembering is, in the first place, a remembering of ourselves, a self-recognition, a recognition of our identity as at once immutable and undergoing continuous change. Pan, cheated of the nymph Syrinx who had changed into a reed to escape his pursuit, reclines in the forest, and through the long hot afternoon consoles himself—as Mallarmé tells us—in the remembrance of other nymphs and goddesses, now long gone— nymphs and goddesses who had succumbed to his embrace. Busying himself with removing the girdles from their shades, he becomes drunk with the recollection. Pan, we see, is making to himself a relation of past incidents—past incidents which concern himself. He is engaged in what we would call autobiography. The philosoper Dilthey has argued that autobiography is indeed the main gate by which we enter into the human world of the past, because autobiography enables the historian to understand human action, so to speak from the inside. Whether this is so or not, the argument enables us to define the historian further, by distinguishing him from the autobiographer. While both are concerned with the past, we can now say that they are concerned with two different pasts. The autobiographer is concerned with his own natural past, while the historian is clearly not so limited. Shall we then call the historian's past not a natural, but a historical past, and shall we add that this historical past is not the remembrance of things past? For remembrance is a recollection of what has happened to one, or of what one has heard or been told. But history manifestly cannot be limited to any one single person's recollections, nor is it a mere collection of a large number of individual reminiscences.

Before we consider this further, let us return to Pan pursuing his autobiographical musings. In summoning his nymphs to the 'sessions of sweet silent thought' he was, Mallarmé tells us, *avide d'ivresse*, eager to become drunk. Pan was, then, using the recollection of his former conquests as consolation and substitute for the pleasure of which the *maligne* Syrinx had, by her flight, cheated him. Pan's purpose, we may say, was a practical one. Here, then, is yet another past to add to our list, as there is a natural and a historical past, so there is a practical past. The practical past is that which we evoke in order to satisfy a current need or purpose—a need or purpose connected with our present circumstances or actions, and with the manner in which we set out to justify or to shape them.

Jews and Christians possess as their Scriptures works which purport to deal with the past, works which can be described as 'relations of incidents'. But these incidents are not related simply for their own sake. They are related in order to provide examples and guidance to the faithful, to instruct them in the ways of God with man, to transmit to them divine commands. These Scriptures, rightly called sacred, enable men to lead a godly life and to attain, or to receive, salvation. The Scriptures are, of course, not the only writings which are concerned with a practical past—a past which is intimately and urgently connected with present praxis; nor is the praxis with which the Scriptures are concerned the only kind of praxis which accounts of the past may seek to facilitate or promote. In the *Peloponnesian War*, a governing object is clearly to show the workings of human nature as it is, always and everywhere. Thucydides uses the incidents of the war in order to draw a lesson and point a moral for his readers—a practical preoccupation. Tacitus' *Annals* and *Histories*, very different from Thucydides' masterpiece, are equally preoccupied with practice. 'His professed purpose in writing', says a commentator, 'is to hold up signal examples of political vice and virtue for posterity to execrate or to admire, and to teach his readers ... that good citizens may live under bad rulers; and that it is not mere destiny or the chapter of accidents, but personal character and discretion, dignified moderation and reserve, that best guard a senator of rank unharmed through time of peril ...'. Livy's *Annals*, again, show the same practical preoccupation. Livy sees the history of Rome as culminating in the rule of Augustus, and to be full of instructive lessons for the Romans

179

of his day who, by reading of their ancestors' mishaps and misfortunes, their exploits and triumphs, would be fortified in their resolution to preserve Roman greatness, and would be better armed for their task. The *Annals* stand out in any record of historical literature, but equally they may be looked upon as the prototype of a host of books few of which approach Livy's excellence—books with some such title as *Our Island Story, The Pageant of British History, Great Heroes from Charlemagne to Charles de Gaulle, Israel from Kind David to David Ben-Gurion, The Arab Struggle for Liberation from Muhammad to Jamal Abd el-Nasser.* We may detect the same practical concern in Herodotus, who begins his great work by saying that great deeds have value in retrospect, whether done by Greeks or others,and that such deeds should be exhibited for the instruction, edification, and admiration of his readers.

Is it here then, in this concern with the practical past, that we may identify the role of historiography in relation to the future? Praxis, by definition, is concerned with future-directed action—action to preserve or defend or improve one's situation—and the practical past may be considered as a help towards this end. Here, then, is one answer at any rate to our question. In this manner, we shall say, historiography will equip us with lessons and warnings, will raise our morale and self-confidence, will fill us with self-esteem and with pride in our inheritance—and in these various ways will enable us to fashion a better future for ourselves. Future-directed action is a venture. The action may or may not contribute to, or have influence over, the success of the venture. The Bible provides a pre-eminent example of a practical past which has captured the imagination and inspired the actions of successive generations. On the other hand, as Eliot wrote in his poem, 'Gerontion':

> History has many cunning passages, contrived corridors
> And issues, deceives with whispering ambitions,
> Guides us by vanities

The practical past may lead those who seek its guidance into a blind alley or into disaster—witness the numerous political ventures which, in the nineteenth and twentieth centuries,

inspired by a nationalist historiography, were intent on resur-
recting past glories and vanished power, and which suffered
shipwreck and ended in ruin.

We have so far identified the character of the practical past
and its equivocal relation to the future. But we had begun by
distinguishing between a natural past, and a past which went
beyond the personal recollection which constitutes the natural
past—and this other past we have called historical. How does
this historical past stand in relation to the practical past?
History, it is commonly said, is a modern European invention.
Such a statement does not mean that history, taken simply as a
relation of incidents, was unknown before the modern period
in Europe. This would be absurd since Thucydides and Livy
and Tacitus and innumerable other writings are manifestly
historical works in this sense. What the statement rather
means to emphasize is that, beginning in the eighteenth century, a current of ideas spread in Europe which ended by
presenting a novel and quite original view of man. This current
of ideas is that which Meinecke, in delineating its first appearance and subsequent development, called *Historismus*; and
which Dilthey (in whom Meinecke found inspiration), seeking
to work out a critique of historical reason, was the first
attempt to describe, articulate and systematize. If we are to
sum up this new picture of man in the briefest possible manner,
we may say that for it man's nature is his history, that man is
fundamentally a historical being. The idea that man is a
historical being implies that he is not an essence which his
existence in due course unfolds, that he is not governed by an
appointed end which gives meaning and coherence to the
whole of his existence, and that he is not endowed with a
changeless and uniform nature which his actions simply serve
to exemplify. In this view the key to history—if we may speak
thus—lies in history itself, and to try and go behind history is
impossible, indeed meaningless. History is the record of
human actions—those actions which constitute man's nature,
and by doing which man makes or constitutes himself, provides himself with an identity and a personality. This identity
is not a fixed quantity, it is one which, facing, coping with,
mastering contingencies, and all the while reflecting on itself in
the process, finds and recognizes itself in the very flux of

continuous change. To use Hegel's formulation, 'What the subject is, is the series of his actions'. But the series is not programmed or foreordained: every contingency evokes a decision, an action, spontaneous and, before the event, inconceivable. This is what is meant by human freedom. As the narrator in Proust's novel, *Jean Santeuil*, puts it: 'And I saw my future before me like a stranger whom one meets in the night'.

The historical past is the concomitant of this new vision of man's historicity, of man's nature being his history. The historical past, it ought thus to become clear, has nothing in common with the practical past. It will exhibit men at a certain time and in a given place, responding to their circumstances as they understand them, setting sail, steering, hauling, veering, tacking, coasting, turning, on a voyage with no known starting-point and with no appointed destination. Such is the historian's past. It affords no guidance for the future. Like the deliverances of the oracle, it is ironically ambiguous. No rules of conduct or laws of behaviour can be extracted from it.

But how is history possible? How can the historical past be known? The past is dead and gone, and the historian in his present cannot directly survey or inspect it. But from this past there has survived, somehow or another, less by design than by accident, a heap of remains and relics which to the unhistorical eye are a mere heap, from which, as need or occasion offers, one may select a document proving title or lineage, or an object attracitve in its beauty, or alluring in its strangeness.

This heap, however, the historian transmutes into evidence—present evidence from which a past is inferred. Herodotus called his work *History*. The word *istoria*, which has become our *history*, originally meant, in the Ionian dialect in which it is found, 'enquiry'. Herodotus uses many kinds of sources: written records, hearsay, the witness of his own eyes. But these sources he submits to, and verifies by, enquiry—*istorie*—and criticizes by common sense. He is not a compiler at the mercy of his sources, rather he is their master. He accepts and rejects evidence, and submits it to the question. He does not look upon the sources as authorities, but precisely as evidence. This character of the historian's activity is mirrored in the dictionary's definitions. He is, we learn, 'one who relates a narrative or a tale, a story-teller', but he is also, which is more to our purpose, the 'writer or author of a history; especially one who produces a work of history in the higher sense, as distinguished from the simple annalist or chronicler of events, or from the mere compiler of a historical narrative'. And if we should enquire what this 'history in the higher sense' is, the dictionary will also oblige: it is 'a written narrative constituting a continuous methodical record, in order of time'. The method which makes the record methodical is precisely the enquiry, the question by which the historian, moved by a desire to make sense of the fragments which have survived from the past, transforms these fragments into evidence.

But, it may be said, the detective, the lawyer, the genealogist, also deal in evidence. They also seek to interrogate the clue, the title-deed, the parchment. But they do this simply in order to find and convict a criminal, to establish who is the rightful owner of a property, or the legitimate heir to a title of nobility. Once the judge has pronounced according to the law and the rules of the court, the file is closed. But for the historian, no file is ever closed. There is no saying what will start him on a particular enquiry, no determining through which by-ways and meanderings it will lead him, or how he will end it. How did the war of 1914 start? What led the British Government to consider Belgian neutrality a vital interest? What was Britain's view of the European balance of power? What did the idea of the balance of power mean in European politics? Did it always mean the same thing? Who invented and articulated it? By the time the historian is dealing with this last question, we are very far indeed from the guns of August. A mere sampling of the historical literature surrounding the outbreak of the 1914 war will show how utterly various, indeed inexhaustible, are the questions which this event has provoked (and will no doubt continue to provoke) and how impossible to have specified in advance those which historians have deemed worth asking.

I have described the outbreak of war in August 1914 as an event, and this way of speaking seems both clear and legitimate. But what is this event? Once ask the question, and the notion begins to seem problematic and obscure. Where does the event begin, and when exactly does it end? If we reflect for a moment, we begin to see that the event is something which the historian makes of the evidence he has gathered. He begins by knowing something incoherently, in fact by barely knowing it; Kaiser Wilhelm, Franz Joseph, Grey, Cambon, Iswolsky: they are names, mere labels. Out of these names, with the evidence he interrogates and on which he reflects, he, the historian, makes the event which his readers come to know as the outbreak of the 1914 war. This is what Dilthey has called the hermeneutic circle, in which knowledge, abstract and incoherent to start with, constitutes itself in due course as ever more concrete and coherent. One crucial operation by which intelligibility and coherence are attained—and this attainment, be it remembered, is precarious, always threatened and perupetually subject to questioning and revision—is by the historian placing an event in its context. And the only possible context for an event is that provided by other events. Thus he will show Grey and Berchtold and Cambon and Foch and Moltke and the rest, acting, choosing, deciding in response to contingencies which themselves are the outcome of actions, choices, responses for which other agents are responsible— and these other agents similarly in their turn. And the historian will show this, as the dictionary says, 'in order of time'. By doing this, then, the historian will have shown and thus will have explained, how the Europe of Edward VII and of Franz Joseph became the Europe of Lenin, Masaryk, and Pilsudski. What is true of political is also true of economic, social and intellectual history. In all these fields, equally, to explain is to recount, to narrate, to show how one contingent event elicits, gives rise to another (equally contingent) event, and so on ad infinitum. If one were God, one might see all events stretched in a mighty and complex chain, event linked to and giving rise to event. As Leibniz wrote in a sentence adapted from Hippocrates, which Meinecke quotes again and again, almost as the very motto of *Historismus*: *Tout est conspirant*. But historians of course are not omniscient: the chain will sometimes extend only for a short distance, it will be broken over many stretches owing to paucity of evidence or the historian's failure of intelligence and imagination.

Just as no event is coherent or intelligible except in the context of other events, so no event can be specially privileged by the historian as being the sole key to, or the crucial

184

explanation of, history or some stretch thereof. Some such implication, among many others, is to be derived from Ranke's famous statements that every epoch is directly before God and that before God all generations of mankind are equal. This must be so, since the historian qua historian does not dispose of a standard or measuring rod, independent from and external to the events, which might enable him to declare one epoch more crucial, or one generation more important, than another. To be able to do so, the historian must possess an independent and invariable unit of comparison. But he, in fact, does not possess it. It might be objected that historians are always making comparisons. Why, they ask, is the British parliament different from the French *parlement*, and this in turn unlike the Spanish *cortes*? They do this, however, in order the more keenly to put the question to the evidence and thus the better to understand the parliament, *parlement*, or *cortes*, as the case may be. If the comparison in this particular case does yield questions which would not otherwise have been asked, this is surely because all these institutions are part, in some sense, of a common legal and political tradition. Historians compare, in other words, for heuristic purposes, not in order to establish the character of an *Urparlament*, of which these institutions are specimens, or to discover a law governing the appearance, evolution, and disappearance of representative assemblies. Heuristic, in any case, is not a systematic and articulated science. Rather, like the wind, it bloweth where it listeth. In seeking to make sense of his evidence, then, the historian will call upon whatever intellectual and imaginative resources, whatever knowledge and experience he can muster, and a particular heuristic will never by itself produce or guarantee good or reliable history. Some like to compare, others find this a bore. The proof of the pudding will lie in the eating.

If comparison between events in any real sense is out of the question for historians, if every epoch is directly before God (for who is to say whether or in what sense twentieth-century Europe is preferable to the Roman Empire under the Antonines?), if the idea of norms (and consequently of deviations therefrom) cannot be accommodated in historical discourse, the notion of cause is likewise misplaced here. To privilege a particular event as the cause of another event or series of events is at once to plunge into a morass of imprecision.

An event, we have said, becomes intelligible and coherent in the context of other events: we are able to follow a conversation because we understand the interlocutors as responding to one another, and we make sense of a battle, a diplomatic negotiation, the fluctuations in the price of a commodity, the functioning of a parliament, say, or a university, as being the outcome of decisions which could have been other than what they were. But if we try to describe events in the language of causality, we are quickly overtaken by logomachy. For in a conversation, or a battle, or an artistic movement, what is cause, what is effect? An event is now a cause, now an effect, or simultaneuosly cause and effect.

But if we somehow overcame, or disregarded this confusion, could the language of causality, systematically employed, open for us a way to make historiography useful in coping with the future? For, after all, a cause is always a cause and an effect always a necessary effect. Cause and effect, in other words, are linked by, are the exemplification of a law. If we could somehow establish a nexus of past causes and effects, then precisely because a law is timeless, what was true in the past, would be equally true in the future. If historical study can establish law-like regularities, then undoubtedly historiography will have a role in relation to the future. The difficulty here is that history deals with events which by definition have taken place at a given time and in a particular place. To make them amenable to the language of casuality, events have to be transformed and homogenized in a manner such that they become specimens or cases which can be analyzed into the requisite components by the causality machine. The French Revolution, the Russian Revolution, the Chinese Revolution, the Iranian Revolution, have to be liquidized and poured into the centrifuge which will separate the revolutionary essence from its purely accidental French or Russian or Chinese or Iranian admixtures. The metaphor brings out the paradoxical and self-defeating implications of a timeless and a literally utopian historiography.

The last few decades, however, have seen the spread and

wide acceptance of a historiographical mode in which this paradox is latent, and even occasionally quite manifest. This mode is associated with the so-called school of the *Annales*. The founders of this school, Marc Bloch and Lucien Febvre, were extremely dissatisfied with the state of French historiography as they encountered it during the first two or three decades of this century. The dominant fashion stressed political and diplomatic history, and thus, they came to believe, was profoundly mistaken. Social and economic history they thought far more important. There is of course no reason why a historian should not study social and economic issues which are just as legitimate, as interesting, and as important as any other subject of historical enquiry. And there is, equally, nothing to object to in a historian following his bent in pursuing one kind of enquiry rather than another. But this particular preference soon came to be justified and dignified by a theory which was elaborated not so much by Bloch as by Febvre, and later on by Fernand Braudel, Emmanuel Le Roy Ladurie, and other members of the Sixième Section of the École Pratique des Hautes Études, established in 1947 with an initial grant from the Rockefeller Foundation, which became, in effect, the headquarters of the new movement and the guardian of its orthodoxy.

The reason, briefly, for which this theory gave the primacy to economic and social history was because political history dealt with superficial things, with things on the surface, with epiphenomena, as one might say. Economic and social history, on the other hand, with underlying reality, with the structure which underlay the surface manifestations of politics and diplomacy. The influence of Marxism on this doctrine is *prima facie* obvious, and is confirmed, in any case, by Febvre himself. But this metaphor of structure and superstructure is quite inappropriate for the historian, who will be at a loss how to decide if one particular event belongs to the structure, and another to the superstructure. Is Lenin's leadership of the Bolshevik revloution superstructural? Is Cleopatra's nose structural? If changes in the price of gold are structural in sixteenth-century Europe, are they also structural in the twentieth-century world—and if not, why not? The difficulty with structure and superstructure is the same which confronts us in historical cause and effect. The amibition to divide events between structure and superstructure was further encouraged and reinforced by the admiration of *Annales* historians for the achievements of linguistics, psychoanalysis, and structural anthropology. *Langue* and *parole*, unconscious and conscious, social structure and social relation, are all distinctions which point in the same direction, distinctions which claim to unveil the mystery of human behaviour, to organize the chaos of appearances which confronts the scientist, and to provide a sure guide through the thickets of data and facts.

Such distinctions, the *Annales* school believes, will be the instrument by which a global, or total history can be constructed. Thus Braudel divides history into three layers: the structural, the conjunctural, and the *événementiel*, and the ambition is to relate all three layers, or all three sub-systems, into one comprehensive system, into a total history. This ideal is, however, misconceived on two counts. If history is an enquiry which any obscurity, any puzzlement can initiate, and if the enquiry can lead the historian through unexpected paths to vistas he had not suspected when he started on the enquiry, this attempt to regiment happenings into categories of the structural, the conjunctural, and the *événementiel* will soon seem a procrustean, an arbitrary enterprise. It will also break down for another reason equally serious. As an admirer of the *Annales* school, Traian Stoianovich has pointed out (*French Historical Method: The Annales Paradigm*, 1976, pp. 97ff.) the distinctions advocated by Braudel are by no means the only ones which have to be attended to. In the interests of a total history, Braudel has taken over from Claude Lévi-Strauss a communications theory whereby communication proceeds at three levels of expression: the exchange of women, the exchange of goods and services, and the exchange of other types of messages. Like Lévi-Strauss, Braudel also distinguishes between conscious and unconscious forms of communication. Since, further, he distinguishes between three units of temporal measure—the time of structure, the time of conjunctures and the time of events, the systematic analysis of the general communications system of a given collectivity would require the identification of at least eighteen ($3 \times 2 \times 3$) sub-systems. But this is very far from being the number of sub-systems which a total history must comprise. Stoianovich points out that there are other message systems which have to be added to Lévi-Strauss's three, and when all of these, in all their possible combinations, are taken into account, the total number of sub-systems will amount to no less than 16,777,216. 'With the aid of the computer', remarks Stoianovich, 'it should be possible to analyze even 16,777,216 variables. One problem remains, however. Who would read the enormous number of printouts?'

In the historical hierarchy of the *Annales* school, there is absolutely no doubt that structural history has the primacy. It is at the opposite pole from *histoire événementielle*, which deals with the mere froth of events, with things which our gossip-column writers think worthy of attention. *Histoire événementielle* Braudel contemptuously dismisses as '*cette petite science de la contingence*'. 'Down with occurrences!' he exclaims. What is worthy of attention is that which lies in the depths, which goes on, perhaps for centuries, unchanged or hardly changed. Le Roy Ladurie, indeed, goes so far as to speak of 'history without people', a history, say, of climate, which is 'free of anthropocentric preoccupation or presumption'. History is emptied of people for the further reason that the historian is now concerned with systems and subsystems, with signals and factors, with series and index-numbers. Another *Annales* historian, Pierre Chaunu, in fact, looks forward to the quantification of the past, to the transformation of all history into *histoire sérielle*. This *histoire sérielle* will, ideally, link, in a chain of statistics and statistical projections, the past to the present, and the present to the future. But can history without people, a dehumanized history, in effect a table of functions and variables, support the notion of past or future? Lévi-Strauss, whose work, as has been said, has inspired the historiographical theory of the *Annales* school, has drawn the only possible conclusion from this state of affairs. From his own structuralist perspective, history is seen as either informing more and explaining less, or explaining more and informing less. The first alternative is the so-called *histoire événementielle*, which is no more than an inventory or storehouse of examples, while the second is structural history. But what gives structural history its intelligibility and its power to explain is biology, psychology, anthropology, and the physical sciences. Why, then, not got the whole hog and abolish history?

Arnold J. Toynbee
History as Paradox

ARNOLD TOYNBEE (1889–1975) retired from Chatham House in 1955. In the two decades which followed he continued to publish works which attest to the vigour of his mind, the width of his interests, and the facility of his pen. His career as a writer began before the First World War, and the books by and about him amount now to a small library. Toynbee was not a mere academic historian writing for a mere learned audience. He was, rather, a popular writer, but not because he set out to write what are called popular books. On the contrary, the work which established his world-wide reputation, *A Study of History*, is of such length and complication that it requires a great deal of leisure to follow, comprehend, and digest its author's reasonings. As G. R. Urban told Toynbee in a recorded coversation:

> ...Your popularity in America astounds me, for your *Study* is very exacting reading; it demands a grounding in the classics which is not one of the qualities American education favours. Yet your *Study* is not only read but definitely fashionable. The same goes, to a lesser degree, for Germany, where the classical background is, of course, much more firmly established. (*Toynbee on Toynbee: A Conversation between Arnold J. Toynbee and G. R. Urban*)

Urban is undoubtedly right, Since the appearance of its first three volumes in 1934, *A Study of History* and its abridgment by D. C. Somervell have been reprinted many times, and the continuing popularity of the work is shown by the publication of a lavishly illustrated, one-volume edition, revised and abridged (in collaboration with Jane Caplan) by Toynbee himself.

In his foreword to this abridgment, Toynbee declares that he had been working on *A Study of History* from 1920 to 1972, and indeed not the least interesting aspect of his work is the way in which Toynbee never ceased to reflect upon his enterprise, to explain and justify his historical method, and to modify—in small and great things alike—the grandiose panorama which he began to unfold before us fifty years ago. Anyone who reads consecutively the ten volumes of *A Study of History* will easily discover changes in mood and tone, as well as in argument and classifications between the first six volumes published in two batches in 1934 and 1939 respectively, and the last four volumes published in 1954. These ten volumes were followed by another, published in 1961, entitled *Reconsiderations*, where Toynbee bent once more over his work, endeavouring to modify it in the light of further reflection and reading, and to respond to objections made by his numerous critics. And the abridgment of 1972 shows that the author continued to brood over his handiwork, seeking to improve its appearance, increase its cogency, and make its message clearer and more forceful.

But substantial as are some of the changes which *A Study of History* underwent from 1934 to 1972, Toynbee still adhered to a view of history which first occurred to him as long ago as August 1914, and on which he built his imposing and complicated edifice:

'The year 1914 [Toynbee tells us in his foreword] caught me at the University of Oxford, teaching the history of classical Greece. In August 1914 it flashed on my mind that the fifth-century B.C. historian Thucydides had had already the experience that was now overtaking me. He, like me, had been overtaken by a fratricidal great war between the states into which his world had been divided politically. Thucydides had foreseen that his generation's great war would be epoch-making for his world, and the sequel had

192

proved him right. I now saw [Toynbee adds] that classical Greek history and modern Western history were, in terms of experience, contemporary with each other. Their courses ran parallel. They could be studied comparatively.'

This passage is crucial for understanding Toynbee's enterprise. His starting point was an analogy between the Peloponnesian War and the War of 1914–18, and it was the pursuit of analogies between different periods and places which would seem to have made Toynbee into a universal historian. *A Study of History* is thus perhaps better entitled, by analogy with Bishop Butler's famous book, *The Analogy of History*. This urge to compare—and to classify—clearly means that the ideal of Toynbee the universal historian is not a narrative, based on all the available evidence, showing how all events are related to all other events. Events Toynbee seems to consider a veil behind which lies the true reality for which the historian is searching. Again, what men have suffered and done, infinitely various and perpetually surprising as it is, does not seem to interest Toynbee in itself. He is (he tells us) in search of 'underlying permanent and uniform facts of human nature'. He believes in 'the uniformity and constancy of human nature', and considers this to be the 'objective criterion' by which the historian must endeavour to be guided. For Toynbee, it follows therefore, a man is not (as Hegel believed) the series of his actions—actions which he has the choice to take or not to take. He does not believe that man's nature is his history. Man for Toynbee rather exemplifies the workings of a uniform and constant human nature, of which his actions are specimens or instances.

> Où sont des morts les phrases familières
> L'art personnel, les âmes singulières?

But, in this perspective of Toynbee's, Valéry's question remains unanswered. The specificity of a human act, the singularity of a human life, must somehow be drained of their substance and significance. This perhaps accounts for what in other historians would be a dismissive and insouciant attitude to historical evidence. Discussing with Urban the *Survey of*

International Affairs, which he edited from many years for
Chatham House, Toynbee declared:

> I have had the curious experience of having written, in the
> '20s and '30s, about events on which the documents have
> since been published. Certainly when the inside material
> becomes available ... things look very different.

To an ordinary historian this gap between what he had written
and the actual evidence would be very disturbing, if not utterly
devastating. Toynbee, however, shrugs off the discrepancy
with a pyrrhonism: '...do you ever', he asks, 'get the full
story?' Together, then, with a firm belief in 'objective' laws at
work in historical events, Toynbee evinces great, if not radical,
scepticism about our ability to know the actual course of the
events. This scepticism seems reinforced by his belief that 'We
can't help having unconscious axes to grind to some extent.'
An ordinary historian might think that in historical discourse
what counts is the evidence, and the arguments derived from
the evidence, and that about these there can be nothing
'unconscious'; in short, that it is what the historian says which
signifies, not his motive for saying it. But for Toynbee, it seems
that the evidence is, because always incomplete, of not much
consequence, and the historian's motive is always suspect. Can
history under these conditions ever be a respectable enterprise?

The reader of Toynbee's works is perplexed by other paradoxes. *A Study of History*, we remember, has its origin in a
comparison between the Peloponnesian War and the First
World War. This comparison did not remain a hermeneutic
guess, opening new vistas of enquiry, and serving to inspire
and illuminate. It becomes rather the foundation on which
Toynbee erected his gigantic analogical construction, in which
'models' are built and tested, and 'specimen' compared with
'specimen'.

The purpose of these operations, we are told, is to discover
'whether or not there is a standard type to which [these
specimens] conform, notwithstanding their individual peculi-
arities'. The specimens which Toynbee believed to constitute
intelligible and comparable entities are those societies known
as civilizations. Toynbee argued that they are constant and

absolute objects of historical thought, that each one of them is an objective 'intelligible field of historical study'. This language serves to impress us with the idea that civilization are more real, more tangible, more dependable than other subjects of historical research. On this point Toynbee was very emphatic:

> Such political communities (national states, city-states, and the like) are not only narrower in their spatial extension and shorter-lived in their time-extension than the respective societies to which they belong, but their relation to these societies is that of inseparable parts to indivisible wholes. They are simply articulations of the true social entities and are not independent entities in themselves. Societies, not states, are 'the social atoms' with which students of history have to deal.

But we soon discover that these large and solid entities, these ultimate 'atoms', these wholes which are said to be indivisible, have, paradoxically, no more (and no less) substantiality that other historical individuals—a state, or an idea, or a tradition —which historians fashion out of their evidence.

On Toynbee's own showing these indivisible wholes turn out to be eminently divisible. In 1934 he counted nineteen civilizations. By 1961 these had proliferated to no less than thirty-two, and in the one-volume abridgement the total stands at thirty-four. To an ordinary historian there is here nothing surprising, for his work consists precisely in making historical identities (which can never be exhaustively listed), and in specifying their *differentiae* according to the evidence, which is never a fixed quantity, and always equivocal. 'Civilisations', for such an historian, are not more real or 'objective' identities than states or churches or corporations or statesmen. History is no doubt a seamless web since all events somehow or another touch all other events. But life is short and seams have to be made. There is, however, nothing to prove that one seam is more privileged than another, that a history organized in terms of civilizations is inherently sounder than histories which adopt some other organizing principle.

Is the historian of Cromwellian England, or of First World War diplomacy *ipso facto* inferior to the historian of any of Toynbee's civilizations, for instance the 'Egyptiac' or the 'Syriac'? Again, is it really the case that (as Toynbee claims) a larger unit is more intelligible than a smaller unit or a panoramic view 'a less misleading reflection of reality than a partial view'? There is, on the face of it, no reason why this should be so, or for speaking as though history is a mirror-image of 'reality'. In *Auguries of Innocence* Blake gives a rather deeper and truer account of the relative significance of the large and the small, and of the infinite shining through the finite:

> To see a World in a grain of sand,
> And a Heaven in a wild flower,
> Hold Infinity in the palm of your hand
> And Eternity in an hour

The civilizations which Toynbee has listed and classified are in any case studied not for their own sake, but only so that comparison between them may disclose the laws of human nature. This results in the events which Toynbee studied being transformed into categories or ideal types, with other paradoxical consequences. Thus, the history of the Roman Empire inspired Toynbee to fashion the concept of 'internal' and 'external' proletariat, and to use it for explaining the decline and downfall of other civilizations. But the notion of proletariat, which in fact has its origin in Roman history, abandons its historical moorings in the end, and becomes a free-floating category to be applied as and when the needs of classification require its presence. Thus we find Toynbee declaring—in the conversation with Urban—that Tolstoy, though a wealthy aristocrat who was privileged to do what he liked, was in reality a proletarian because he was 'alienated' from the Czarist régime. Similarly, the South African whites who are opposed to *apartheid*: 'Aren't they part of the proletariat—alongside of the blacks of South Africa? Many of this white minority are eminent intellectuals, some of them are wealthy, but from this spiritual and psychological point of view they are part of the proletariat.'

The demands of Toynbee's classificatory system result in

many other paradoxical statements which, if taken *au pied de la lettre*, must bewilder the historian—let alone the common reader. Thus Toynbee argues that universal states engender universal religions. This argument is clearly inspired from Roman history where Christianity spread as a religion of its spiritually famished 'internal proletariat'. But Toynbee must needs generalize from this 'specimen', and we are therefore invited to believe that the Caliphate (which was itself the outcome of Islam) did for Islam what the Roman Empire did for Christianity. Again, universal states are broken up by barbarian invasion—and therefore the Ottoman Empire, but for 'the mightier march of Westernization', would have been broken up by 'incipient barbarian invasions'. Who were these incipient barbarian invaders?

The Ottomans provide yet another puzzle for the readers. Toynbee explains that the growth of civilization is the outcome of a succesful response to a challenge. But if response is not adequate to the challenge, a society may become 'arrested'. The Ottomans, like the Spartans, are an example of arrested growth. They 'leaped' from being a pastoral Nomadic community to being an imperial Power:

> They faced the unprecedented challenge of having to govern vast populations, and, trying to cope with this novel political problem, they created intractable and inflexible institutions which precluded any further social developement.

Now it is well known that among empire builders the Ottomans were not unique in having pastoralist origins; nor is it the case that their transformation into the rulers of an empire was a sudden 'leap'. Such a description would fit the Arabs much better. It is also well known that the Ottoman state lasted for some six centuries, which is quite a long time, that from first to last its institutions underwent a prodigious amount of change, and that on the whole they managed quite well the problem of governing 'vast subject populations'. What sense, then, are we to give to the epithet 'arrested' when it is applied to the Ottoman Empire, and how are we to establish that is was more or less 'arrested' than the Roman, or the Abbasid, or the Austrian, or the British Empire? 'Inflexible', 'intractable', and 'arrested', when used to describe societies and political institutions are mere metaphors; as a *jeu d'esprit* they may be stimulating, but by themselves impart little of substance. May we not even go further and ask (with the author of a recent appreciation of Toynbee's *oeuvre*):

> Who can gainsay Lord Palmerston's dictum that 'Half the wrong conclusions at which mankind arrive are reached by the abuse of metaphors'...? (*Arnold J. Toynbee: History for an Age in Crisis*, by Roland N. Stromberg)

The needs of his system led Toynbee to a judgement which, of all the paradoxes in *A Study of History*, will perhaps most bewilder and disorient his readers. For Toynbee asserted, flatly and sweepingly, that the Western genius in architecture, sculpture and painting in the half-millennium since Giotto has been 'afflicted' with 'sterility'. It has been sterilized by a 'Hellenising renaissance', the evil effects of which were not thrown off until the nineteenth century, when Hamlin Hall built on the shores of the Bosphorus in 1869–71, and the Halle des Machines in Paris in 1889 first showed us what the Western genius could do when it was not smothered by the ghost of a resuscitated Hellenism. This extravagant and exorbitant verdict is a mechanical application of Toynbee's theory about growth, arrest and decline. Growth expresses the strength of native genius; therefore to be inspired by the achievements of a dead civilization is a dangerous raising of ghosts, a sinister trafficking with the dead. Therefore Cyrus Hamlin is better than Brunelleschi.

Toynbee's wholesale dismissal of five centuries of Western art, eccentric and paradoxical as it is, raises fundamental issues about the character of human life itself. Man is a being who is aware of himself, and aware that his world is a mind-affected world. It is because his world is such that he is all at home in it. To say this is to say how vitally man depends on legacies and traditions, on the transmission of modes of thought and behaviour, on artefacts and institutions, without which he would be unable to survive, or at best become simply an animal or a savage. It is for this reason, among others, that man's nature is his history. Toynbee's depreciation of legacies and traditions, his dismissal of them as a dead hand and an incubus, does not tally with our experience and historical knowledge. And if this depreciation is systematically adopted as a maxim or a rule of action, then it must result in making men aliens in their own human world, in increasing their insecurity and 'alienation'.

Such feelings of instability are, in any case, usually disagreeable. To show this we need go on further than *A Study of History* itself. Readers of the original ten volumes know how stable and immutable the position of the Jews and Judaism was in Toynbee's scheme. The Jews were fossils who had survived from the dead Syriac civilization. Their religion was characterized by fanaticism and intolerance and arrogance, and from it the West had derived these detestable traits. These views almost disappeared from the one-volume abridgment which even went so far as to state that in all three religions of the Judaic school, 'God the sovereign legislator has been seen to be God the merciful and compassionate synonym for love'. Toynbee went even further. This fossil of a dead civilization, now a scattered diaspora, is declared to be 'the wave of the future', and this because the 'transformation of the world into a cosmopolis favours social organisation on a non-local basis'. Verily, to adopt the Psalmist's words, the fossil which the builders have rejected is now the headstone of the corner! But this is none the less puzzling. For the Jews are now still what they ever were, and no new historical discovery has occured to warrant so radical a reappraisal. It is disturbing to come upon so great and so unexplained a change in the seemingly solid and 'objective' fabric of Toynbee's scheme.

As Professor Nathan Rotenstreich pointed out some years ago, the attention which Toynbee devotes to Jews and Judaism is out of all proportion to the place which he allots to them in world history.[1] This remark is as true of the abridgment as of the original work. Toynbee was much preoccupied with the past, present, and future of the Jews. He discussed the two options which have been open to them (which he called Herodianism and Zealotism), and attempted to fit Zionism and anti-Zionism within these categories. He pointed out that

---

[1] Nathan Rotenstreich, *The Recurring Pattern: Studies in Anti-Judaism in Modern Thought*, p. 76.

in terms of these two options, the Zionist position is ambivalent, and he concluded: 'At all events, the attempted Israeli–Jewish responses to the problem of 'peculiarity' will all of them fail unless the policy of national and religious exclusivity is renounced forthwith.' Zionism, as is well known, is a nationalist movement, no different in its ideological assumptions from other nationalist movements in the Middle East and elsewhere. Why it should have been singled out for such a peremptory monition is obscure. Furthermore, the reader may wonder whether the historian is in a position, *qua* historian, to offer advice so confidently, and so imperiously. Supposing the Israelis proceeded 'forthwith' to follow Toynbee's advice, and in consequence came a cropper? Or supposing they disregarded it, and thereafter flourished exceedingly? What, in either case, would be the historian's apology?

But it does not seem that such dangers worried Toynbee very much. On the contrary, the history which he wrote had an avowed practical purpose. *A Study in History* was there to inculcate a lesson and to point a moral. The lesson was that of the 'senseless criminality' of human affairs hitherto; and the moral was that mankind had to grow 'into something like a single family', or else destroy itself. It is to drive this point properly home that Toynbee embarked on a universal history. 'A study of human affairs', he tells us, 'must be comprehensive if it is to be effective.' Toynbee clarified this argument by means of a quotation from Polybius whose influence on him was (he told Urban) 'enormous':

> The coincidence by which all the transactions of the world have been oriented in a single direction and guided towards a single goal is the extraordinary characteristic of the present age, to which the special feature of the present work is a corollary. The unity of events imposes on the historian a similar unity of composition in depicting for his readers the operation of the laws of Fortune on the grand scale, and this has been my own principal inducement and stimulus in the work which I have undertaken ...

We are puzzled how we are to understand this passage in the context of Toynbee's own work. Was it that he, too, believed

all the transactions of the world to be oriented in a single
direction? And did he, too, want to depict 'the operations of
the laws of Fortune'?

In this passage Polybius, we know, is looking forward to
and celebrating the beneficent spread of Roman dominion. But
Toynbee was far indeed from eulogizing any earthly state or
dominion. On this issue he was perfectly categorical. 'The so-
called "civilised" state is', he affirmed, 'simply an imposing,
high-powered version of the primitive tribe.' This, of course, is
simply not true. A tribe is held together by blood and kinship, a
civilized state by law. In a tribe there can be no distinction
between private and public, while on such a distinction all
civilized states must rest. A tribe is primitive because it lacks
the institutions which mediate between the multifarious interests of its members, while a civilized state is civilized
precisely because it can discharge these mediatory and re-
medial duties. But it is easy to see that the achievement which a
civilized state represents is, paradoxically, of little consequence to Toynbee. 'Paradoxically', because an historical
study is concerned with human actions, and the evidence will
simply not allow us blithely to dismiss as insignificant the
establishment and maintenance of a polity, or to condemn all
political actions as hopelessly tainted with criminality.

But for Toynbee all the political arts are pernicious and in
the end vain and useless. The stimulus of danger or a cold-
blooded calculation of expediency are inefficacious for salvation. The power to save ourselves can only come from love:

> In virtue of this love which is equally human and divine, the
> Kingdom of God has a peace of its own which is not the
> philosophic peace of detachment, but the peace of life lived
> by men in and for God ... That is the palingenesia which
> Jesus proclaimed as the sovereign aim of his own birth in the
> flesh.

Again, we are told:

> If this is a soul's recognised aim for itself and for its fellow
> souls in the Christian Church on Earth, then it is evident
> that under a Christian dispensation God's will *will* be done

on Earth as it is in Heaven to an immeasurably greater degree than in a secular mundane society.

In respect of these passages too we are perplexed. And for this reason: that in his conversation with Urban Toynbee declared that he was not a believer, that he did not know whether there was a God, and that when he was an undergraduate he had ceased to believe in the doctrines of Christianity. How then are we to understand these references in *A Study of History* to God's will and to divine love and to 'the palingenesia which Jesus proclaimed'?

But however we may understand them, is it anyway the case that in our fallen condition it is love (and only love) which saves? What is love? Love is a feeling which moves the lover to promote above everything else the good of the loved one. Is this feeling, even though it were universal, enough to maintain the state of the world? The world with all its denizens, we know, is various, changeable, and even treacherous. What the lover may look upon as good the loved one may consider simply hateful. And does it follow that if you want the good, you will have enough prudence to bring it about? And even if your action is faultless, may the course of events not in the end mock your benevolence, and out of good in fact produce evil? Love is not enough.

Toynbee also uttered exalted words about conscience. He saw a conflict between it and the 'ecclesiastical "Establishment"', and his language shows clearly enough that he believed the promptings of conscience always to be better than the wisdom of the 'Establishment'. But the individual conscience, acting strictly on its own, spurning the help of institutions and traditions, is as likely to counsel evil as to prescribe the good. Eichmann, we remember, pleaded that he did what he did 'for the sake of conscience', and he may not have been lying.

Where will love and the dictates of consciene take us? Paradoxically, they will take us to a super-establishment, an all-engulfing institution. For Toynbee looked forward to the unification of mankind in a world-state. What would a world-state conceivably look like? Will it not have to be some kind of gigantic EEC in which Love will have to be codified in 'community regulations', and whose managers will be infinitely more remote than any State or Church which has hitherto existed? But it may be that Toynbee did not think so, for the model which he seemed to commend to us was that of Communist China. The caption below a picture of an athletic display in China (drafted by Miss Caplan but approved by him) declares:

> Westerners tend to see in China a repulsive modern Leviathan, but behind the ceremonial lies an ideal of mutual solidarity and co-operation from which a fragmented world may learn.

The caption appended to the reproduction of a Chinese propaganda poster (it shows Chairman Mao visiting a factory) invites us to consider the possibility that here is 'a deliberately controlled attempt at a felicitous synthesis' which might be 'a wholly new cultural departure for civilised Man'. Toynbee was clearly much attracted by Mao's China (as his conversation with Urban shows):

> TOYNBEE: This is a possibility—a rule of technocrats, with the state acting as Confucian paterfamilias, demanding and receiving, as you say, filial obedience from the workers. The extremism of the Cultural Revolution shows that Mao must have perceived this as a very real danger. This extraordinary purge, not only of the ruler's enemies, but of his bureaucracy—the transmission belts of his system —is, I think, unique in history, and is totally unlike the Stalinist terror. Mao made fools, in public, of the Mandarins, but then, instead of having their heads cut off, he put them back in office, and the people, having had the Mandarins guyed and seen through, will perhaps now not kowtow so abjectly as, according to tradition, they would be inclined to do. I think this was in Mao's mind.
> URBAN: If one could set aside the appalling cruelties that preceded (and partly also accompanied) the Cultural Revolution, one might applaud, anyway, Mao's intention. I would personally rejoice at the thought of Italian bailiffs, French social security administrators, and even some

British customs officers being given a taste of the Maoist whip.

TOYNBEE: I think it would be a salutary exercise for all bureaucrats—they ought to be put through it at fairly short intervals.

It may be that we too, if we desire the 'felicitous synthesis' of Maoist China, should arrange for our First Division civil servants (should we call them practitioners of 'institutionalised violence'?) to make quarterly public confessions before the multitude in Trafalgar Square.

Toynbee, as we have just seen, contrasted favourably Mao to Stalin. But his judgement of Soviet Communism was by no means unfavourable. Its founder, Lenin, he put in the same category as Christ, the Buddha and Gandhi. Lenin was 'a creative personality [who] feels the impulse of internal necessity to transfigure his fellow men by converting them to his own insight', and whose emergence 'inevitably precipitates a social conflict, as society struggles to cope with the disequilibrium produced by his creative energy'. Lenin's transfigurative activities were inspired, as is well known, by Marxist doctrine. This doctrine (Toynbee tells us) is 'the classic exposition of the social crisis that accompanies the disintegration of a civilisation'. The Marxist schema, he believed, is true, 'as a matter of ascertainable historical fact'.

> The phenomenon of disintegration, as it is revealed in history, does exhibit a movement that runs through war to peace; through an apparently wanton and savage destruction of past achievements to fresh works of creation that seem to owe their special quality to the devouring glow of the very flames in which they have been forged.

What is so lyrically described here Toynbee called a movement of 'schism-and-palingenesia'. Palingenesia is the word he had used to describe what Jesus proclaimed. Are we to understand that what Lenin effected was a palingenesia?

As a matter of ascertainable historical fact the Bolshevik Revolution was accompanied by a great deal of violence. But this violence was evoked by, was a response to, a disintegrating Western industrial society which, in Toynbee's pages, is depicted throughout as greedy and aggressive in various ways. The West has presumed to take possession of the whole world as though it was 'in the gift of some war goddess of private enterprise'. Commerce and industry, material welfare, Toynbee denounces as Western cultural aggression, as though humanity had before then been utterly innocent of buying and selling. We are shown a contemporary Nigerian shop sign showing a man in Western clothes and proclaiming: 'SEE THE MANAGER IN CHARGE'. This, we are told, 'is a signal of the West's successful cultural aggression, which has transformed the patriarchal chief of a tribal society into the ubiquitous managerial boss of Western commerce'. A few pages further on, we come upon a sketch—a caricature really— reproduced from a left-wing French periodical of the beginning of the century and purporting to show a European in a solar topee sitting in an easy chair, with revolver in hand and drink at his side, receiving the obeisance of grovelling and cowering natives. As though this picture depicted ascertainable historical fact, the caption declares: *'unprofitable or dangerous natives must be exterminated like vermin: a nineteenth-century French colonialist does his bit for civilisation.'* The West is guilty of 'atrocities' in Korea, the Americans in Viet Nam, the French in Algeria, and the French police in Paris in 1968. These 'atrocities' are the sign of breakdown, and 'moral responsibility for the breakdowns of civilisations lies upon the heads of the leaders'. This passage occurs on page 166 of the one-volume abridgement.

As I have said, Toynbee was not a popular writer, and made no concessions to his audience. We may assume that the readers who had the diligence to persevere so far would be educated enough and knowledgable enough to know that those against whom the Western forces were fighting in Korea, the Americans in Viet Nam and the French in Algeria were ruthless and unscrupulous enemies fully capable, as a matter of ascertainable historical fact, of committing the most chilling atrocities. Would this reader then wonder why the North Koreans, the Viet Cong, and the FLN are not denounced with the same stern and prophetic accents? If it is right to assume that some such thought would revolve in such a reader's mind, then not the least paradoxical in this budget of paradoxes is Toynbee's continuing popularity in the Western world to which Urban has attested, and to which the illustrated edition of *A Study of History* constitutes such weighty testimony.

Religion and Politics
Arnold Toynbee and Martin Wight

THE YEARLY commemoration of Martin Wight by means of a lecture is doubly appropriate. An annual lecture keeps his memory green among his friends and pupils. And in the second place, it is a peculiarly fitting celebration because Martin Wight was a teacher whose greatest and most seminal influence was in large measure exercised in lectures, tutorials, seminars and discussins groups. Exercised that is by means of the spoken, the living, word transmitted directly person to person, mind to mind. When it is contrasted with, say, a book, mere speech is thought to be something fleeting and evanescent, not to be compared with the tangibility, fixity, durability of the written and the printed word. But this is the merest superstition, for that which is fixed is also dead and inert. If the written word has power to speak to us, to move us, this is because it is the emanation and the embodiment of the living spirit. I am, here, put in mind of a striking passage which occurs in that most moving of Plato's writings, the writing known as the seventh epistle—a passage where Plato describes how his teaching is transmitted. This teaching he declares is not to be found in anything written down. The knowledge with which he is concerned is of the kind which 'after long-continued intercourse between teacher and pupil, in joint pursuit of the subject, suddenly, like light flashing forth when a fire is kindled, it is born in the soul and straightway nourishes itself'. The light of Martin Wight's discourse, its *rayonnement*, an irradiation now felt by many who never

knew or met him—it is this which brings us together in
commemoration and which illuminates the issues I am about
to consider—issues which we have reason to believe interested
him closely, and in more ways than one.

I met Martin Wight in the spring of 1950. It was by accident.
I was staying in Cumberland Lodge in Windsor Great Park
trying to do some reading in peace and quiet for my finals. In
the house was also staying a party of LSE undergraduates
together with some of their teachers. One day after lunch, in
the hall, by the main staircase, I do not know how, I found
myself standing together with some of these students in a circle
round someone with whom they were carrying on a discussion.
The centre of that circle, as I was soon to learn, was Martin
Wight. I cannot now recall the exact subject of the conversation but there still remains with me the vivid impression made
by this tall handsome man with the thoughtful eyes and
courteous attentiveness, who considered with slow delibera-
tion the speech of his interlocutor, and whose incisive response, when it came, was accompanied by a smile which
hovered, diffident and a shade ironical. One's initial impression—an impression which deeper acquaintance only confirmed—was of a pleasing, a satisfying harmony between
physiognomy, countenance and mind.

Though I do not remember the exact topic which drew me to
the circle gathered round Martin Wight, I do remember that
the talk eventually turned to modern European history and
historians, and it was this which became the subject of our first
conversation. For this too I also remember vividly, as one
remembers those occasions in one's own intellectual history
(few and far between as they are) when a thought, a word, a
sentence is enough to change henceforth the whole aspect of a
question, to stretch the mind and permanently enlarge the
understanding, to enlighten, to illuminate. To the undergraduate that I was, what Martin Wight had to say about the
imperial temptation which was a legacy from Rome to modern
European politics constituted an organizing idea which at
once introduced order into a jumbled multitude of events, and
provided a guiding thread for future enquiries. Talk about the
character of European history led to talk about historians.
Among those mentioned were, as I remember, Ranke—and

Toynbee. It was on that occasion that I think Toynbee and his book *A Study of History* first made an impression on me.

It was my good fortune that this conversation at Cumberland Lodge was followed by other exchanges both oral and epistolary—his letters written in that unmistakable and elegant Italic hand—, an informal and most fruitful converse, converse of a kind which, much more than the regular tuition of lectures and classes, helped to teach me what it means to be an historian. And, to judge by the devotion to his memory of so many friends and pupils, I could not have been the only one for whom to know Martin Wight stands as a memorable landmark.

A few months after the first meeting I have described I got married, and as a wedding present Martin Wight gave us the first six volumes of *A Study of History*, then all that had so far been published. On the fly-leaf he inscribed three quotations, one from G. M Young, one from Anatole France, and one from Kenneth Clark, all in one way or another expressing his high admiration of the work he had chosen as a gift. The quotation from Kenneth Clark referred to Burckhardt's famous work on *The Civilization of the Renaissance in Italy*. 'Like all the greatest historians (Mommsen is another example),' Clark wrote, 'Burckhardt selects his material with an imaginative power which gives his work an almost prophetic character', and it is clear that, *mutatis mutandis*, this is what Martin Wight thought of the historian Toynbee on the strength of the work which had already made him world-famous.

But of the remainder of the work, the four volumes published in 1954, Martin Wight's opinion was not so high. To me in conversation he said, I think about that time, that the book would have been more grandiose and more striking had it remained an unfinished torso, and there is evidence in unpublished writings that this remained his considered view. Particularly apposite here is a judgement which figures in the script of a broadcast on 'Arnold Toynbee at Eighty' given on Radio Baden-Baden in September 1969. In this broadcast Martin Wight declared that Toynbee was 'theologically naive'.

What makes this judgement highly interesting to us is that we cannot but relate it to the exchange between Toynbee and Wight which occurs in volume VII of *A Study of History*—one volume, that is, of the batch published in 1954. The exchange occurs in the footnotes and appendices to the section on 'Universal Churches' which forms part of this volume. And my purpose here is to elucidate, with the help of this exchange as well as of other writings of Toynbee's and Wight's the meaning of the judgement that Toynbee is theologically naive, and to bring out some, but by no means all, of its implications.

In the section of volume VII on universal churches Toynbee is concerned to describe the relation, the necessarily complex relation, between religion and civilization. His object, however, is not exclusively historical. It is also practical. He wants not only to establish the historical relation between civilizations and churches: whether civilizations are the chrysalises of churches and whether the function of churches is to make possible the rise of new civilizations and nurture them in their infancy. But also arising out of this historical concern is his—equally prominent—practical preoccupation with the place of religion in the conduct of one's life, and its contribution to the welfare of societies which have been brought into contact with one another through the scientific inventiveness and the economic enterprise of the West. Thus we see the section on 'Universal Churches' concluding with a sub-section on 'The Promise of the Churches' Future' where, among other subjects, Toynbee discusses: the promise of overcoming discord, the promise of revealing a spiritual meaning in history, the promise of inspiring an effective ideal of conduct, and the promise of exorcising the perilousness of mimesis. This intertwining of historical concerns and practical preoccupations is equally evident in some of Toynbee's other writings which apeared after the last four volumes of *A Study of History*, namely *An Historian's Approach to Religion* which appeared in 1956, *Christianity Among the Religions of the World* which came out in 1958, and *Hellenism* which followed in 1959. In point of volume and extent, Martin Wight's writings come nowhere near Toynbee's, but there is enough substance in them for us to discover a counter-vision to that of which Toynbee seeks, at such length, to persuade us.

In common, then, with the books just mentioned *Hellenism* combines a historical and a practical argument. Toynbee is not an admirer of the *polis*. In this he belongs to a well-defined (albeit not a popular) tradition of classical studies. To this tradition, many historians, some quite respectable, and some very distinguished, have belonged: William Mitford, Fustel de Coulanges, Jakob Burckhardt. For Toynbee, as for these, the city-state is a demanding and oppressive tyranny. But within this particular tradition Toynbee is distinctive in the manner in which he describes and explains this tyranny. For him it is an outcome of idolatry, of man-worship. 'The tutelary goddess [of a city-state] stood for the collective power of a city-state's male citizens.' And he adds that one might say, to use the language of modern psychology, that in worshipping this deity, the citizens were worshipping their own collective anima. Toynbee also gives another explanation which goes considerably further, and which also has far-reaching, implications for the modern world and for contemporary politics. He quotes the well-known saying of Protagoras that man is the measure of all things and interprets it to mean that 'the Hellenes saw in man "the Lord of Creation" and worshipped him as an idol in the place of God'. This, for Toynbee, is what is to be understood by the term, Humanism.

Whether he is right in so identifying the cause of the tyranny of the polis, in so characterizing Greek religion and in so interpreting Protagoras' saying—all this is debatable, but what is more to the point in our present context is that Toynbee believes that, following the Italian Renaissance, this Hellenic collective self-worship has become 'the dominant religion' of the world, only thinly disguised 'by a veneer of Christianity, Islam and other higher religions'. 'It is' Toynbee categorically asserts, 'manifestly the dominant religion' in the Western world today.

Such a judgement is sweeping and categorical. It unfits us for making the necessary distinctions, it prevents us from discriminating between various modes of social life, of aspirations and ideals. To say that the tyranny of the polis or, as Toynbee also describes it, the 'pagan Hellenic ideal of political absolutism' is the ancestor of modern despotism is to fail to see, as Martin Wight pointed out in his debate with Toynbee, that 'Paganism came nowhere near the combination of political fanaticism and spiritual coercion which is the essence of a Modern Western "totalitarianism".'

211

Toynbee, again, contrasts this 'pagan Hellenic ideal of political absolutism' with the 'Christian ideal of individual liberty which was a corollary of a Christian belief in the value of every human soul in the sight of God'. But as Martin Wight also observed, it is 'very disputable' whether Christianity can make an exclusive claim to the ideal of individual liberty. This ideal did of course arise and flourish in Western Christendom; but in Eastern Christendom, he pointed out, the reverse was to be observed, for here, Christianity 'provided the milieu for the flowering of the older bulb of sacred monarchy, in which the unbiased reader of the Old and New Testaments and of the Fathers would be much more likely to see the natural political expression of Christianity than he would be likely to see it in any form of individual liberty'.

Toynbee's identification of the modern European state with the polis and its tyranny, not only makes it impossible for us to distinguish modern tyranny from ancient, it also obscures the fact that the ideal of personal liberty is one which emerges as something new, something unknown before the coming to be of modern Western society. This society, we can now clearly see, is made up of individuals the diversity of whose beliefs, capacities and aims is literally infinite, individuals who have to co-exist with one another, and hence have to be not mere solitary individuals but also fellow citizens, citizens whose political institutions have to facilitate and not to hamper the pursuit of a multitude of different satisfactions, and to conform, as well, to the sense of what is fit and what is right, entertained by the members of such a society with all their diverse and peculiar views. These values are encapsulated in the modern Western state and the history of Western Civilization, as Martin Wight wrote in his essay, 'Western Values in International Relations', is to be seen as 'primarily the development and organization of liberty especially in the form of the tradition of constitutional government'. To say, therefore, that the modern state is a form of collective self-worship in imitation of the sinister example of the polis is to make it impossible to account for and describe a form of life which is at the opposite pole to the Hellenic city-state.

This modern liberty, if it is to exist, calls for life in a state which, as we know, has been and indeed could be nothing else but a constitutional state—an original political arrangement invented in the modern (as much as in the medieval) West, and which could not have been invented, let alone sustained, if collective self-worship had been the ethos of this society.

For Toynbee, modern Western civilization suffers from yet another *damnosa haereditas*, the 'Judaic' (as Toynbee calls it) legacy of a 'jealous God' who is a 'man of war'. Christianity, he considered, had been perverted by this other sinister element which it had incongruously and inexplicably readmitted, 'after having taken a decisive new departure from Judaism by recognizing that God is Love'. For Toynbee, then, genuine Christianity, all of it, is and ought to be comprised in this seemingly uncomplicated and transparent statement that God is Love. Two distinct questions are, however, posed by such a view of Christianity. Christianity is an old and doctrinally complex religion. In the first place, then, is Toynbee's characterization of it adequate to the historical and theological record? The answer to this question is eloquently—unanswerably—set out in Martin Wight's essay 'The Crux for an Historian Brought up in the Christian Tradition' printed as an annex to Volume VII of *A Study of History*. 'The central declaration of Christianity' as he told Toynbee, 'is not that God *is* something, but that God *has done* something', that 'God *has done* something in history. He has acted *in history* to show the meaning of history'. To conceive of God exclusively as Love is, again, historically and theologically deficient. For, as Martin Wight wrote in the same essay, 'God's love is not a mere benevolence: it is a love that is identical with Holiness and Justice'. This complex and paradoxical idea of God it is that one has to come to grips with if one is to have an adequate understanding of the Bible and its religious vision. The difficulty and the paradox make for intellectual tension—and theology may be described as the study or discipline which explores (among other things) the meaning of this paradox, and its bearing on human life and conduct. Theology, it follows, must be a rational discourse, a series of intelligible and coherent propositions. If it is not, then the mystery with which it must deal will remain inchoate, invertebrate, given over to uncontrollable fancies and perilous imaginings. But that theology is a rational, a philosophical discourse is, as

213

Toynbee objected to Martin Wight, precisely its vice. Toynbee would distinguish intellect from intuition, and make intuition the organ by which 'the truth of the Heart' (which for him *is*, exclusively, religion) is apprehended.

But what kind of society would it be, a society which lived by 'the truth of the Heart'—whose God was exclusively the God of Love? Here I would like to refer to a writing in which the implications and consequences of a belief that love is the sole, exclusive value are explored in the most acute and original fashion. As is well-known, the young Hegel was a student at the Tübingen seminary. His theological studies there left him unsatisfied, left him indeed highly contemptuous of the intellectual qualities manifest in the theological works he had been required to study. Having renounced a career in the ministry, he spent some eight years as a private tutor in Bern and Frankfurt. It was during those years, from 1793 to 1801, that he managed to work out for himself an original philosophical position on which, it is no exaggeration to say, much of his later work was to be founded. The intense intellectual life of those years revolved precisely round theology. The young Hegel wanted to work out for himself why the dominant Protestant theology of his day was defective, and whether a more convincing, a more satisfying position could be worked out.In the course of these attempts, he came to compose in 1796 a long piece to which the editor of his early writings gave the title, 'The Spirit of Christianity and its Fate'. In the course of this writing, Hegel reflects on what befell the group of Jesus's followers after his death. I am not concerned here with the historical basis—or the lack of it—for Hegel's speculations, but rather with the way in which he delineates the working out in actual life of the particular principle by which men choose to live. After Jesus's death, Hegel tells us, his disciples kept together as a group, and the essence of this group was '(a) separation from men and (b) love for one another'. 'The friends of Jesus kept together after his death; they ate and drank in common. some of their brotherhoods wholly abolished property rights against one another ... They conversed about their departed friend and master, prayed together, strengthened one another in faith and courage.' Many engaged in spreading the faith. Here, then, was a

214

community bound not by interests, or by mutual fear, but only by love. 'In love's task', Hegel says, 'the community scorns any unification save the deepest, any spirit save the highest . . . But the community cannot go beyond love itself'. It cannot do so, since were the members to be engaged 'in that prodigious field of activity' which lies beyond praying, eating in common, believing, hoping and proselytizing, they might 'put themselves in jeopardy of clashing against one another's individuality', and this would destroy the community of love. Here then is the predicament of a community the exclusive principle of which is love, that any of the diverse and marvellous activities which engage the energy and ingenuity of men will put love at risk and this danger, says Hegel, 'is warded off only by an inactive and undeveloped love, i.e., by a love which, though love is the highest life, remains unliving. Here the contranatural expansion of love's scope becomes entangled in a contradiction, in a false effort which was bound to become the father of the most appalling fanaticism, whether of an active or a passive life.' Love as the exclusive principle of social life must stultify and hamstring, must turn into its opposite.

But the love to which Toynbee calls is even more problematic in its consequences than the love which binds a small community. For he preaches a world-wide love, calling for 'a wider synthesis' beguiling us with the 'great dream of a world society with a universal religion of which the historical faiths are but branches.' But as Hegel sensibly pointed out in the writing from which I have quoted, 'the grand idea of a universal philanthropy' is shallow and unnatural; 'the love which a large group of people can feel for one another admits of only a certain degree of strength or depth and demands both a similarity in mind, in interest, in numerous relationships of life, and also a diminution of individualities.' In the nature of things, these are impossibilites. If we attend to what men are (and what they are is what they have done) we have to dismiss these ideas as simply fanciful.

But perhaps not simply to dismiss them, since to do so would be to remain unaware of the inhuman and nightmarish world which a universal religion, taken in earnest, bids fair to conjure up. Toynbee believes in a universal religion, or in the equivalence and interchangeability of all religions because he

215

believes that there is one essential truth which lies behind the myriad of rites and practices which men have adopted and followed, but which of themselves are inessential and accidental. To be attached to a traditional form of ritual, of law and worship is not only not to worship God, it is to give oneself over to man-worship. Toynbee therefore, invites us to look forward to a time when Religion 'could cease to be an accident of birth and become a matter of choice'—a world to imagine which is to imagine an arid desolation in which souls, lost, lonely and unattached, float about perpetually shopping in the heavenly supermarket, yearning for this or that creed to appease their disquiet. The world would indeed become the alien and unbearable wilderness which gnostic visions have described and where, as Toynbee indeed believes, incarnation is incarceration.

This arid vision would brush aside, and dismiss all human activity, politics included, as hopelessly futile, indeed as evil, and only look forward to a world where spirit is liberated from flesh. But a world such as this would not be the human world. In the human world, as we all know, spirit is not alive unless it is incarnate. If body is separated from soul death supervenes. In this world of flesh and blood, men strive to build for themselves refuges with a little light and warmth where they may, in some tranquillity, enjoy their powers, and exercise their energies and their inventiveness. These havens of light and warmth are the religions which men have followed, religions which may not be cavalierly divorced from their specific rituals, laws and modes of worship; they are also polities and states which confer protection and secure liberties. To preach mere love is to be simply impatient and dismissive of our world, the world which is lighted by the light of common day, is to lose the desire and perhaps the ability to cope with, and understand politics—which is not and cannot be love.

States to be sure may, do, come to grief; they may be guilty of great oppressions, but they are not for all that to be condemned in principle and in advance as demonic idolatries, as monsters engendered by human cupidity, arrogance and savagery.

It is only when they are not thus condemned, that it becomes possible with open-eyed and sceptical shrewdness to take the measure of those bodies which, now beneficent and now destructive, are yet necessary to the maintenance of life, to attend patiently to their mutual relations, to what Martin Wight has called 'the intractable anomalies and anfractuosities of international experience'.

If, taking him as our guide, we were to do so, what he would show us in the Western state system, to the study of which he devoted so much of his energy and his subtle intellect, is a human world, tension-ridden and equivocal, but intelligible and manageable; not a Manichaean world of absolute evil and absolute good confronting one another, but that *juste milieu* which he illustrated by a saying from Grotius to the effect that 'a remedy must be found for those that believe that in war nothing is lawful, and for those for whom all things are lawful in war'.

The moral delicacy, the nicety of judgement evident in this passage of Grotius's is exactly Martin Wight's own. Those qualities are evident in the very first writing of his on international affairs, the essay on *Power Politics* which appeared in 1946, and we find them sustained, enriched, deepened throughout the rest of his life. The writer who tells us in 1946 that honour is an ambiguous word now meaning pride and now ⁓allegiance to accepted standards of conduct, that morality is not a matter only of a civilized tradition but also requires a feeling of security to sustain it, that powers do seek security without reference to justice, but that in the fraction that they can be deflected from this 'lies the difference between the jungle and the traditions of Europe'—the same writer twenty years later surveying the same *Europe aux anciens parapets*, with all its sanguinary conflicts and its ruinous civil wars, sums up its ambiguous achievement of a political morality—an achievement which seems peculiarly its own. As Martin Wight expressed it, felicitously theorizing the practice and experience of centuries, this political morality is not so much the imposition of 'a dramatic moral veto on political action ... as the discovery of an alternative positive policy which avoids the occasion of the veto'. This moral sense, again, 'assumes that moral standards can be upheld without the heavens falling' and that 'the upholding of moral standards will in itself tend to strengthen the fabric

217

of political life'. In this subtle and exact summation speaks the voice itself of a beleaguered and fragile, but a still living tradition.

Religion under Stress

IN THE LAST century or so Scriptural religions—and perhaps all traditional religions—have had to face the challenges and dangers of 'secularization.' The onslaught has come from many directions. A scientific world-view has gained ground which on the face of it is incompatible with the Bible or the Koran; a new ideal of moral autonomy for the individual, irreconcilable with the authority of divine prescriptions, has become increasingly attractive; and the pervasive influence of Marxism has diminished all religion into a mere illusion, an 'opium', used to lull the pain of alienation which men must suffer in a class-ridden society.

Religious responses have varied a good deal. Some of them have been uncompromising in rejecting modernity root-and-branch. But most have been anxious to appear broadminded and up to date. In his recent Reith Lectures, Dr Edward Norman, for example, has forcefully argued that Christianity has absolutely no business with politics, and is not a religion of social service. But as other writings of his have established, commitment to the ideology of a liberal intelligentsia has been rife for decades now in the Church of England. Such a commitment whether it stems from conviction or from the prudent pursuit of a defensive strategy of accommodation with what is taken to be 'the spirit of the age', was manifest in reactions to the Falklands war. There was reluctance to acknowledge that a victory was a proper occasion for thanksgiving by the national Church; an eagerness, almost, to treat both sides with a distant impartiality; and even a fastidious distaste for the profession of arms. The same commitment is also patent in the activities of the World Council of Churches, as it is in the outlook of large numbers of Roman Catholic clergy. The Mexican priest 'on the run' in Graham Greene's *The Power and the Glory*—a poor and scared creature, with his craving for alcohol, and terror of the authorities hunting him down, who yet at the peril of his life is driven to go from place to place secretly saying the Mass and administering the sacraments, because God must be brought to the faithful and only a priest can do so—is a figure from another world. Today he would be schooled in 'Liberation Theology', able and ready to discourse fluently to television journalists on the Third World, Neo-colonialism, Multinationals, and the charms of urban guerrilla warfare.

Secular ideas and attitudes have also affected Islam deeply, albeit in different ways. Secular notions came to the Muslim world charged with all the prestige which a powerful and prosperous Europe possessed. Their attraction derived from the belief that modernity (of which secular notions are part) would enable the Muslim world, which had come to be dominated by the European Great Powers, to defend itself and attain the same degree of prosperity and power. This was particularly important for Islam, since from the earliest times it had come to consider worldly success a proof and validation of its truth. But by the same token secularization was bound to lead to strain and tension in the life of Muslim societies. For traditional Islam had been associated with the idea that it was a religious duty for the subject to obey the ruler, whether bad or mad. The principle of individual autonomous judgement associated with the secular outlook made this unacceptable. Again, non-Muslims had their own, subordinate and inferior, station in a Muslim society: and this too was incompatible with secularity. Also, a secular outlook includes the notion of a society of states whose sole formal characteristic is the equal possession of sovereignty, and whose intercourse is, in some fashion, regulated by international law. An international order of this kind is at variance with a doctrine which saw the world as divided between the abode of Islam and the abode of war.

The strains might have been eased and the tensions alleviated if secularization had borne the fruit which its advocates expected. But secularization has not served to make Muslim world visibly more powerful or more prosperous. And from the very first it gave rise to great opposition on the score that it was a betrayal of Islam, and a sure way of delivering it into the hands of its traditional enemies. Even when the prestige of Western civilization was at its highest, and hence also the power and influence of the secularizers, this opposition was never completely silenced. With Khomeini in Iran and the Muslim Brethren in Syria and Egypt—with Pakistan officially enforcing the Islamization of the judiciary, the economy and other public activities—with Malaysia and Indonesia harbouring powerful Islamic movements—what has been called 'fundamentalism' is in full and seemingly irresistible flood.

But irresistible as it seems, fundamentalism may have a secret canker at its heart. For it is intimately affected by the secularization it so sincerely rejects. The ideals of equality and social justice which it proclaims are really inspired by the popularity of Western ideologies which have disseminated these ideas all over the world. In this respect, the fundamentalist divines and those fashionable clerics of the Western world who equate Christianity with 'social justice' may be brothers under the skin. In another respect, fundamentalism is caught in a dilemma. Muslim countries can no longer do without motor cars or telephones or all the other products of Western science. the argument now is that these things can simply be 'imported' as they are required, that they need not make it impossible to found purely Islamic commonwealths, and lead a life similar to that of 'the first Muslims'. There is a desperately theoretical air about such arguments, since it was precisely the importation of Western techniques and Western manufacturers which in the first place led to secularization.

Even more serious, fundamentalism will have to stand or fall by its ability to make Islam secure and powerful—which the secularizers failed to do. Can *power* and *security* today be attained without the weapons which the Muslim world does not develop or make—a state of affairs which the fundamentalists are least likely to remedy?

Judaism has also been profoundly touched by secularization

and the strains this has set up are as serious as they are unresolved. Secularization has offered Jews two alternative self-views, both of which are at variance with the traditional self-view: but neither of which is, in the end, satisfactory in providing a transparent and unproblematic account of the place of the Jews in the modern world, and in making them feel fully at home in it.

In the tradition self-view, the Jewish situation is simple. The people of Israel are bound by a Covenant with God. They are collectively responsible for abiding by the terms of the Covenant; but this collective responsibility in no way diminishes the responsibility of each single Jew to see that the Covenant is kept. To break the Covenant is to disobey God: and this sin brings punishment to the transgressor himself and to the whole people. Punishment for transgression culminated in Exile and Dispersion for the people. God is just, but He is also merciful, and in the course of time He will take pity and pardon. The exile and dispersion will end and the Messiah son of David will sit on his throne in Jerusalem.

This traditional self-view is unproblematic. Divine anger and divine mercy are the two poles which govern the course of Jewish history, all its vicissitudes, horrors and catastrophes included.

Another characteristic of this traditional self-view seems to have been established early on in Jewish history. In this history, almost from the beginning there was a dichotomy between prophethood and kingship, between, so to speak, spiritual and political authority, with kingship considered decidedly inferior to prophethood. From the very first, therefore, there was a depreciation of the political, and a profound scepticism about its efficacy. Of the many differences between Athens and Rome on the one hand, and Jerusalem on the other, this is probably the most striking and most far-reaching. Earthly power and its pride were nothing—and powerlessness, which marks so much of Jewish history, and which modern man so much resents, was not a particular concern to the traditional self-view.

This traditional self-view came in modern times to be considerably eroded by a rival one, which saw the Jews not as the object of divine election—which involved duties rather than privileges—and not as agents in a providential history the unfolding of which is set out in Scripture. Rather, the Jews are seen here as simply one group among the many which together constitute humanity. Like all of them they have progressed from Superstition to Enlightenment, and are now set to enjoy equally with their fellow men all the rights and duties of citizenship, in a world where the inevitable spread of universal education will eradicate ignorance and its two products, fanaticism and despotism. Jews now take their place in the general society; they are bidden to be men abroad, but Jews only at home.

It is no doubt possible to see the course of Jewish history in these terms. In those Jewries where the European Enlightenment found lodgement, this self-view became popular, indeed dominant. But Nazism, to which a people hitherto considered to be in the van of civilization gave overwhelming support—and the Holocaust which ensued—threw grave doubt on the notion of historical progress which the Enlightenment had invented, and on the particular Jewish self-view derived from it. For if this self-view is acccepted, then there is no possible accounting for the disasters which befell the Jews after 1933. If, in large parts of Europe, Jewish citizens suddenly found themselves outlawed, their property and lives wholly subject to the arbitrariness of their own governments and at the mercy of their fellow citizens then surely there was something quite wrong with this modern self-view. By contrast, the traditional one, so long derided as reactionary obscurantism, now reveals unexpected strengths. What Enlightened Judaism cannot explain, traditional Judaism has the spiritual resources to cope with. But, for good reasons, neither the one nor the other self-view can secure complete dominance in the Jewish world—and it is not simply that some give allegiance to the one, and some to the other. It is rather also that often, within one and the same breast, the two self-views dwell in strenuous contention or uneasy coexistence.

There is yet another rival Jewish self-view which has appeared in modern times. It is now just as influential as the other two. This is Zionism. Like the Enlightened self-view, it is the outcome of the Jewish encounter with moderm Western thought. Nationalism is one of the most powerful and influential ideologies invented in the modern West. It holds that humanity is naturally divided into nations, each one of which has its own specific and peculiar character. If national values are to survive, nations have to live on their own territory and enjoy self-government. Zionism is the adaptation of this doctrine to the Jewish condition. Only in a country of their own, Zionists hold, can the Jews survive and preserve their identity, their lives and their culture. If Judaism is deprived of a territorial base it becomes ghostly and insubstantial, and fails to satisfy the spirit. On this analysis, homelessness is the central Jewish predicament. The establishment of Israel is, in a sense, the fulfilment of the Zionist aim.

But how different the circumstances in which Israel was established and exists today from what the founders of Zionism had in mind! If homelessness is indeed the central Jewish predicament, Israel has proved no remedy. Far from Israel resolving the dilemmas of Jewish existence in the Diaspora, the Diaspora is today essential to the welfare, and perhaps to the survival of Israel. The so-called 'Canaanites' and others in Israel have, however, taken the line that there is and ought to be a fundamental distinction between Jews and Israelis. This is an untenable paradox since it is as Jews, and because they were Jews, that the original settlers came to Palestine and laid the foundations on which Israel was built. Even if this were practically possible, it would still be highly uncomfortable for their descendants to cut themselves off from their past, and rather bizarre to think of themselves as not being part of Jewry.

Far more prevalent today is the idea of the centrality of Israel in Jewish life and history. But this notion too is not without its difficulties. To put the state of Israel at the centre of Jewish history, or consider it as the terminus and fulfilment of Jewish history, would be to look upon two millennia of Jewish life in the Diaspora as a mere preface and preparation for the establishment of a Jewish state. But the fact is that Jews, scattered throughout the world, without benefit of political sovereignty, indeed frequently the victims of unfriendly and oppressive rulers, did succeed, in a most remarkable and original way, in creating and preserving a network of communal institutions; and these became the buttresses and carriers of their tradition and identity.

The Jewish self-view which Zionism promotes has by no means superseded or cancelled the other two. Hence an additional cause for inner fragmentation and strain. Equally with Christianity and Islam, Judaism testifies, thus, to the ravages which modernity has wrought on traditional religions and on the traditional societies for whom they provided solace and coherence.

To a greater extent perhaps than in the other two religions, modernity has disrupted Jewish patterns of communal life and communication. Hence the existence of a Jewish state can serve to protect and promote institutions working for the survival and continuity of Judaism. But whether Israel— which has successfully absorbed and adapted Western values and norms, but which has not so far proved religiously innovative —can succeed in fashioning a Judaism intellectually able to challenge modernity (better say, than U.S. Jewry, so much more numerous and incomparably wealthier) remains a moot point. Also, the character of Israeli politics since 1948 means that religious parties have taken shape which are deeply involved in the bargaining or haggling which government-by-coalition entails. *Mystique* descends to *politique*, and this is not compatible with the aloof detachment from political quarrels which is necessary for authority in religion.

In its aims and assumptions, Zionism may seem to hold an eccentric view of the course of Jewish history and be hard put to it to account for the present state of affairs. But does Israel as it is now depend on the truth, or cogency of the doctrine which presided over its coming to be? However it came about, here is a society which is now a going concern, in all its variety and complexity, its tensions and complications. It does not need to justify its existence by appealing to some ideology. Nor can the ideology make Israel immune from the chances and changes to which all states are necessarily subject, or save its rulers from mistakes and blunders. And, given the differing self-views which coexist in the Jewish world, it is not easy, or indeed even practicable, to have recourse to one single ideology in order to explain and justify the nation-state.

But it is really the very predicament in which Israel has

found herself since 1948 which leaves contending self-views and ideological warfare behind.

Since its foundation Israel has been in a state of war with its neighbours. This international conflict has been the direct consequence of a strategic decision taken by the leaders of the Palestine Arabs long before 1948. In their uncompromising opposition to Zionism these leaders decided to call in the Arab and Muslim worlds to the support of their cause. To judge by its results, the strategy has not so far been notably successful in protecting the interests of the Palestine Arabs. What it has done is to widen immeasurably, and to increase enormously, the gravity of what started out by being a local and limited quarrel. This ceased to be simply a matter of a Jewish 'national home' or a 'Jewish state'. The whole Arab, the whole Muslim, world has now become involved in this contention, and consequently the whole of Jewry as well. Israelis have found themselves inexorably treading the treadmill of power and violence, enmeshed in the dialectic of political conflict and armed struggle which few Zionists can have envisaged when the movement began. And the uncompromising stance, the 'maximalist' language which has been throughout a hallmark of the conflict, has conjured up forebodings of catastrophe and nightmares of expulsion and extermination, the reverberations of which, as is only natural, affect most intimately the Jews of Israel. An inkling of what these can be may be gathered from post–1948 Israeli poetry and fiction, some of which has explored quite subtly such mental and spiritual states, and how they can coexist with military efficiency, courage, and prowess on the battlefied.

But the effects of such forebodings and nightmares are not confined to Israeli Jews. They spread to, and deeply affect the Jewish world, and their power is enhanced by the memory of past disasters—which stretch back at least to the Roman Empire's sack of Jerusalem. Just as the fortunes of Judaea touched in the end the whole of Jewry, in which the Diaspora (then as now) was by far the largest component, so willy-nilly the fortunes of Israel, good or bad, will do so similarly, and in ways now unexpected and not to be foreseen.

The Jews between
Tradition and Modernity

WHEN THE Jewish Historical Society of England was
founded in 1893, its first president, Lucien Wolf, declared that the work of the Society constituted 'a religious and
moral task'. It was religious, according to Wolf, 'because
Judaism can have no distinctive existence apart from its great
historic sanctions. It was 'a specifically moral task' because
'beside cultivating historical knowledge we shall cultivate
historic spirit'. There was 'nothing more essential to the moral
well-being of a people', Lucien Wolf asserted, 'than the historic spirit'. This spirit bore the same relation to the community as 'personal repute' did to the individual. The historic
spirit, he argued, is 'the sense of national honour, the consciousness of a high level of conduct to be maintained, a
standing proscription of mean actions'. The historic spirit, in
short, was 'destined to make clear to the meanest of us the
sacred mission of Judaism, and to fit us for its accomplishment.'

This evocation and celebration of 'historical knowledge and
the historic spirit' by Lucien Wolf should make clear that,
when it was founded, the Jewish Historical Society of England
constituted a local Jewish manifestation of a wide and powerful European intellectual movement—a movement which,
together with that which led to the establishment and the
development of the natural sciences, has, since the end of the
eighteenth century, transformed our view of the world and of
our place in it. This movement took its rise from the belief that
there was great value in the historical study of the past—value

which in turn stemmed from the view that the truth about men is to be discovered by examining what they do and what they make, their actions and utterances, their products and institutions in all their ceaseless change and immense variety. The study of the historical past, in other words, is predicated on the assumption that there does not exist a uniform human nature which is the same everywhere and at all times, that human nature is in continuous change, and that the intelligibility and coherence of human activity are to be sought, not behind or above this ceaseless changing, but in the very change itself. If such are the organizing ideas of the historical enterprise, then it should not surprise us at all that the traditional Jewish outlook—shaped and maintained by the rabbis who, until the Enlightenment, were the exclusive guardians of Jewish learning—should have been indifferent to history and generally incurious about historical change. For the rabbis, revelation, whether written or oral, handed down to 'Moses our rabbi' on Mount Sinai, was the only truth. It was to be studied in every generation and its furthest implications explored and pondered. The Torah, however, was not subject to change, and its norms and injunctions applied at all times, everywhere. When, therefore, at the beginning of the nineteenth century, Zunz, his friends and disciples began to write what is recognizably Jewish history, this was positive evidence that the Jews of the German-speaking lands were now becoming part of this European intellectual movement which was to enlarge so remarkably men's understanding of themselves. The foundation of the Jewish Historical Society of England at the end of the nineteenth century, within a community appreciably smaller than that of the German-speaking Jews, and where academic and intellectual concerns were somewhat less prominent, is witness to the continued vitality and attractiveness of this European intellectual current.

If the rabbis attached no importance whatever to the study of historical change—might even have dismissed it as on the whole a vain and useless occupation—this is not to say that there is necessary or inevitable conflict between the study of the historical past and what the rabbis study and teach. Everyone knows how much time, energy and ingenuity were consumed on both sides in the so-called conflict between

228

science and religion. After a century and more of discussion which now seems in large part otiose, it ought to have become clear to us that what scientists—basing themselves on the always provisional assumptions and hypotheses of their various sciences—may say, for example, about the physics and chemistry of the human body will not settle questions worth raising about conduct, or resolve moral dilemmas, or still feelings of spiritual inadequacy or dissatisfaction. If the case had been otherwise, religion would long ago have been banished to the remote and superstitious parts of the globe.

The same is true of historical research. What the historian does is to consider actions, institutions, or artifacts simply in respect of their pastness. From what he has present before him—whether a building or a painting or a document—the historian attempts to evoke a past. His activity, therefore, is one of abstraction. Confronted, say, with a building, the historian qua historian is concerned not with its aesthetic quality, or with the engineering or architectural problems which it poses, or with the uses to which it can be put, or with its value as a piece of real estate; rather he is concerned with the building solely as evidence of the outlook and the purposes of its builders, and of its successive inhabitants and owners. And what he has to say on this score can provide little guidance to the student of aesthetics, to the architect or engineer, to the estate agent or economist. Nor is what he has to say either superior or inferior to what is said by those whose concern is art or science or the making of money, each one of whom similarly abstracts from the one building that aspect which is of particular concern to himself. We can say that, like science, historical research is tangential to the concerns of religion—inasmuch as religion is engaged in exploring the meaning of an ever-present and changeless divine revelation, and in providing guidance for believers in the conduct of their lives.

But when Lucien Wolf, in addition to historical knowledge, invoked the 'historic spirit' and enjoined his audience to cultivate it, what he had in mind, as his words clearly show, was somewhat different from history as I have tried to describe its practice and significance since its appearance within the circle of European culture during the last two hundred years or so. It is also, in a way, considerably older and more familiar.

229

Wolf's invocation of the historic spirit is, in some respects, not without analogy to Joshua ben Sira's 'Let us now praise famous men and our fathers that begat us.' Ben Sira's words express a universal human need for a self-identity which finds satisfaction in the establishing of one's antecedents and the identification of one's ancestors. The genealogies of which the Bible is full do, among other things, serve such a purpose. But what Wolf was looking for in history seems to go beyond this traditional quest—seems, in fact, to be the reflection of a tendency which had become prevalent in the Western culture of his day, and which has since spread to almost every part of the world.

This is the tendency to seek validation for one's values in the past as such. On this view, the past, simply because it is one's past, is seen to give rise to, to sustain, and to validate one's present way of life. The memory of a shared past, Ernest Renan argued, is what holds a nation together. It is this state of mind which is responsible for the extraordinary florescence of national histories which were believed to provide proofs of national existence and to buttress claims of national rights. That of course was not what Wolf himself was trying to do—not that, but something similar. He was appealing to history to establish 'the sacred mission of Judaism.'

But the rabbis, as guardians of 'the sacred mission of Judaism', were indifferent to history—and rightly so, since the revelation they studied and expounded was divine, extra-historical, timeless. And the quest for historical knowledge in the new European mode would have no bearing to speak of on their own concerns, just as rabbinical concerns should have been seen by historians of Jews and Judaism as tangential to their own particular pursuit. For, after all, their mutual relation is similar to that of lawyer and legal historian. The lawyer is concerned with devising ways in which laws, the existence and forms of which he takes for granted, can be applied to a variety of situations which the lawgiver may or may not have foreseen; his, in other words, is a present and practical interest. The legal historian, by contrast, seeks to elucidate when and how laws came into existence, and how their scope and meaning changed with the passage of time; for him, whether a law is operative or obsolete is beside the point.

But if between rabbi and historian there is, if not mutual indifference, then at any rate no ground for conflict, it is otherwise when history or the past is called upon to illustrate and validate the 'sacred mission of Judaism'. To search for such validation is to concede that the values of Judaism are not self-validating, that the truths of Judaism require propping up by the help of an ancient pedigree. This appeal to the historic spirit would strike the rabbinical mind as difficult to reconcile with its traditional outlook. The reason is not in doubt. This desire to seek certainty and self-identity in history is yet one more result of the hold which secularization has achieved over the European mind and, to a greater or lesser extent, wherever European culture has been received and accepted. The secularist outlook, whatever else it is, cultivates and thrives on the conviction that our world is open and unmysterious, that all that happens can be fully analyzed and accounted for. But, paradoxical as it may seem, when revelation has ceased to carry conviction, there still remains a need which craves satisfaction and which seeks satisfaction and fulfillment in the past as repository and guarantor of values—the past which here, therefore, becomes a substitute for religion. Whether the substitute can really yield the satisfaction or still the craving which religion is now thought incapable of doing is a matter for debate.

What is not open to doubt is that before the nineteenth century no Jew would have been found to invoke the historic spirit to illustrate and defend 'the sacred mission of Judaism'. This is not to say that before then the Jews did not have a very vivid consciousness of their past, or that this consciousness did not suffuse and colour their self-view. It is only to say, rather, that before modern times there would have been no need felt to substitute a presumed truth about the Jewish past for the truth of revelation, or to seek to prove or buttress the truth of revelation by the help of historical truths. But, in fact, from the very earliest period of their existence Jews had a firm and clear view of their self-identity—a self-identity defined by the transactions which they believed had taken place between God and their forefathers. With the passage of the centuries this self-view persisted, but other self-views came to be added to, and perhaps to modify, the earliest one. So that today Jewish self-

231

identity is complex, not to say complicated, to the point that a modern Jew may find it extraordinarily difficult to hold in view and accept all the successive self-identities which have resulted from a varied and troubled history. It has become so difficult that many attempts have been made, and others will no doubt continue to be made, to fasten on one self-identity or another and to declare that it alone expresses authentic Jewishness—that for which Jews stand and which should guide them in the future.

The oldest self-identity is no doubt that which affirms that Jews are 'sons of the Covenant'. Once upon a time, that is, Jews were the object of divine election, and it is this momentous event which gives meaning to their subsequent history, and should serve them as a guide always. This particular view of the Jewish past is extraordinarily complex, and its reverberations down the centuries are no less astonishing. Jews, according to this particular account—an account which has shown a tenacious power of endurance—are the descendants of Abraham, who left his native land and became a wandering stranger in obedience to divine command. God's covenant with Abraham, in which he was promised a land which his seed would inherit, was renewed at Mount Sinai and became a bond between God and each individual Jew. In connection with both covenants the theme of exile and alienation is prominent. Thus, for example, Genesis XV:13, 'Know of a surety that thy seed shall be a stranger in a land that is not theirs, and shall serve them, and they shall afflict them four hundred years.' Or Deuteronomy XXVIII:64, where one of the punishments for transgressing the Sinaitic Covenant is that 'the Lord shall scatter thee among all people, from one end of the earth even unto the other'. Bearing in mind the long centuries of dispersion and political powerlessness which followed the clash with Rome, one is not surprised that these past encounters with the divine and the predictions associated with them should have had such a tremendous evocative power for successive generations of Jews, should have provided them with an explanation of current predicaments, and guidance as to how they should be confronted and surmounted.

Another piece of the past which was endowed with scriptural authority and which formed part of the traditional

Jewish self-view is that relating to the exercise of power by a Jewish ruler in a Jewish polity. In contrast to their neighbours, the Jews did not entertain a belief in the divinity or sacredness of the ruler. Even more, the version of the past which generation transmitted to generation included many episodes the lesson of which inculcated scepticism, not to say mistrust, of political power and the life of politics. Pre-eminent among these episodes is that so powerfully described in I Samuel in which the Jews ask Samuel for a king—a request which leads to an itemized description of the oppressions that such a king will practice and which ends: 'And ye shall cry out in that day because of your king which ye shall have chosen you; and the Lord will not hear you in that day.' Again, in so many other episodes relating to the kingdoms of Judah and of Israel, there is shown a duality of authority between what we might call temporal and what we might call spiritual authority—between king and prophet. Not only is duality assumed, but also antagonism is exhibited between prophetic values and kingly values, with the prophetic values emerging invariably as the superior and the enduring ones. This is a great contrast to the caesaropapism—to borrow a term from Christian history— which in one form or another characterized the politics of the ancient world, and of Byzantium and Islam. The view of their past encapsulated in these biblical narratives, like the stories of the Covenant and the references to exile as the fate which Jews would suffer for their sins, seems to have been reinforced by the political experience of the Jews in the Dispersion, while, in turn, it gave coherence and meaning to this experience. Political scepticism, mistrust of power and of its exercise, an awareness of the narrow limits of what politics can really achieve are recognizable features of the traditional Jewish ethos which the lessons of this transmitted past inculcated.

By the late nineteenth century there had occurred a great change in the self-view of European Jews—at any rate in the self-view of the Jews of Central and Western Europe and of North America. The change may be exemplified by the short description of the Jewish Historical Society of England's aims quoted earlier. These included the promotion of the study of the history of 'the Jews of the British Empire', and of the 'historical role they played in this country and the Commonwealth'. Or to put it in the words used at the celebration of the Society's semi-jubilee in 1920, the Society believed that it was the 'paramount duty of the Jews of England to record with all possible fulness the story of their life in this country ... to narrate their services to the State ... and to describe that struggle for toleration which culminated in the full admission of English Jews to national rights and obligations.' These words signal a universe of discourse far removed from that of the biblical narratives and the rabbinical glosses upon them. What underlies these words is a self-view in which exile and dispersion do not loom very large.

But apart from exile and dispersion, the traditional self-view had another component which derived not so much from the Bible as from later experience, and from the theory which the rabbis derived from this experience. In this later experience, the Jews—exiled, dispersed, and politically powerless—not only entertained great scepticism and distrust concerning political action and the life of politics; they were also taught—and experience confirmed the teaching—that they were apart from the nations and kingdoms of the world, and that the only proper, indeed the only safe, stance to adopt toward these nations and kingdoms was one of passivity and withdrawal. To speak of the 'Jews of the British Empire', to seek to 'narrate their services to the State' therefore argues a considerable revolution in the Jewish self-view.

This revolution may, in brief, be described as twofold. It meant, in the first place, that religion was now seen as a private affair, having little or nothing to do with public activities. This distinction signalled a break in the traditional outlook in which religion governed both public and private life and could not but do so. For Jews to see themselves as citizens of a modern— usually European—state different from their fellow citizens only in the religion which they practised at home and in the synagogue was problematic. Problematic because it effected a hiatus between Jewish existence, as it was now supposed to be, and the traditional vision of its past as well as its future. It was to see Jews, not as especially subjects of divine election and a divine plan of salvation, but as only yet another group taking its due place in the unfolding of universal history. Between this new vision (the creation of the European Enlightenment) and

234

the traditional one, the strains could be quite considerable and the differences not easily reconcilable.

In the second place, the new vision was predicated on the assumption of what might be called a social contract between Jewish citizens and their fellow non-Jewish citizens—a contract decreeing equality in rights and obligations and making religion irrelevant to civic and political action. In this veiw of things, politics and political action were the prerogative of the citizen, something not to be shunned with fear and suspicion, but to be practised with confidence as the means of providing for both private and public welfare. It is in this perspective that it makes sense for Jews to 'narrate their services to the state' and to commemorate the role they have played in country and commonwealth. For a lengthy period few, if any, doubted that this social contract would hold, would indeed become ever firmer. But, as we know, beginning in the 1930s all over the European continent the contract was unilaterally, arbitrarily, violently broken and for a decade and more, Jews were treated not as fellow citizens, but as outlaws whose lives and possessions could be seized and destroyed at pleasure. A merciful Providence prevented such an outcome in the English-speaking world. But the experience of the thirties and the forties is not easily accommodated within the historical scheme of the Enlightenment which the Jews of the West adopted when they took their place in European political society. It is, on the other hand, much more easily accommodated within the traditional self-view, with its accent on exile and dispersion, and with its scepticism and mistrust of politics.

Meanwhile, another historical self-view has vied with the one derived from the European Englightenment for the suffrages of modern Jews; it is that constructed and propagated by Zionism. This self-view has elements in common with the traditional one. It, too, speaks of exile and redemption; it, too, looks upon the Jews as a separate people with their own special destiny. But this destiny it sees in purely mundane terms. It is to form a sovereign European-type state, and to attain this end by political action, 'like all the nations'—in the words the elders used to the prophet Samuel. But between this self-view and the traditional one the strains are hardly less

235

great, and their coexistence, lest alone their merger, hardly less problematic. For in the Zionist self-view, trust in the efficacy and beneficence of political action is central, and the redemption comes about by human action. Such human action is to inaugurate the return of the Jews to their ancestral land and to secure their continued presence there. Since, in such a vision, only life on the ancestral land can preserve and foster Jewish values, it becomes a puzzle how Jewish life and Jewish values were secured and preserved—as in fact they were—in the long centuries of exile and dispersion. Modernity, then, whether in the guise of the Enlightenment or in that of Zionism, seems to involve puzzles, ambiguities, and tensions in the way in which Jews view themselves and their history—puzzles, ambiguities, and tensions from which the traditional self-view seems largely immune. But whether this traditional self-view can speak to modern men and command their acquiescence is itself problematic.

These competing self-views, their mutual tensions and ambiguities, constitute the (ever shifting) framework and distinguishing landmarks of Jewish history. They provide that which will engage the interest, not only of mere historians, but also of anyone who has ever asked himself what it means to be a Jew.

The Character
of Jewish History

THE NINTH of AB in the Jewish calendar (which usually but
not invariably falls during the month of August in the
Gregorian calendar) has been observed by Jews, for the last
two thousand years or so, as a fast day. It is a day of mourning,
commemorating two remarkably similar catastrophes, separated by some six centuries, which befell the Jews and
Judaism. The first, in 586 B.C.E, was the handiwork of
Nebuchadnezzar, king of Babylon, who destroyed Jerusalem
and carried off its surviving inhabitants into captivity. The
second, in 70 C.E, was that of Titus (shortly afterwards to be
proclaimed emperor in Rome), who likewise destroyed
Jerusalem and its Temple, carried off the people into captivity
and encompassed their dispersion. Titus's exploit was com-
memorated by a triumphal arch, which still stands in Rome as
a landmark for tourists to gape at and Classical scholars to
study. What Titus and his soldiers did is also still visible in
Jerusalem in the Western Wall. This relic of Herod's Temple,
which the Romans looted and burned, was thought until
modern times to be all that had survived the destruction. But
unlike Titus's Arch, which though unscathed is now no more
than dead and inert stone, the fragment of a wall that escaped
the Roman scourge is instinct with the devotion of Jews who
believe themselves to be the descendants in an unbroken line,
of the people whom Nebuchadnezzar conquered, and Titus in
his turn subdued and dispersed. At the service on the eve of the
ninth of Ab there is recited at the Western Wall (as it is in

synagogues the world over) the Book of Lamentations, which was inspired by the first destruction but which, since the second, is read to refer to both catastrophes. The Jews are the only people now living who recall and lament inflictions suffered at the hands of Powers whose pride bit the dust a thousand and two thousand years ago.

The lamentation on the ninth of Ab is not only on account of the fire, the rapine and the slaughter suffered on both occasions; nor is it because, on both, princes 'were hanged up by their hand' and foxes walked on the desolate mountains of Zion; nor because the terrible famine made the skin 'black like an oven', and

> They ravished the women in Zion And the maids in the cities of Judah

Rather, and much more importantly, it is because both visitations are taken, in the perspective of Judaism, to have the selfsame cause. It is true that Babylon's and Rome's were the hands that destroyed and killed. But Babylon and Rome were only agents sent on their mission by the Lord, who in his anger against Zion had 'swallowed up Israel', 'cast off his altar', 'abhorred his sanctuary', and 'given up into the hand of the enemy the walls of her palaces.' However, just as His anger had been called forth by the transgression and rebellion of His people, so His mercy and goodness will be extended to those that wait for Him, to the soul that seeks Him. Hence the Book of Lamentations is more than a sad, backward looking commemoration. For the descendants of those who were carried off into captivity and Exile, it is meant to impart a lesson, and the import of which is ever present and ever urgent, while Nebuchadnezzar and Titus, through whose instrumentality this lesson was driven home, have been long dead and gone.

By the time the Jews clashed with Rome they already had, and were aware that they had, a long history. In the course of this history they had come into contact, and been involved in contention, with many of the peoples and Great Powers of Antiquity, among others, Pharaonic and Ptolemaic Egypt, Assyria, Babylon, Persia, the Seleucids. Compared with such Great Powers, the Jews were politically puny and insignificant. But all these Great Powers—the loyalties they instilled, the ways of life associated with them—are now dead, while the Jews have lived to transmit from generation to generation a tradition in which Moses is seen as leading their ancestors out of slavery in Egypt, in which the Assyrian descends like a wolf on the kingdom of Israel, a tradition recalling those who by the rivers of Babylon sat down and wept, whom Cyrus the Great allowed to go back to the land of their fathers and on whom Antiochus vainly tried to impose a false idolatrous worship. The Jewish year is punctuated with solemn occasions and festivals, which keep alive the memory of these contacts and transactions: not only the ninth of Ab, but also Passover, which celebrates the signal deliverance from Egyptian bondage; the festival of Purim, when the Book of Esther is read, which, with its story of Haman and his unsuccessful plot to exterminate the Jews in the dominions of King Ahasuerus, is set in the context of Jewish life under Persian rule; and the festival of Chanukah, which commemorates the successful resistance of the Maccabees against the attempt by Antiochus Epiphanes to impose paganism.

The peoples and Powers of Antiquity with whom at one time or another the Jews became involved have now all disappeared. The history of each one of them has a beginning and an end, to be sure more or less clear, more or less defined. That they are wholly past makes them a more manageable object of study than their one-time contemporaries, the Jews, whose history goes back to remote times, but also extends to the present day. What is just as remarkable is that this small group, politically and militarily insignificant, has had an influence on the course of civilization which only Greece and Rome, among the peoples of Antiquity, have equalled. And while Christianity and Islam eventually absorbed large elements of Classical culture, this happened, so to speak, indirectly, since both these religions (which were to penetrate and largely dominate the world except for the Far East) decisively rejected the pagan gods: the God they acknowledged and worshipped as the one true God was the God of Abraham, Isaac and Jacob. Christianity (which claimed in due course to be the *verus Israel*) arose among Jews, and was to define and elaborate its dogmas by reference, and in opposition, to Judaism. The Prophet Muhammad's religious universe (as the Qur'an attests) was wholly that of Judaism and Christianity, and the divine message, of which he announced himself to be the bearer, in his eyes only continued and completed the Revelation that mankind had received through the intermediary of Moses and Jesus. The Judaism out of which Christianity and Islam developed was essentially the same Judaism that has come down to the present day, with its biblical canon already established, with its Oral Torah supplementing the Written Torah and equal to it in authority, with the same rabbinical cast of mind, outlook and methods of argument already largely formed. It is this rabbinical Judaism that Christianity and Islam held to be both antagonist and point of reference. The Jews and Judaism, then, by reason of their position in world history, may be looked upon as the *trait d'union*, the buckle, which at once separates and unites ancient and modern in those societies to whose history such a periodization is applicable.

If Judaism 'gave birth' to Christianity and Islam, Jews had, following their clash with Rome and the catastrophe that ensued, to lead their lives in societies and states dominated by Christians and Muslims—societies where they were held at arm's length and where they were powerless. Their continued survival as a group in these dominant, attractive and yet very frequently hostile societies, where other groups sooner rather than later were lost without trace—as, for instance, the pagans of Greece, Italy and Western Europe, or the Christian populations of Anatolia and North Africa—must be adjudged remarkable. That such a group, utterly powerless as it was, did manage to survive for two millennia in a distinct and identifiable fashion is, on the face of it, a puzzle which calls for elucidation. The elucidation is to be found not so much in the conditions that the Jews faced in different times and places, with all their great variety, as in what Jews made of these peculiar conditions, what social arrangements they devised for the preservation of their group and the carrying on of their tradition. This is to say that the understanding of Jewish history requires that its divisions and articulations should follow its own autonomous movement, and be faithful to its own self-shaping spirit.

The disasters recalled by the Book of Lamentations were

national disasters of the kind to which any polity, through mismanagement or bad luck, can fall victim. In this respect the Jews were no different from any other people. Nor were they different from the other peoples of Antiquity in closely linking religion and politics. For example, the polis and its tutelary deities formed a unity such that the prosperity of the citizens depended on the gods receiving due worship and propitiation. But the values enshrined in the religion of the polis were, so to speak, exclusively political. A defeat of the polis was, ipso facto, a defeat for its gods, and the destruction of a polis not only put the lives and possessions of its members wholly at the conqueror's mercy, but also left them spiritually naked and disoriented. Classical culture overwhelmingly put its trust in the life of politics and therefore had no defence against the inevitable vicissitudes of politics. But the Jews who wandered in the land of Assyria or wept by the rivers of Babylon or were taken by Titus into captivity, though their fate was as hard as that of any *polites* or *civis* whose polity suffered destruction, could draw on spiritual resources which enabled them to withstand, individually and as a community, the chances and changes of politics.

Their religion was marked by peculiar features which distinguish it sharply from other religions of Antiquity. For one thing, from the beginning, exile seems to figure in it as a leading motif. Abra(h)am, whom the Jews considered as their ancestor, breaks with his family and his ancestral religion and leaves his country in obedience to a divine injunction: 'Now the Lord had said unto Abram, Get thee out of thy country, and from thy father's house, unto a land that I will show thee' (Gen. XII:1). Later on it is foretold to him that his descendants will also experience exile and humiliation 'Know of a surety that thy seed shall be a stranger in a land that is not theirs, and shall serve them, and they shall afflict them four hundred years' (Gen. XV:13). What Abra(h)am did was in response to a divine message of which he personally was chosen to be the recipient, and his election by God was ratified by a Covenant in which his seed was promised a land of their own. But there is another, later, Covenant standing at the beginning of Jewish history which is of even greater significance. This later Covenant followed the departure of Abraham's descendants from

Egypt, and in it God signified that He had chosen them for His people. This Covenant is between God and the children of Israel, each one of whom is responsible for keeping its terms. If the terms are not kept, we are told in Deuteronomy, various punishments will follow, and one in particular, that 'the Lord shall scatter thee among all people, from the one end of the earth even unto the other' (Deut. xxviii:64).

Another theme in the traditional Jewish self-view serves to distinguish the Jews even more sharply from their neighbours and contemporaries. As the scriptural account has it, after Moses had led them out of Egypt the children of Israel were governed by elders and judges. In due course, Samuel received the divine calling and led the people. When he grew old, he appointed his two sons judges over Israel. But they proved unworthy, taking bribes and perverting judgements. The elders then applied to Samuel saying, 'give us a king to judge us.' The Bible hints that Samuel was taken aback and displeased by such a demand, but God told him to accede to it 'for they have not rejected thee, but they have rejected me, that I should not reign over them.' Such a passage is indicative of an outlook which considers not only that kings are not divine— divinity of the ruler was an idea common among the neighbours of the Jews—but also that divine rule is preferable to kingly rule. The biblical narrative also manages strongly to hint that this hankering after a king is somehow wrong and disreputable. When Samuel tries to persuade the elders that a king may prove to be a scourge rather than a blessing, they respond by insisting, like people obstinately bent on their own perdition: 'Nay, but we will have a king over us that we also may be like all the nations.' That a king was only a man capable of wrong-doing and crime, and subject to Divine Judgement and punishment is a theme that recurs more than once in the Bible. The best known instance concerns David, whom the prophet Nathan rebuked harshly and to whom he promised retribution for committing adultery with Bathsheba and encompassing her husband's death (II Sam. xii:1–12). The arguments by which Samuel tries to deflect the elders from their purpose are remarkable. Samuel recites a whole catalogue of oppressive and despotic acts which may be expected from a king—and the Bible declares that in so doing Samuel was conveying the very words of God. The king will conscript the sons of the poeple to fight and to work his land, he will take their daughters for his service, he will levy taxes and appropriate land, 'and ye shall be his servants. And ye shall cry out in that day because of your king which ye shall have chosen you; and the Lord will not hear you in that day' (I Sam. VII:10–18). These emphatic words about the disappointments, the mishaps and the disasters of politics are cast in the prophetic mode. The theme is repeated many times elsewhere in the Bible, where we find prophets using argument and exhortation at various critical junctures when internal disorder or external threat called into question the ability of the king or his judgment.

All through, then, we find expressed in the Bible mistrust of merely political authority, a questioning of its legitimacy and scepticism about the ability of rulers as such to act justly or safeguard the common weal. The prophets maintain a distance from current political arrangements, and deal with political power at arm's length: the attitude they articulate is that the body politic, a human contrivance and thus necessarily subject to decay and failure, is not that which gives meaning and coherence to human life. On the contrary, politics is perpetually under judgment, God's judgment revealed through prophets.

This peculiar duality, without parallel either in Classical Antiquity or among the Jews' immediate neighbours, paved the way for a situation quite as remarkable. The prophets spoke as the agents of Divine Revelation, the authority of which was supreme. This Revelation, the Torah as it came to be designated, was held to have been given to Moses on Mount Sinai. This Written Torah was complemented by an Oral Torah, declared to have been revealed to Moses at the same time. This Oral Torah was of co-equal authority with the Written, and was transmitted like it to later generations: 'Moses received the Torah from Sinai and transmitted it to Joshua, and Joshua to the elders, and the elders to the prophets, and the prohets transmitted it to the men of the Great Synagogue' (Mishnah, Sayings of the Fathers). Of this Oral Torah the guardians and expounders were the rabbis, whose decisions and conclusions were declared to be linked by an unbroken chain leading back to 'Moses our rabbi', so that what Akiba or Hillel or Shammai or their successors and their successors' successors expounded is all held to have formed part, *ab initio*, whether Moses knew it or not, of the original Mosaic Revelation. It is possible to go further. These rabbis, the heirs of the men of the Great Synagogue, who had received the Oral Torah from the prophets, who had received it from the elders, who had received it from Joshua, who had received it from Moses, were the ultimate authority as to the meaning of Revelation—a meaning to be clarified and ascertained in the course, and by means, of debate, disputation and commentary. A famous and remarkable passage in the Talmud records that in a disputation between rabbis, one of them, Rabbi Eliezer, sought to support his view by appealing to miracles. A carob tree was uprooted a hundred cubits from its place; his opponents said: 'No proof may be brought from a carob tree.' A stream of water flowed backwards; his opponents said: 'No proof may be brought by a stream of water.'

> Then he said: 'If the *Halakhah* [i.e. the decision] agrees with me, let the walls of the school house prove it'. Thereupon the walls of the school house began to totter. But Rabbi Joshua rebuked them and said: 'When scholars are engaged in *halakhic* dispute, what concern is it of yours?' Thus the walls did not topple, in honour of Rabbi Joshua, but neither did they return to their upright position, in honour of Rabbi Eliezer; still today they stand inclined. Then he said: 'If the *Halakhah* always agrees with me, let it be proved from Heaven'. Thereupon a heavenly voice was heard saying: 'Why do you dispute with Rabbi Eliezer? The *Halakhah* always agrees with him.' But Rabbi Joshua arose and said (Deut. xxx:12): 'It is not in heaven'. What did he mean by that? Rabbi Jeremiah replied: 'The Torah has already been given at Mount Sinai [and is thus no longer in Heaven]. We pay no heed to any heavenly voice, because already at Mount Sinai You wrote in the Torah (Ex. xxiii:2): "One must incline after the majority."' Rabbi Nathan met the prophet Elijah and asked him: 'What did the Holy One, blessed be He, do in that hour?' He replied: 'God smiled and said: My children have defeated Me, My children have

defeated Me.' (Translation in Gershom Scholem, *The Messianic Idea in Judaism*, 1971)

Intellectual poise and self-confidence are apparent in this passage, and the Talmud, the Midrash, the aggadic literature, the codes of law, the *responsa* and the commentaries upon commentaries which went on being written well into modern times indicate that this self-confidence and implicit belief in the high worth and relevance of their discipline continued to be the rule in rabbinical circles. Nor was the enterpise looked upon as simply academic. Following the disastrous clash with Rome, and the destruction of the Jewish polity in Palestine, the Jews became a collective of communities all over the Mediterranean basin and further afield. They were dispersed, small in number and politically powerless. With the official conversion of the Roman Empire to Christianity, and the subsequent rise of Islam, their position deteriorated further. In these new, far-flung political structures, membership of the body politic depended on professing the official faith, while those who did not do so were subject to various disabilities, the severity of which in practice varied from time to time and place to place, but which remained, until the nineteenth and twentieth centuries, part of the public law of Christian and Islamic states. But these scattered communities managed to survive for centuries on end in these adverse and unpropitious circumstances. Not only to survive, but to maintain their cohesion, and, so far as they could, to govern themselves by means of communal organizations that were recognizably similar, however distant they were from one another in time and space. These communities, furthermore, were linked to one another by social, mercantile and scholarly networks which eventually became world wide. They constituted, and were aware that they constituted, a distinct group among the peoples of the world—a group which kept alive the traditional belief that it was the object of divine election.

It is the rabbis who, without benefit of state of power or territorial base, provided and kept in repair the framework of belief, custom and law which allowed these small, dispersed communities, always vulnerable, often oppressed and occasionally terrorized, to maintain in unpromising conditions social cohesion and spiritual coherence. Nothing remotely comparable can be seen elsewhere in history. The Written and Oral Torah originated in and referred to a state of affairs in which the Jews formed a polity in a territory of their own. By submitting these materials to a centuries-long dialectic of interpretation and counter-interpretation, by engaging in detailed textual commentary and, eventually, by codifying the conclusions of debate and commentary, the rabbis built up a structure of law and custom, of injunction and prohibition, which regulated social, economic and religious life in conditions unimaginably remote and alien from those obtaining in say, King David's time or that of the Hasmoneans—eras which form the original historical context of the Torah. This structure of communal regulation, which was in effect self-regulation, was maintained and transmitted over large areas and long periods. It has been the achievement of contemporary historians, such as Simon Dubnow, Salo Baron and most recently S. D. Goitein, to convey to their readers a detailed and vivid picture of the complex institutions and the sophisticated arrangements which enabled these communities to subsist for so long in such precariousness. And some of these communities continued to live in the traditional manner and according to the traditional arrangements set up and developed by the rabbis up to within living memory. One such community is that of Marrakech, the inner life of which, in the two or three decades preceding the Second World War, José Benech has so strikingly and with such penetration depicted in a little-known work, posthumously published shortly after the war, *Essai d'explication d'un mellah*.

As has been said, exile figures from the earliest times as a *leit motiv* in the Jewish self-view. Following the destruction of the Second Temple and the ending of Jewish autonomy, the fact and the consciousness, of exile naturally became even more prominent. Through their own sins, successive generations of Jews were taught, they had brought this punishment upon themselves. But God is a merciful God, they were also taught, who will in his own time send the Messiah to redeem them and to restore them to the Holy Land. The redemption here in question was an earthly one: it did mean that when redemption came the Messiah, the Anointed One, would once again sit in Jerusalem on David's throne, at the head of a divinely regulated polity when scarcity, famine, envy and war would disappear. In the words of the ancient blessing recited after the reading in the synagogue of the weekly portion from the Prophets:

Rejoice us! O Lord our God, in the coming of thy servant Elijah the prophet, and in the kingship of the house of David, thine anointed. May he come speedily to gladden our hearts. Let no stranger sit on his Throne and let others no more claim his honour for their inheritance; for Thou hast sworn unto him by Thy holy name that his lamp shall never be quenched. Blessed art Thou, O Lord, the Shield of David

The blessing invokes God's ancient promise and supplicates for its fulfilment. It does not of course indicate when the Messiah will actually come. But, as may be suspected, the temptation to announce the tidings of his coming, especially in times of trial and suffering, was great. The rabbis, however, were firm in warning against such predictions. the Talmud and the Midrash forbid calculating the End, that is, forecasting the advent of the Messiah, or pressing for it, forcing its coming through human action. Jews are likewise enjoined not to revolt against the kingdoms of the world, and not to come up from exile 'like a wall', i.e. in a mass. In the twelfth of the Thirteen Principles of the Faith, which Maimonides codified and which are recited at the end of the prayers on the eve of the Sabbath, Jews profess their belief in the coming of the Messiah who will redeem those who await his final salvation. But Maimonides lays it down in a commentary that one must not determine a time for him, and he repeats the curse pronounced by the rabbis against those who calculate the End.

Belief that the Messiah must one day come to redeem Israel from exile and sit on Daivd's throne in Jerusalem thus implied a concomitant political quietism which, inculcated by rabbinical teaching generation after generation, became, it is not too much to say, the ingrained attitude towards political action characteristic of Jewish communities everywhere. It is a surprising and unexpected sequel to a turbulent pre-Exilic history in which political issues had loomed so large—whether the issues had to do with reconciling political action with divine injunctions, or whether they had to do with negotiating the dangers posed by the ambitions of Great Powers. This is not to say that political passivity was always and invariably the rule. If that had been the case, there would have been no reason for reiterating the prohibition of calculating the End. From time to time belief in the imminent arrival of the Messiah would grip some community and plunge it into effervescence. One such Messianic movement which, in modern times, affected the whole of the Jewish world is that associated with Sabbatai Zevi (1626–76). Gershom Scholem has shown in his masterly study of Sabbatai and Sabbatianism, how the movement developed in an autonomous fashion out of kabbalistic doctrines. He has also shown how, within a year or so of Sabbatai's proclamation as Messiah in 1665, there was hardly a Jewish community in Asia, Europe or North Africa which was not more or less profoundly touched by the Messianic hope.

Sabbatai was proclaimed Messiah in May 1665; he was arrested in Constantinople by the Ottoman authorities in February 1666, and in the following September he turned Muslim. He thus disappointed the hope of redemption which had swept the Jewish world, and his followers were eventually confined to a group of outwardly Muslim secret believers chiefly in Salonica, and some others in central and Eastern Europe. But as Profesor Scholem has argued, the Sabbatian movement is highly significant not only in what it indicates about the outlook and world view of Jewry, but in its intellectual sequels as well. Sabbatianism was antinomian in tendency, and its failure left a residue of disaffection towards rabbinical Judaism and a readiness to dismantle the fence round the Torah which the rabbis had so zealously errected, maintained and guarded for centuries. The fence was eventually, in large part, dismantled and destroyed. The role of Sabbatianism in this should alert us to the possibility that autonomous intellectual changes within Jewry had a role to play here as much as did the European Enlightenment and the policies that characterized Enlightened Absolutism and the Democratic Revolution—as the historian R. R. Palmer has called it—which followed.

During this latest period of Jewish history the main centres of Jewry were central and Eastern Europe, and subsequently the U.S.A. The political passivity which marked Jewish life under the aegis of the rabbis was increasingly abandoned. The democratic states and the democratic aspirations which became increasingly prominent in the nineteenth and twentieth centuries offered a new promise and imposed new requirements. Democratic politics seemed to offer the prospect of Jews taking their place as citizens *à part entière* in a secular order where religion was a private matter, not an affair of state. This indeed has so far proved to be the case in the English-speaking world, and most notably in the United States. The Messianic vision of a *novus ordo saeclorum* seems to have received here a measure of realization, denied as yet to that which Jewish prayers have, these many generations, enshrined; and in this *novus ordo* Jews, like other citizens, sustain, indeed themselves are, the political order. Democratic politics elsewhere have proved more disastrous for Jews than Nebuchadnezzar or Titus had ever proved to be. In the decades following the First World War the Jews of Central and Eastern Europe found themselves far worse off in polities deriving their legitimacy from the popular will than they had been in the dynastic regimes the war had destroyed; indeed the regime that encompassed the holocaust issued from universal suffrage and continued to enjoy popular support to the very end. The Sabbath synagogue service includes a prayer for the ruler. As is well known, the Tsarist regime oppressed and persecuted Jews in various ferocious and ingenious ways. A certain rabbi in the Tsar's dominions, however, always insisted on saying this prayer with great fervour, explaining that one should always wish long life to the Tsar, since the next one was sure to be worse. This may apply, *mutatis mutandis*, to the promise and temptations of the life of politics as Jews have encountered it in so many places during this century.

Zionism is the other guise in which the life of politics has presented itself to the Jews of the modern world. Zionists hold that the Jewishness of the Jews demands the safeguard and the fostering care of a Jewish state. Considered historically, such an approach would reduce two millennia and more of life in the Diaspora to a mere hiatus between Solomon's kingdom and its restoration in the shape of the State of Israel; and this restoration, brought about as it has been by mundane means, may not perhaps be thought identical with the Messianic restoration the advent of which, the rabbis taught, may not be forced. However, the State of Israel exists, and in it lives a sizeable portion—though by no means a majority—of world Jewry. Israel came into existence in a world profoundly different from that known by the founders of Zionism; and it continues to exist amid circumstances which they did not envisage or even imagine. Their hope was that a Jewish state, by doing away with 'Jewish homelessness', would 'solve the Jewish problem' then becoming acute in a populist, and hence nationalist, Europe. But Israel has not, of course, abolished the Diaspora, which in fact is necessary to support and sustain it. In the thirty-six years of its existence so far, Israel has experienced with an ancestral fortitude the long forgotten splendours and miseries which attend the life of politics. As it continues to do so, it will be watched over with anxious solicitude by those kings of Judah and Israel, by those Hasmonean princes and those High Priests who, in their generation, had to deal and contend with Assyria and Babylon, with Seleucia and Rome.

Index

251

Index

Index